COME OF AGE

COME OF AGE

Angus Buchan

MONARCH
BOOKS

Oxford, UK & Grand Rapids, Michigan, USA

First published in the UK in 2011 by Monarch Books
(a publishing imprint of Lion Hudson plc),
Wilkinson House, Jordan Hill Road, Oxford OX2 8DR.
Tel: +44 (0)1865 302750 Fax: +44 (0)1865 302757
Email: monarch@lionhudson.com
www.lionhudson.com

First published in South Africa in 2010 by Maranatha Christian Publishing.

ISBN: 978-0-85721-021-0

Distributed by:
UK: Marston Book Services Ltd, PO Box 269, Abingdon, Oxon OX14 4YN;
USA: Kregel Publications, PO Box 2607, Grand Rapids, Michigan 49501

This book has been printed on paper and board independently certified as having come from sustainable forests.

British Library Cataloguing Data
A catalogue record for this book is available from the British Library.

Printed and bound in the UK by CPI Cox & Wyman, Reading.

This book is dedicated to those who have lost their way.

Also by Angus Buchan

Books

Faith Like Potatoes
Aartappelgeloof
The Seed Sower
Jesus... a farmer... and miracles
Is Jesus Enough?
Hard-core Christianity
Passing the Baton
A Farmer's Year
Daaglikse geloof
A Mustard Seed
'n Mosterdsaad
Fathers and Sons
Pa en seun
A People Saturated with God
MMC 08 Coffee Table Book
MMC 09 Coffee Table Book
Grassroots Volume 1

DVDs

Faith Like Potatoes
MMC series
Grassroots series

Contents

Acknowledgments

I want to thank God for Ann Roux who, once again, has edited this book to the best of her ability, even in the face of really trying times with her husband Pete not being at all well. Thank you so much, Ann. Thank you for your standard of excellence that has made it possible for this book to be printed.

I also want to thank God our Heavenly Father for Yvonne Ashwell, who has once again painstakingly typed out the rough manuscript of this book for me. Well done, Yvonne! Thank you for being a true friend and for always finding the heart in the book. I really appreciate you, Les and Duane.

My thanks to Patrick Royal for the magnificent photographs you have provided. As always, the quality of work that you produce, time after time, is truly wonderful.

I would like to express my heartfelt appreciation to Rod and Lyn Samouilhan of Pinetown Printers, who are becoming more friends of mine than business partners.

Thank you, Jilly Hull (my youngest daughter), for your painstakingly hard work, and for your ability to finish the things that your dad starts. I don't know what I'd do without you.

Lastly, I want to say to my dear wife, Jill. Thank you, Jill, for believing in God in me. Surely I would not even be alive – I don't think – to write this very book if it had not been for your love and your commitment to God to look after me, and to try and tie me down to rest. I really do love and appreciate you. As I have come of age, I appreciate you so much more now than I did when I first met you all those decades ago.

Most of all, I thank the Lord Jesus Christ for giving me the privilege of being able to share this story with His children, many of whom are still groping with that coming-of-age phenomenon.

Foreword

"Hi, hello, hello! That you, Tortoise? Where you been? Haven't been able to get hold of you!"

"Hello Buchan-Hare, I've been here all the time. Good to hear you!"

The Buchan-Hare saga started many years ago. Buchan-Hare always in a hurry; Tortoise trailing behind, being told to get moving.

Angus and I have travelled this road together over many years, from soon after we met at the church we were both attending.

Angus and Jill were soon to be hailed as a couple of worth, Angus rising to the rank of elder soon after joining. The leadership quality in him was soon recognized.

On Angus' second campaign, which was to Port Elizabeth, I went along as a member of the team with not the foggiest idea of what was expected of me, or what I had to do. I think that applied to the rest of the team as well. We were put out onto the streets to learn many lessons, which prepared us for all the other campaigns that Angus conducted.

It's amazing, the first attempt is the one by which you learn the most. Probably because that's where you experience the hard knocks!

The road we travelled sometimes reminded me of an old Ford car going over smooth roads, then hitting the rocks and the dongas (large potholes) with many bangs, squeaks and splutterings. Then hitting the slippery uphills, but always reaching the top – always a climax to end with. People being saved, healed, and encouraged. It did as much for the team as it did for the people being prayed for.

Yes! God's hand has truly been with Angus. To stand by as an observer of the miracles that have taken place has been a lifetime experience for me. I wouldn't have missed it for anything the world could offer me. I have lived in a different dimension, for which I thank my Lord and Saviour.

I attended the 2009 Men's Conference on the Sunday. We were in a car parked a distance from the platform, but could see and hear clearly. The two screens were in full view. I saw Angus approach the microphone and I heard him say, "I have come of age." It was a statement he made. It hit me like a ton of bricks, because then and there I realized that I too, like Angus, had come of age.

I pray that this book, written from the heart of my spiritual son, Angus, will change the heart of every man and woman and child who reads it. It is written through real-life experiences.

TO GOD BE THE GLORY!

Peggy O'Neill

Preface

This has been a very exciting book for me to write! It's almost like scales have fallen from my eyes since the incident where I collapsed under the stage at the 2009 Mighty Men Conference on Shalom Farm. It's like "a strange warmth has come over my heart" (John Wesley) and I have seen life and the preciousness of life in a completely new dimension. I can honestly say, maybe unfortunately, that there is no short cut to getting this view of the real savouring and taste of precious life, except by going through hardship and literally staring death in the face.

I thank God for every experience that I've had which has brought me to the stage of my life where I believe I have really come of age.

What a fearful thing it must be for someone who's maturing in life and yet has not met the Master face to face! When I was lying, totally immobile, on that lawn and could not move and could not speak, I could see everything and I could hear everything. There was no fear in my heart.

One of the greatest compliments my family has been paid came from the paramedic Hans Hartmann, who was on the scene at the time with the doctors and many others. He said that he has never, in all his twenty-odd years of medical crisis work, seen such peace and calmness and total control upon a whole family that is standing by and watching their loved one coming as it were, to the end of the road. Again, we give all the praise to our blessed Saviour, Jesus Christ.

As I write this preface, I'm walking around the farm which my sons now own and run. I am truly and utterly fulfilled. I am ready at any time to meet my Maker. But I am also quite content to stay on earth for as long as He needs me here. Paul said: "I am crucified with Christ: nevertheless I live; yet not I, but Christ liveth in me: and the life which I now live in the flesh I live by the faith of the Son of God, who loved me, and gave Himself for me" (Galatians 2:20, KJV). Very humbly, I want to say that that's exactly how I feel at this time in my life. I've come of age and am ready for whatever Christ has in store for me and for my family.

My prayer is that you'd read this book, and that you too would find that peace, that joy and that fulfilment that comes from knowing Jesus Christ in a very intimate and personal way.

Angus Buchan
Shalom Farm
January 2010

Chapter 1
Come of age

There is a word whose full meaning I never knew. I really do understand it implicitly now. It is brevity; particularly the brevity of life. I looked up the dictionary definition after my wife Jill explained to me what it means. The *New Collins Concise Dictionary* says that the word "brevity" means a short duration. It comes from the word "brief", so in other words, the briefness of life.

I have, in the last three weeks, come to the full realization of the meaning of the words "brevity of life". I'm sixty-one years old as I write this book and it's taken me sixty-one years to come of age. It's a funny thing, you can go on preaching and teaching about the importance of life, tell your children, your congregation, your friends, the world, but unless the Holy Spirit reveals it to you in a very drastic way, you never really understand what it means when you hear that life is but a vapour. It's like the grass of the field. It's here today but gone tomorrow. Especially when you are a young person, you think you're going to live forever. It really saddens my heart more and more each day as it seems as if there are more young people dying than older people, especially in our beloved continent of Africa.

David Kain is an old gentleman I respect immensely. I remember well the day that he remarried. His first wife had passed on and he was well into his eighties. He invited me to his wedding. I purposely arrived at the wedding a little bit late, hoping to sneak into the back and sit there and just be a part of the celebration, which was held on the premises of African Enterprise. It was a huge turnout of people. His sons were there, some of them preachers of the Word themselves.

As I walked in, he was standing at the altar, about to make his vows. He gave me the thumbs up, and there was a twinkle in his eye. The ushers came and literally arrested Jill and me, marched us right up to the front, in front of everybody, to sit in the front row. He had told me a week or two before that he wanted me to come to his wedding. And, if the Lord laid a Word on my heart, just to share it with the congregation… That was all he said.

Jill was not amused at all, because she thought I'd set this thing up. I hadn't. I had tried to play it really low-key. So there we were, sitting in the front row next to all the family and the many visiting ministers. He's a very popular man. His son Russell, who was conducting the service, said, "We're now going to call upon Angus Buchan to bring the message." One thing I learned many years ago was always to carry a sermon in your top pocket. I had to get up and bring the full message!

David Kain is a man who has come of age. He and his dear wife Winks enjoy life to the full. They are both well into their eighties and probably have more life in them than most youngsters under the age of twenty-one. They appreciate every day and I'm sure they enjoy every sunrise and every sunset.

David came out to the farm to encourage me once to keep on preaching the Gospel for Jesus. He said something that I've never forgotten. He said, "Angus, I can't go down the well any more but I can hold the rope." In other words, even as I have to keep going down the well, he can stabilize and assist me by holding the rope at the top. That's a statement made by a man who has come of age. That's why God has blessed him so much and is still using him so powerfully in his day-to-day living.

I think that many of us, when we were younger, thought that we'd come of age, only to realize at a much later date – for me, at the age of sixty-one – that we've only now come of age.

I love going to Israel. One of my favourite places there is Peter's Landing. It's the place where nothing has changed. It was from the shores of Lake Galilee that Jesus conducted most of His ministry, a place called Tabgha, where seven springs come out of the ground and flow into the lake at that spot. Being a farmer and a naturalist, I can understand why the fisherman fished that area, because all the nutrients out of the ground and all the food sources would have flowed into the lake right there.

I think of Simon Peter, the big fisherman, the son of John. After the crucifixion the disciples had all scattered and basically betrayed the Lord through fear. They were sorely distressed because their hero, their champion who was going to deliver them from the oppressors – the Romans – had been killed. They had lost hope and had gone back to doing the only thing they knew how: fishing. They were fishermen by trade.

Peter's Landing is where Jesus stood on the steps on the Sunday morning following the crucifixion, and they are still there, cut into rock. I've been there. I got very emotionally involved because I believe the Lord challenged me in my heart in that same place.

Jesus stood on the steps and shouted out to the men who were fishing maybe fifty metres off the shore. I can only assume it would have been a misty morning, because they obviously didn't see the Lord's face or His silhouette very clearly. They heard the voice shout out (John 21:5): "Boys, have you caught anything?"

"No."

"Throw your nets on the other side."

They obeyed, and caught one hundred and fifty-three large fish. Those tilapia are beautiful fish. They're a type of bream and have a beautiful white flesh. I've eaten them myself.

John recognized Jesus and said, "That's the Lord!"

The Bible says that at that moment Simon Peter, the big fisherman, took off over the edge of the boat, half putting on his clothes. He must have half run, half swum to the edge of the lake. There was Jesus!

He had prepared breakfast for them, like He always did. He had baked fresh bread and roasted some fish. He always took care of all of their needs. And He still does.

When they'd finished eating, Jesus asked Peter, "Simon, son of John, do you love Me?"

"Yes, Lord."

"Feed My sheep."

He asked this three times. I think Peter must have been sorely vexed and troubled by the third time. I can imagine he was weeping. He'd also denied the Lord three times. He said, "Lord, You know everything."

Jesus said, "Feed My sheep."

I firmly believe that Peter, the big fisherman, had come of age at that moment, because his life was totally transformed. Before then he'd been the braggart. He'd been the one who said to the Lord, "I'll die for You!" He was the leader of the pack. He had the big mouth. He was probably the hard-drinking, rough and tough man.

But after he had let the Lord down so badly by denying Him three times, he was a changed man. After Peter was baptized in the Holy Spirit on the day of Pentecost, his life took on a totally different outlook. He then went on to preach his first sermon and three thousand souls came to Christ that day. Jesus Christ was the Head of the church but Peter became the leader.

Legend tells us that he was eventually caught in Rome and crucified. This is a man who could not even own up to being an associate of Jesus Christ before he'd come of age. He asked to be crucified upside down because, he said, "I'm not worthy to die like my Saviour." They crucified his wife before him. While she was dying, he kept saying to her, "Remember the Lord." Peter had come of age.

We need to come of age, because there's no time left for fooling around. David Kain said he can't go down the well any more but he can hold the rope. He has come of age.

Charles Haddon Spurgeon was regarded by the Baptists as the Prince of Preachers. When he was twenty-one years old the Baptists built the London Tabernacle for him. It could seat ten thousand people. A man who, though uneducated – he had never been to Bible College – wrote more Christian books than any other man, ever. Yet, when he was in his late fifties and got sick, Spurgeon said, "By attempting to do less, I hope to achieve more."

There comes a time in every person's life when we have to face up to facts and realize that we are not here forever, that while we are here we have to do something constructive with our lives. I thank God for the turmoil, the pain and the tribulation I went through a short while ago, because it made me come of age. The tragedy is that some people never come of age. My dear friend reading this book, I hope you are not one of them.

I heard of a man who was being divorced for the sixth time. As he came out of court, he was overheard to say, "Well, I'm so sorry. She tried her best to please me but she just couldn't quite get it right." Have you ever heard anything as childish as that? A man who had already had five wives, who was getting divorced for the sixth time, and who was still saying, "She tried so hard, but she couldn't make me happy." It sounds like a two-year-old speaking, not a fully-grown man.

There are some men who have so much in terms of finance, reputation and power, and yet they will not share it with anybody. God gave me a picture one day of a two-year-old little boy sitting on a carpet surrounded by hundreds of toys that he could never play with in a year. Another little boy came to visit him and he would not let him play with one toy. I have a grandson of that age and I thank the Lord that he's not like that.

Such a childish attitude; and yet how many times haven't we seen grown-ups act the very same way? A man who has so much money that if he were to live three lifetimes he would never spend it all, yet he will not give it to anybody, will not help anybody. Of course, he is the loser in the end.

A few weeks ago I had the most amazing experience of my entire life to date. Every time God does something in my life I say, "Well, Lord, You can't do better than this." Yet He does.

Six years ago, God called me to cancel all my preaching appointments, all my evangelistic outreaches and to concentrate on mentoring young men. He showed me that there are so few spiritual fathers in this nation, and indeed in the world, at this time. I was up at the Mkuze Game Reserve in Northern Zululand, having a rest with my wife, Jill. God rebuked me very severely, saying, "You have left your first love" (Revelation 2:4). God was saying to me that he wanted me to get back to my first love. The passage goes on: "remember therefore from where you have fallen; repent and do the first works, or else I will come to you quickly and remove your lampstand from its place" (verse 5). The lampstand means light, so, light being the Holy Spirit in my life, I knew exactly what that meant.

I duly went back and did what God had told me. The first miracle was that no one was angry with me, although some of these men had booked me a year, two years before. They had even begun some of the advertising for the meetings. But one thing I realized is that when you do something God's way, it always works out.

I started out at that stage, in 2004, with the first men's conference. Two hundred and forty men came, which was a huge miracle for us because we did no advertising. We sent out one e-mail letter, and that's what happened. The next year six hundred men attended; then the numbers increased to one thousand and sixty; then to seven thousand, four hundred; then to sixty thousand plus; and then to one hundred and fifty thousand plus men – between one hundred and fifty thousand and two hundred thousand men – which was the hugest event I've ever addressed. This wasn't just for one meeting; it was for a complete weekend.

Although it was due to start on the Friday evening, we'd opened the gates on the Monday before so that there wouldn't be such traffic congestion. By the Thursday we already had over a hundred thousand men camping.

It was the greatest moment of my life. In preparation, we

had hired the biggest platform we could find. The pylons reached eight storeys high. We had big screens where we could be clearly seen from two hundred and forty metres away. The screens were not only around the stage but also a hundred metres out from the stage so that the next group of men could also see everything happening. It was a most amazing happening.

Eight kilometres of 15 cm (six-inch) piping was put in the ground for water, showers and toilets. Twenty-three thousand toilets were built especially for the event. Three hundred and forty thousand litres of water an hour were needed for the men to just shower.

We had an earth-moving company that was on the farm for a solid month just building roads. I remember a few years back when, as a young farmer, I would almost have had a nightmare hiring one grader for an hour because of the cost. Here we had graders, back actors, bulldozers, cranes, compactors and JCE riggers literally resident on the farm for a month. They built proper hardened district roads right through the three farms to accommodate the coaches coming from Cape Town, Johannesburg and all over Southern Africa.

Six months before the conference, Joe Niemand, one of my spiritual sons, who has become an amazing Gospel singer for Christ, flew down especially from Johannesburg to tell me that he had been fasting and praying, and God had showed him that the glory of God was going to come down on this particular Mighty Men Conference, the sixth conference we were going to host in the sixth consecutive year. He was weeping when he told me. We just sat at the little airport in Pietermaritzburg for a couple of hours, and then he caught the plane straight back to Johannesburg.

He wrote a special CD, which was ready for the conference. It had taken him twenty-eight days to make, instead of his customary three years for a CD. A full string orchestra and three choirs were employed. That music is truly an amazing soundtrack which God made through this young man Joe Niemand.

He said that the glory of God was going to come down and I agreed with that. We didn't know how. We didn't know whether it was going to come through the music, whether it was going to come through the camp-fires at night, or whether it was going to come through the preaching, but we knew that the glory of the Lord was going to come down. It was so exciting!

From a week before the conference began, I took my food and my Bible, got in a car, and literally went and hid in a forest every morning for a solid week, spending time waiting before God, weeping, laughing, crying out to God, seeking God's face, not even so much in preparing the messages as in preparing my heart. Then, as the end of the week approached, I started hearing the echo through the forest of the cars, the jeeps, the 4x4's, the caravans, tents, trucks and pantechnicons pulling onto the farms every day. It was so exciting!

It was a time when I went through my personal Gethsemane – my olive press. Remember, Gethsemane was where Jesus spent the night before the high priest's soldiers arrested Him.

We had just gone through Easter a couple of weeks before that. I had preached at home, which I very rarely do. I haven't preached there for ages. I spoke to young Marc Porée, also one of my sons in the Lord and the pastor at our church (which is doing so well), and his wife Mandy, and said: "I really feel that I need to bring the message on Good Friday." I really felt very strongly about it. To me, that is the most important day in the Christian calendar.

That morning I was very emotional, as were the congregation, when I shared what God had laid on my heart. God had impressed upon me that the hardest thing that Jesus ever had to do was not so much the flogging, or even the crucifixion. It was in the Garden of Gethsemane, because, at that time, He could still have pulled out! He even prayed, "Father... not My will, but Yours, be done," (Luke 22:42) when He had to drink of the cup of suffering, the cup of pain. However, once He'd made His decision, once He'd made up His mind, there was no turning back and He went through with it. Up to that time, though, He could have pulled out.

That's exactly where I was in that forest. On the Monday it started raining. Remember, this whole event was open air. It wasn't just Shalom Ministries who were involved; it was also the young farmers who had put all their money, all their faith into this project, who were believing God for the men to arrive and for the weather to hold. On the Monday before the conference began, it was pouring with rain and the temperature plummeted right down to five degrees. Jill and I were jogging one morning and there was what felt like sleet against our faces.

It was almost like everything was going wrong. The bookings for the registrations for the camping were done with *iTicket* and they had a special system whereby they would call me every day on our cellphones to tell me how many men had booked in. The men were just not booking in. I think we had barely fifty thousand bookings, and we were catering for two hundred thousand men. I really

24

experienced just a very small – a very, very, small – part of what Jesus must have gone through in the Garden of Gethsemane. Every time He wanted the disciples to help Him, they were sleeping.

While I was in that forest, the devil was saying to me very clearly and distinctly, "This time I'm going to expose you for the fraud that you are. This time you are going to fall. This time Jesus can't help you. This time you've committed yourself and you are going to slip right into a lake of fire." Remember, the men had laid out money, they had given out the concession for food to a group of Christian men, who had by faith brought in thousands and thousands of rands worth of food to be sold at the event, and the news media had been informed. I had the biggest wrestling match of my life in that forest. But I never thought about pulling out, because I couldn't. We were totally committed.

On the Friday there was a breakthrough. The men were coming in by the thousands. By Friday night we had well over a hundred and fifty thousand men already camping there, camping nearby at campsites, on other farms, in school hostels, in hotels, in bed-and-breakfasts. It was absolutely amazing. Men came from all over the world. There were aeroplanes flying in from everywhere. More than eight helicopters were there that weekend.

Friday night came and indeed the atmosphere was electric. They had made a special walkway for me to get from the house onto the platform without being thronged by all the well-wishers. We had ushers who went with us, good men who escorted me to each meeting. Everybody was ecstatic. Everybody was expecting God to do something special.

Again, Jesus had made a decision at Gethsemane. He

was going to go through with it. If we backtrack just a few days, remember when Jesus came into Jerusalem they were waving palm leaves in front of that little donkey and throwing their garments and robes on the road in front of Him. Everyone was shouting out, "Hallelujah; Glory to God in the highest!" It was a time of celebration.

We really felt that. That Friday night was electric. Everything worked well. The sound system was impeccable. The lighting was fantastic. The *God Channel* had agreed to televise all four services – Friday night, Saturday morning, Saturday night and Sunday morning – live to the whole world. Something I never even dreamed would have happened ten years ago.

I got up, preached my heart out that night, and then saw something I've never seen thus far in my life before. When I prayed for a recommitment, every one stood to their feet as one man, like a soldier in a regiment, and repented before God. I asked the question: "If this is the first time in your life that you have publicly accepted Jesus Christ as your Lord and Saviour, please, will you raise your hand?" Over a third of those men raised their hands.

I've been preaching the Gospel for thirty years. Never in my life have I ever seen anything like that. It was absolutely mind-blowing what God did that night. There was weeping. We prayed for the sick – and as I looked out over the sea of faces, the crowds literally disappeared from sight. It was dark at night but there were lights, banks of lights. You just saw men, and men, and men, and men, going right into the distance.

That night was the most amazing night and I couldn't sleep. Maybe many men didn't sleep, because it was so exciting. I couldn't wait for the next morning. But that night I came down with a fever. I was lying there in a pool of perspiration. Jill was concerned for me. I asked her to pray for me and by the morning the fever had left me.

I got ready, I had my sword (my Word of God), my black hat, the cowboy boots that I'd been given as a beautiful gift by the men of Australia at the beginning of their Men's Conference just a few weeks before, I put my western shirt on, and off we went. It was absolutely thrilling to see the joy and the happiness in men's faces; definitely a "God time".

I got up and preached that morning to the "sons of promise" on: How do you get more faith? I'll never forget it. How could I? There were three main points: Number one, by spending time in the Word; number two, by being prepared to go through hardship, tribulation, if necessary, to grow. Little did I know what was going to happen literally an hour later! And number three, to know Him more personally and to know the person of Jesus Christ.

When I'd finished, we again saw multitudes of men responding to the Gospel; we saw joy, we saw weeping. I went down the stairs, off this huge platform. Huge – sixty metres by sixty metres! Underneath the platform they had cordoned off a special area with double-thick shade cloth drawn around the poles for a bit of privacy, a place where we could just wait and rest before preaching.

I'd asked some visitors, thirty-three of them to be exact, who had come just for that weekend all the way from Australia, the other side of the world, to come and meet me underneath the platform so that I could have a word of prayer with them for a few minutes, and to say thank you for coming all that way. They came in. I was hot. It was very, very hot at that time and there wasn't very much air inside the enclosure. It wasn't just a prayer the men wanted; they wanted me to anoint them, they wanted the mantle that God had given to me, just like Elisha asked Elijah for the mantle. They were weeping, as I was. It was an emotional time.

I finished praying for each one and said, "Chaps, I've got to go now, because I've got to get ready for the afternoon message." I started to walk out of that room and suddenly felt light-headed. At that very moment Andy, my oldest son, had just come off the platform, down the same steps. They'd played the last song before the men left to go to their camps for lunch, and as he came down the steps, I walked out of the room and collapsed. He caught me in his arms. He thought that I was dying. My eyes rolled back and I didn't know where I was.

When I came to, I was perspiring profusely. I was nauseous, I was sick; I didn't know what had happened. I thought maybe I'd just passed out. They had called in doctors, and I could see that they were very worried. There was a young Zulu doctor, Dr Thobeko Ntuli – a wonderful young man of God and a member of our congregation – and Dr Visser, another wonderful man of God all the way from Tzaneen right up on the South African/Zimbabwean border, who had come to my aid. Not to mention the paramedics, including Hans Hartmann. They gave me oxygen, stabilized me for the trip and put me in the car. I took my mask off and shouted, "Amen! I'll see you guys at five o'clock!"

With that, they took me off to my house, about four hundred metres away. I asked Andy to go ahead and just prepare Jill so that she wouldn't get a fright, to tell her that I'd just fainted but that I'd be fine. I walked down the path to the little garden gate at the back and sat down. She brought me a cup of tea. I drank half the cup and collapsed a second time. This time I wasn't coming around. I lay on the grass.

My dear friend, literally one half-hour before that, I was standing on the platform speaking, preaching my heart out, the thing I love the most, to the biggest crowd of men I've ever seen in the world. Now I was lying on the grass like a helpless, newlyborn babe, unable to do anything but fully conscious of what was happening around me. My eyes were wide open and I could see everything. I could hear everything, but I couldn't do anything for myself.

My dear wife, my best friend whom I love so dearly, came and took hold of my hand. I'm so proud of her! She didn't break down, she didn't become hysterical. On the contrary, she just kept reassuring me. The love that I experienced from my family, from my children, Andy, Rochelle, Fergie, Robyn, Jilly, Greg, Dougal and, later on, Lindy and Ashleigh, who weren't there at the time but came to the hospital – I've never experienced anything like it before in my life.

I was lying on that grass. The men were called straight back from their tents and about two hundred thousand men returned. They'd been told that I'd collapsed and had had a possible heart attack, and they were ready to pray. I heard men singing. I heard men weeping. I heard men shouting: "Amen! Don't worry Angus; God's going to do it!" Thousands upon thousands...

They rigged up a makeshift field hospital right there on the grass and began to monitor my heart, my blood pressure, only to see it start slipping away. In desperation they took raw adrenaline and pumped it into my veins, and it seemed to bring me back again. Then it happened a second time.

In the meantime they'd ordered a helicopter from

Durban, which is two hours' drive by car away from the farm. It landed literally outside our garden. The paramedics – amazing men and women of God, angels, in fact – cut right through the fence of the garden, brought the stretcher in, put me on it, strapped me down, and talked me right through everything.

By this time, my family was very concerned. They thought I was dying, and I think l was. I think I was standing at the Gates of Glory. I want to say to you, to any believer who has any fear of death: Do not be afraid. For a believer, when you die there is no pain. I experienced no pain whatsoever, only peace.

They put me in the helicopter. It took them fifteen minutes to fly me from the farm to the actual hospital in the city. As that helicopter took off, I'll never forget stretching my head up, trying to look at the men, giving them the thumbs up, and seeing thousands and thousands of men weeping and praying, with their hands raised up towards the red helicopter that was airlifting me to hospital. I'll never forget that sight as long as I live.

I firmly believe with all of my heart that in the fifteen minutes it took from the time I left my little house on the farm to the time that I touched down at the helicopter pad in the hospital grounds at Medi-City in Pietermaritzburg, the Lord Jesus Christ healed me miraculously because of the effective, fervent prayers of righteous men and women, boys and girls, all over the world (James 5:16).

At the hospital they put me on a stretcher. That was the time when I felt the most nauseous, because they took that stretcher flat out through the corridor. All I could see was the ceiling spinning past me. Then they brought me into the ICU ward, where I was attended by wonderful nursing sisters.

The cardiologist, the specialist, Dr Baig, is a wonderful man who had a tremendous presence of peace about him. He asked me questions:

"Is there any pain?"

"What did you feel?"

I answered them. I explained there was no pain.

He did tests on those big screens and said, "There's nothing here. I can't see any damage to your heart."

He then got me onto a treadmill. He had me running, walking on an incline treadmill for maybe ten or fifteen minutes. He said, "There's nothing wrong with you whatsoever! I'm going to do some blood tests and you can go back to the farm."

While I was in the hospital, the meetings on the farm had not stopped, and I thank God for that. My son Andy, who was doing the praise and worship, got up on the platform and said, "Dad's not here. But we didn't come here to listen to Dad; we came to hear from God, so we're going to carry on." They had a praise and worship evening, which I believe was unbelievable. Many men had a complete turnaround in their lives that night.

That evening they took me back home to the farm. Jill was just so grateful to God that her husband had come back, because a lot of them didn't think they'd see me again when the helicopter took off. I said to my family that I wanted to preach the next morning. My children asked me very seriously, "Please don't do it; just rest. You've had a heart attack, maybe two."

I said, "Well, I must just greet the people."

The next morning the service was due to start at nine o'clock. At half past eight I was driven in a car (my family would not allow me to walk!) to the platform. Again, I've never experienced anything like that in my life; a human tunnel of men and young boys clapping, whistling, shouting and chanting the name "Jesus! Jesus! Jesus!" and slapping the car, shaking my hand through the window; some weeping; others laughing, pleased to see me back.

I went inside and underneath the platform, the same place where I'd collapsed the first time. Andy said to me, "Dad, get up on the platform, say goodbye to the guys, five minutes. Come down and then we'll start the service."

I said, "No, son, you've got it wrong. You get up on the platform, you lead them in the praise and worship, you can have a testimony from the doctor, then Joe is going to sing his song, and then I'll preach."

I preached for twenty to twenty-five minutes, from my heart. I told the two hundred thousand men, women and children – because women and children, as usual, joined the men on the Sunday morning – that I have come of age and that for the first time in my life I've realized what the brevity, the briefness, of life means. I was very emotional, weeping. I said, "God has given me a second chance." I remember using the Scripture: "Unless a grain of wheat falls into the ground and dies, it remains alone; but if it dies, it produces much grain" (John 12:24).

I told them that this is not the time to have grievances against your family, or your fellowman. I told them how, right at the end of the last chapter of the Bible, in the Book of Revelation, I had written in the margin: "Keep short accounts with God and with man, for the time is now very short." That morning we all got on our knees on the grass and we prayed together. That was a turning point in my life.

Afterwards, I went home. There was a tremendous sense of peace at Shalom as the men began leaving, trekking their way back home, some to the Karoo, others to the big cities, some to the Cape, others to the maize-growing area of North West Province, many to KwaZulu-Natal, and all over. Black, white, coloured and Indian, all going back to take peace with them; to speak to their wives and tell them that they love them – unconditionally; to ask forgiveness; to do the "kneeling thing"; to ask their wives to give them a second chance; and to tell their children how much they love them. We've been inundated with phone calls and e-mails and letters. Thousands upon thousands of lives changed forever, because men of promise have come of age.

Hans Hartmann, one of the paramedics attending to me, has given his testimony, which I want to share with you here:

Impressions of a Medic
MMC 09 – 28 April 2009

Three months ago, the deal was finalized. I would supply the medical cover at this year's event. I was competing against a rival company and was prepared to equal their quote for three vehicles on site. I would promise three vehicles, but would throw in a field hospital; two quads and ten outstations, at the same price. These would be manned from Friday morning to Sunday night. Having done the event last year, I knew what I was letting myself in for. After all, last year we had 65,000 men attending, and we coped with them – with our ten medics, all volunteers. With the 200,000 expected, we would have many more volunteers, and the money we would be paid would cover our disposables and travelling expenses, as well as our meals. I planned to discount whatever we did not spend, as this was an event I would not do for money...

Three days to go. I have not slept very well for the last three weeks. I have searched high and low for medics, but have only three; myself and one ambulance crew that I am standing down from my operations. I phone my stepson, who is one of the ambulance staff, and plead with him to find me more staff. Even the medics who attended last year have pulled out. I have phoned my competitors and asked them to take over the event – assuring them that the exposure they will get far exceeds the little money they will get paid. Again I am turned down.

Then I receive an SMS from my stepson:

"DEPEND ON IT – GOD KEEPS HIS WORD. DOUBT IS A DEMONIC DETOUR. WHEN YOU GET TO WHERE GOD WANTS YOU TO BE, HIS PROVISION WILL ALREADY BE IN PLACE. NO TURNING BACK."

OK, but I have already prayed and asked... I am now in panic mode, and I change my requirements from Christian male volunteers to Christian male medics who will be paid, and eventually to any male medic who is prepared to work for money. This will be financial ruin, but I no longer care.

One day to go. Thursday morning I receive a message that my North Coast manager has managed to find some medics, as has someone in Durban, and five are available in Pietermaritzburg. I proceed to Mighty Men to set up the field hospital for Friday morning. By sunset the first patients arrive, even though we are only on duty from Friday. Already 60,000 men are on site. My ambulance is dispatched immediately to cover the event during the night, and by sunrise six patients have been treated, all minor ailments.

Friday morning dawns, without any sleep. Two medics from Durban do not show up, two from North Coast and three from Pietermaritzburg. I am left with twenty. Not quite what I was hoping for, but manageable all the same. I hate myself for doubting in the first place. However, I am the only paramedic, and should we have to move a serious patient, the event will be left with nothing but ambulance staff. It will just have to do!

By 10 am the patients are starting to arrive: flu, runny tummy, asthma, allergy – silly things that mean a lot to the patient, but are not what we are trained for. We need the serious stuff to make our life worthwhile... A provincial ambulance response vehicle pulls up with a doctor, required by Disaster Management to be in the OPS Centre in case of disaster. This centre is based about ten metres from our field hospital. The doctor strolls in and introduces himself in a heavy Zulu accent. Great, I think, just what I need, an intern who is forced to do his work at a provincial ambulance service. He promptly announces to the organizers and police manning the OPS Centre that should they require him, he will be at the field hospital, and promptly starts to scratch through our equipment. Anyway, I am too busy arranging medics at the outstations to worry about him at this stage.

By the time I have everyone arranged, stations worked out, instructions given, I become aware that the doctor is the only one in the tent treating patients. I wander across for a closer look and discover that he is not just handing out the few medications we have, but is actually examining the patients with their aches and pains, and actually treating them. "This simply won't do," he announces, and drives off to Greytown and returns shortly afterwards with half the hospital pharmacy, handing out antibiotics and medications that you need to study at least seven years just to pronounce. Wow, now this is what was needed in the first place! In addition, he unpacks ventilators, heart monitors, vital signs monitors, etc, from his vehicle. When the going gets really tough, another doctor arrives to help out. Another three doctors treat patients at the outposts. "... His provision will already be in place!!!!!..."

Friday night Angus does an altar call and sees literally thousands give their lives to the Lord. Awesome! Out of the corner of my eye I catch one of my medics holding his hand up high. Wow, and I wanted only Christian medics here! The night offers little sleep. Some patients need hospitalization. There are some broken bones from falls on the motorcycles, some medical cases, all stable, none life-threatening. When things do quieten down, I am amazed to see medics sitting in small groups, Bibles in hand. Words are falling on fertile land everywhere. Another piece of the Lord's way falls into place. God has a plan with everything. His way, not ours. Why is this repeated over and over again – and again I am still surprised by it?

Saturday morning breaks cool and clear. Soon the heat takes over but all runs well. The medics are doing their job, the doctor is amazing. The service is electrifying. Men are called to honour God, to put Him first, to honour their family. Angus talks of the war that the devil is waging against all believers. We need to be fit to fight the war. He does push-ups, runs on the stage, tells us that God loves us and wants a personal relationship with us, and tells us that God talks to us. He tells us to read the Bible, and makes us promise that we will. "Good people don't go to heaven, BELIEVERS go to heaven!"

He tells us how he has had a restless night, with no sleep. He has had a fever, but after his wife prayed for him, the fever has left him. He tells us that he is tired but must fight the war. After two hours he is visibly exhausted, and after praise and worship we make our way back, slowly, between 200,000 men. No sooner do we reach our tent when a marshal rushes over with the news that we are needed urgently at the main stage for a patient who has collapsed. We make our way back through the endless crowds, eventually reaching the stage, only to find one of our ambulances already there.

I find it strange that the patient is under the stage, but push through anyway. Maybe they needed the shade for the patient. Near the entrance I find an elderly gentleman lying on the floor. He is covered in sweat, already has a drip up, and has an oxygen mask on. I kneel down next to him to assess him, and discover it is Angus. Even lying there, he keeps telling us that this is a war; the devil will attack everywhere. He explains that he is exhausted! Whilst still lying on the floor, he makes plans for the night service. He will take it easy tonight – maybe even sit on a chair whilst preaching. We all know that this will be impossible for him. Even so, we remove the drip and help him to his feet. Outside the stage area, men are praying and singing, and shout and clap when Angus appears. He is taken to his house by car, still weak.

Thirty minutes after we arrive back at the tent, another usher appears. We need a stretcher urgently at Angus' house. No other information. Could be someone who has come for prayer, or could be Angus himself... We fly through the crowds. Security men let us through, and we grab the stretcher and jump-bags before rushing into his modest house. The walls are thick, with small windows, and little light. We are spotted and chased out. Once we get out into the light, we are recognized and sent around the house to the front lawn. There we find Angus, on his side, unresponsive – our Zulu Dr and another Dr at his side. The heart monitor is already attached, a new drip running full speed. I ask the doctor for an update. He informs me that Angus collapsed, and glances at the monitor. One look and my worst fears are realized. The rhythm is very abnormal, with an inverted T wave, typically found with a heart attack. I look at the blood pressure monitor. More bad news, it reads 80/40. The oxygen mask is already on, with all holes masked up to try and increase the concentration of oxygen delivered to Angus.

I have seen this many times before. I know what happens next. These are the precious few seconds we are given to prepare for the inevitable. CPR is just seconds away. Angus has already received his Disprin and TNT Spray to dilate blood vessels around the heart and assist with the breaking down of blood clots. He is deeply unconscious. I know the drill, so I pull out my drug bag and break open the resuscitation drugs we will need shortly; adrenaline in one syringe, atropine in another, calcium gluconate in a third. To counteract acidosis that occurs during CPR, I set up the sodium bicarbonate drip, but don't attach it yet. Angus is still going, barely, which gives me a chance to select the tube that will shortly go down his throat to assist in his breathing. I check the equipment to do this with. He is still going, barely. I pull out the paddles from the heart machine, and place the gel next to it. This will be needed to deliver the shocks to his chest to attempt the restarting of his heart. At this stage Angus' blood pressure remains low, despite the drip running full out. I select another, smaller, drip and add four ampoules of adrenaline to it. Sometimes this helps to increase the blood pressure. It seems to be working. His blood pressure climbs slowly to 100/60, still dangerously low, but better.

Now we need to decide on how to move him to a specialist as quickly as possible. A helicopter has already landed, but a quick inspection shows that we cannot lie Angus down anywhere inside the cramped aircraft, and his condition is too critical to take a chance. A medical helicopter is required, and is summonsed. How lucky that I know the manager personally, and can dispense with all formalities of protocols and guarantees of payments. Is this luck? The helicopter leaves immediately.

In the distance, I hear the call over the massive speakers for the men to get together and pray. Tens of thousands heed the call and move in that direction. Thousands more collect around Angus' house. Loud prayers are heard everywhere. I am acutely aware of the chill in the air, the clouds that are suddenly building up. "THIS IS WAR" keeps going through my mind. If this is a war, I am living in the middle of it. This servant of GOD is being struck down.

Angus slowly regains consciousness. His family

is by his side. There is no panic, no fear. I have never experienced this before. They are just by his side, holding his hand. Such peace. There is no doubt in anybody's mind that Angus is about to meet the Lord. The helicopter lands and another paramedic jumps out. Caleb, one of the best paramedics I know – and trust. After a quick handover, Angus is loaded into the helicopter and takes off. I can still see his face, straining to look out, waving with both hands.

I feel exhausted, and spend a long time picking up the medical waste. With a heavy heart, I go back to the tent. I am dismayed at the number of people packing up their tents and leaving. At the same time, I have no doubt that Angus will not be back soon, if at all. However, I know that I am not here to meet Angus. I am here to meet Jesus. That night, rumours spread that Angus has been discharged. However, I know better. I was there, I had seen the cardiac rhythm, had seen the low blood pressure, and had personally infused the adrenaline. Either way, I attend the night meeting, and find peace and joy in knowing God.

The next morning I am summonsed to set up a station under the stage. Angus will preach! How can that be? Obviously he has forced himself out of hospital, and barely clinging to life, will now attempt a sermon in spite of his condition! How wrong I am. He arrives with his family and friends, is full of life, kneels and prays before going up to the stage to present his sermon. He talks of his day lying helpless on his lawn, and asks if we are ready to meet the Lord? He was close to meeting Him yesterday, but he was healed. The cardiologist ran stress tests; they ran blood tests, and every other conceivable test. Final diagnosis: NOTHING. NO ABNORMALITIES DETECTED. No abnormal chemical levels, no traces of heart damage, NOTHING. He is discharged three hours after arriving at the hospital. Either I need to go back to study, because after twenty-five years I have no idea what I am doing, or accept that God is capable of great miracles. Personally, I believe the latter.

Angus preaches, and many more give their lives to the Lord. It is a war, and those that left before Sunday, are the casualties of this war. Those that stayed saw the greatness of our God. Those that came to meet Angus were disappointed. Those that came to meet God met Him.

Sunday afternoon comes, and we pack up. We are exhausted, but feel alive. My body tells me it's been through hell. Every joint aches; every muscle complains. It feels like it's been at war. My soul is alive and on fire. God is mighty, He is good. I pay my medics. Total cost? EXACTLY the amount quoted three months before the event!!! Travelling costs, meals and disposables will be recovered from the few ambulance transfers done by the ambulance. "... His provision will ALREADY be in place" just does not want to get out of my mind.

At the debriefing we hear testimonies of men whose businesses back home improved dramatically whilst they were serving at Mighty Men. We hear of SMSes of impending danger that were received before Angus' collapse, people phoning from around the world with prayers and words of encouragement. What an awesome GOD we serve! We are warned of the devil's attack in the week to come, where he will try and destroy all the good that has been done. Already there is talk of Angus having *been flown to hospital with a stroke; that this is done only for money, etc. The devil is at work, and THIS IS WAR. OUR GOD IS GOOD... ALL THE TIME!!!!*

In total we treated close to two hundred patients. Dr Ntuli was awesome. The experience was great. It allowed me to serve with the gift that God has given me. It allowed me to grow in my faith. Would I do it again? ANY DAY! Should we do it again? The devil will have won the battle in the end if we don't.

Hans Hartmann
Paramedic
Believer

Just the other day Jill was reading that it's only through fiery trials that the salt of a man comes out. It's only through times of severe testing that our character is, in fact, built up. Some people preach that if there's sickness there must be sin. That's not always the case. Even Jesus spoke about it when He healed the man who was born blind (John 9:1–12). When the disciples asked Him who had sinned, the man or his parents, Jesus said that none of them had sinned. Jesus Himself suffered more physically, as well as mentally and spiritually, than any other person who has ever lived.

Just as happened to Simon Peter, I can honestly say that that weekend, the highlight of my life to date, not only brought me to my knees, but also to maturity. Simon Peter realized that without God he could do nothing. When I lay on the lawn that Saturday afternoon, I knew that I could do nothing. There were two hundred thousand men who had come to hear the Gospel. I was incapacitated. I could do nothing. I came of age. I realized in an instant: God, if You don't do it, it's not going to happen.

Of course He did it! Not only did He do it, but He completely healed me. They tell me that when some men have a heart attack – and I had possibly two – they are out of action for up to six months. Some never recover. I was back home within three hours, totally restored. I have come of age. My life is only starting to count now.

As I am writing this book, I have taken a couple of weeks' rest. I am sitting down at the beach in a little beach cottage surrounded by natural trees and bush, looking out at the vast ocean. Most days Jill and I have got up and sat on a deck overlooking the sea, drinking our tea as the sun comes up, literally out of the sea, in the east. It is totally different every day. It is beautiful. Some mornings it is blood-red, other mornings it's camouflaged by the clouds, and then it starts showing rays of light that look like a crown. Yet other days, it comes out of the ocean like a ball of fire.

But I have realized, as have my wife and family, that every single day is a gift from God. Every day that sun comes out of the sky – and it's been doing that for me for the past sixty-one years – and I've only now realized what a gift and what a blessing it is. When you come of age, you stop complaining and start thanking God for every thing that He has given you, indeed for every breath that you breathe.

I have realised that God's ways are not our ways. His thoughts are not our thoughts. When I reflect back on that awesome event, the 2009 Mighty Men Conference, there was a depth of brokenness and repentance and a move of the Holy Spirit which one cannot explain. In fact, when speaking by telephone to a number of men throughout the nation, they have said that when other men, who couldn't make it to the conference, have asked them what took place and how it impacted their lives, they become dumbstruck. They cannot explain what took place.

There are no words to explain what the Holy Spirit did that weekend. All we know is that the fruit that has been borne through that weekend is revival. Newspapers, secular magazines, not to mention Christian magazines, have carried articles where men have said their lives have been transformed. What has touched me, probably more than anything, is that their wives have written in and said that their husbands have come home with a different outlook in life.

Yes, indeed, many have come of age. I'm talking about young teenagers (remember the age restriction to come to the Mighty Men Conference is that if a young man can ride a horse and shoot a rifle he's regarded as a man – the same qualifications as the early settlers and the Voortrekkers); mature men; and older men, who have all come of age through what God did on that memorable weekend of 24–26 April 2009.

I spoke to some of my close confidantes and told them that if I could have preached the four best sermons that I've ever preached in the entire span of my preaching ministry, a period of close on thirty years, I could never have had the impact, or even a part of the impact, that that incident had on our lives that weekend. Everybody has been unanimous about that.

I do not believe that the devil tried to kill me that weekend. I do believe that God allowed that situation to take place so that we could come to a state of brokenness and realization of just how short this life is, and to understand what the brevity of life means.

Peggy O'Neill, that faithful old intercessor of ours who

has been with me since our work began, is a lady who understands what suffering really means. Even as she prays for me now, she prays from a wheelchair because she has had one leg amputated due to diabetes, and the other leg is not strong. She suffers from cancer, from high blood pressure and from many other ailments, and yet she is indeed one of the most beautiful people I have ever known in my life.

She wrote me a lovely card, which I cherish and keep in my Bible, the type of card that older ladies write. It's a card that's got frills all round the side, and lovely sunflowers on the outside, and a little angel with his hands lifted up towards the Lord. In it she says, "Hi, Buchan-Hare." I need to clarify that. We've had a standing joke between the two of us for many, many years relating to the story about the tortoise and the hare. She is a spiritual mother to me and senior in years to me. She has observed my lifestyle and calls me Buchan-Hare because I'm always running flat out all over the place. She's steady and just keeps on faithfully plodding along but she always seems to get there before me.

The card continues: "We serve a faithful God. I understand only too well, Buchan-Hare, when you said you've come of age. The same thing happened to me a short while ago on the trip I had back from the UK. God has given both of us a second chance." Then she said something very interesting. She quoted something that we have said for many, many years at Shalom: "One genuine miracle equals a thousand sermons."

I believe with my whole heart that's exactly what took place on that weekend when we, approximately two hundred thousand men, came of age. The devil also tried to do a very foolish thing. He tried to eliminate me from the Mighty

Men Conference, thinking that it would be destroyed. But through that apparent tragedy, came goodness. It worked in exactly the opposite way, as it always does, because the Bible says that all things work together for the good of those who love the Lord and are called according to His purpose (Romans 8:28). I was taken out of the equation for a few hours and the conference went on from strength to strength. You see, the conference actually had nothing to do with me. It was all about God and He was in full control. He healed me miraculously. And as a result He showed those men – the future leaders of our nation and the world – that He is a miracle-working God.

I read somewhere that the definition of success is failure turned inside-out. God takes a supposed failure and turns it into a success.

The story is told of a man who was sitting at his desk. On the window-sill there was a cocoon. Inside the cocoon was a beautiful butterfly trying to emerge. He looked out and saw the other butterflies flying around in the garden, they were magnificent. The colours in their wings were brilliant, especially when they were caught in the sun. He watched this beautiful insect trying to get out of the cocoon but the opening seemed to be too small. He sat at his desk and watched for hours as this little insect tried to get through the restricted opening.

He thought he would help it a little, so he took a pair of fine scissors and slit the opening, ever so slightly, so that this beautiful butterfly could come out. Within a few minutes, it emerged and started to crawl on the window-sill. It stopped, lay in the sun for a few seconds, then tried to fly but couldn't. Eventually it fell off the window-sill and perished.

The man was quite distraught. He didn't know what had happened until he realized that God has created these insects so that they need to struggle and undergo immense pressure as they go through the opening of the cocoon. The blood is then pressed into the wings through the pressure that the insect experiences while coming out of the cocoon. This is what gives life to those wings, so that it can fly away. This poor man, in his efforts to help the struggling insect, had actually killed it in the process, because the lifeblood couldn't get through to the wings. It couldn't fly and so it died.

Many a time we ask: "Lord, what is going on? Lord, how could You allow this to happen?" That's what they said about Jesus Christ when He died on the Cross. All His followers thought that that was the end of it. But, you see, He had to die for your sin and mine, so that we would have an opportunity to escape the clutches of eternal damnation and hell. That is why Jesus said to His Father: "Father, not My will, but Your will be done." Because He went through with it, that amazing victory took place on Easter morning.

I can honestly say to you that through the trial of coming of age, God has given me new life in my wings. He's given me new insight and I know, trust and believe that He's done that to and for all the men who came to the conference. Many of those men call me *oom* Angus, (Afrikaans for Uncle Angus), a sign of respect. Some of them are even older than I am, and I am deeply honoured by that title. Out of a potential disaster, out of a potential failure of the whole conference, in God's hands, it actually became the tool that changed our hearts, starting with mine, and going up towards every other man and boy who attended that conference, and spreading into their respective families as they went home.

That's the most beautiful thing about Christianity. I've heard some people call it the upside-down Gospel, because the Lord says that if you want to become great, you must become the least. If you want to be blessed, you must be a blessing to others. If you want to be first, you must be last. I've seen that so many times. So often it's not the man on the platform that's the instrument of God, it's the others who are quietly getting on with the job behind the scenes.

Someone I have always esteemed very highly is a man by the name of Brian Oldrieve, who operates out of Zimbabwe. He's a mature man who has also come of age. I've had the privilege of meeting him on a few occasions. He owned a number of farms when the land takeover by the war veterans took place in Zimbabwe. He also had a Bible College and an agricultural college. He was doing tremendous work with the emerging farmers, teaching them how to plough and how to cultivate their crops.

He was thrown off his farm and threatened with death if he returned. Before he left, though, he taught those very people who had thrown him off his farm how to use his irrigation pumps, how to operate his tractors. He literally blessed his enemies before he left. It sounds absolutely ridiculous, doesn't it, but that's exactly what Jesus expects of you and me. Up to that point those people were totally blinded, but that man has sown good seed and that seed will bear, and is bearing fruit.

You cannot bless somebody and think: They will never appreciate it. I used to think that before I became a believer: It's a waste of time. They don't understand. They don't appreciate it. But that is a lie. These are things that God is revealing to me now. It is an absolute lie! They do appreciate it. They will appreciate it. They will never forget the thing you did for them. That piece of bread, a cup of cold water in Jesus' name is never forgotten.

I remember that wonderful film *Chariots of Fire*. It's a true story about Eric Liddell, a young man who was running for Jesus. The other man, his main rival, was running for self-gain and also to try to justify his life and his background.

Eric Liddell became a gold medallist at the Olympic Games. He was the man who would not run on a Sunday, because he didn't believe that was the day for sport. He was severely tested on his belief because the Prince of Wales, the future king of England, put amazing pressure on him and told him he would be running for his king and his country. He refused, saying, "No, my King says that I will not run on a Sunday."

Reluctantly, they put him in other races that he hadn't trained for: the two- and four-hundred metres. He ran those during the week, not even having prepared for them, and came home with gold medals.

The part in the movie that really touched my heart and brought me to tears was when he was about to run the final race for the gold medal. He walked up to each one of his competitors from different countries all over the world, and shook hands with each one. He must obviously have said, "May the best man win!" They stood there with their mouths wide open, amazed at what this man was doing.

If you think about sport today, it's all about "win at all costs; psychologically intimidate your opponent". If you look at the All Blacks rugby side when, for example, they're facing the Springboks (and, by the way, I love rugby), and the All Blacks do that *haka*, it's to intimidate the opposition. If you look at boxing, Cassius Clay, also known as Muhammad Ali, one of the greatest athletes of all time, would continually taunt and speak to his opponent and psychologically wear him down while he was fighting him in the ring. Even if you look at tennis today, you'll see that they are continually psyching themselves up.

Yet here was a man who went up and in all sincerity shook hands with every one of his opponents, and said, "May the best man win!" Before the gun went off, one of the famous American contenders at the one hundred metres, who was obviously not running against Eric Liddell in that race because he had pulled out of the Sunday final, walked up and slipped a little piece of paper into his hand. He opened it up and it was a Scripture (Isaiah 40:31), encouraging him, telling him that God was with him: "Those who wait upon the Lord..." With that, the gun went off. Eric Liddell just ran with that beautiful music playing in the background and, as the saying goes, won the race by a country mile.

So often we don't understand why things happen at the time. But, when we look back in retrospect, we can see God's hand in everything. I know, and will continue to believe this until the day I die, that the Lord Jesus Christ had the perfect plan for the glory of God to come down on that Mighty Men Conference. He showed us just how fragile life is. He showed us just how irrelevant man actually is in His plan of things, although He loves us so dearly that He gave His only begotten Son to die for us on the Cross of Calvary. What an honour, what a privilege it is to be just a very small part of the huge plan which God has for our lives!

It's not for us to ask why. It's not for us to question God. Think of Job when he was angry and confused, fearful and unsure. He started to talk to God and to ask questions. God asks him (Job 38):

"Where were you when I laid the foundations of the earth?

"...Have you commanded the morning since your days began, and caused the dawn to know its place?

"...Have you explored the springs of the sea? Or who can pour out the bottles of the heavens?

"...Have you entered the treasury of snow,
Or have you seen the treasury of hail,

"Which I have reserved for the time of trouble?

"By what way is light diffused,
Or the east wind scattered over the earth?

"Who has divided a channel for the overflowing water,
Or a path for the thunderbolt,

"To cause it to rain on a land where there is no one,
A wilderness in which there is no man;

"To satisfy the desolate waste,
And cause to spring forth the growth of tender grass?

"...Can you bind the cluster of the Pleiades?

"...Do you know the ordinances of the heavens?

"Can you set their dominion over the earth?

"Can you lift up your voice to the clouds that the abundance of water may cover you?

"Can you send out lightnings, that they may go,
And say to you, 'Here we are'?

"Who has put wisdom in the mind, or has given understanding to the heart?

"Who can number the clouds by wisdom?

"...Can you hunt the prey for the lion? Or satisfy the appetite of the young lions?"

This is when I realise that in the sight of God we are so small, yet He loves us so much.

Through fiery trials, through the salt coming to the surface, we are able to understand that our future and that of our family, our loved ones and the nation is held in God's hand. When we can understand that, then peace comes upon us. Peace which is indescribable. Peace like a river that just flows over us and gives us that deep joy.

When I lay on that grass, helpless as a babe, there was a peace in my innermost soul, because I was totally out of control. I could see everything, hear everything that was happening round about me, but I could do nothing for myself. Yet I knew that I was in God's hands, because I have come of age!

Chapter 2

There's no fool like
an old fool

I wish to clarify that statement right at the beginning of this chapter because the Bible is very clear that we are not to call any man a fool. In our society today, so often we think that because a man has white hair, because he's a senior citizen, he's automatically wise. Unfortunately it doesn't work that way. I've seen some young men who are mature well beyond their ages, simply because of the lives they've had to live. They've had to grow up quickly because of circumstances in their homes.

I think of my own boys. When we started farming at Shalom in South Africa, Andy was only seven years old. Fergie wasn't born yet. By the time Andy was nine he was already driving a tractor, taking the pick-up, collecting things for me on the farm, not because I was trying to teach him anything, but out of sheer necessity. We just didn't have the manpower. The same thing happened to Fergie. When he came of age he was milking cows, dipping cattle, driving tractors, etc. That tends to mature a man well beyond his age. I don't think there's anything wrong with that. In fact, I think it's commendable. Even now, I see my boys' friends are normally men who are a good ten years older than they are, because a lot of the young men of my sons' age group are still very immature in many areas. Maybe they just didn't have the exposure to responsibility and pressure at a younger age!

I heard a tape-recording of a very powerful sermon preached many years ago by a Scottish preacher with a very broad accent. I don't even remember his name – possibly McGregor. He spoke about a gentleman who owned a mill, run in the old days by a water wheel. Two big grinding stones would grind the corn. All the farmers would bring their corn into the water mill, and the miller would charge them so much a ton, or whatever it was, to grind the corn for them. Of course, as the mill was grinding the corn, the money was coming in.

The gentleman was old and he got sick. He asked his family to put his bed right close to the millstones so that, as the mill wheels were turning and grinding the corn, he could hear them working. Some Christians, who were very concerned for his life – knowing that he was coming to the end of his lifespan and was about to die – came and sat next to his bed and asked if they could pray; whether he had peace in his heart; and did he know where he was going if he were to die that night?

Because of the noise of the old grindstone milling out the corn and making money for him, the old man kept saying, "I can't hear you. I can't hear you!" What that foolish old man didn't realize was that he was going to die that night and the mill and the grindstones, the corn, and especially the money, would all remain behind. Unless he knew Jesus Christ as his personal Lord and Saviour, he was going to hell. But he was too busy making money to be concerned with listening to the people who were worried about his soul. All he kept saying was, "I can't hear you!"

There is a similar story of a man with a concrete mixer. He was mixing concrete and making driveways. He got very old and sick, and was about to die. Exactly the same thing happened with him. They came to visit him. He was sitting right next to his concrete mixer that was churning out the concrete. They were concerned about his soul and asked, "Do you know where you will be if you die tonight?"

He said, "I'm sorry, I can't hear you. The concrete mixer is making such a noise." Such childish greed!

Jesus spoke to the rich young ruler and said, "I want you to give all your money to the poor and come and follow Me, and I will make you a fisher of men." The young ruler declined and walked away. As one man explained to me, he was walking to eternal death and damnation. He was actually going to the grave, but all his money and his riches would be left behind on earth.

One thing coming of age teaches someone is to realize that he's not as strong as he used to be, and he can't do the things he thought he could do before. It is very sad and very distasteful for me to see a middle-aged man trying to mix it, as they say, with the young men, or to see a woman trying to compete with young girls – mutton dressed up as lamb, as the saying goes – rather than growing older with grace and stature. There's nothing nicer than to see a mature lady, well-dressed and conducting herself in that manner, and to see all the young women gather around her, to learn from her.

It's in trying to get through the hard knocks of life that we become patient and realize our limitations. I'll never forget the movie in which a middle-aged truck driver in his mid-fifties, early sixties, who was doing long-distance truck driving, pulled into a diner, an off-road restaurant, to get himself some supper. He had a huge thirty-ton rig, one of these massive American Mack trucks, fully laden.

He walked into the diner and ordered his supper. He was sitting there quietly having his supper and a cup of coffee, probably on the phone to his dear wife, when he heard a tremendous noise outside.

About ten or fifteen motorcyclists – Hell's Angels as they were called – arrived on their big Harley Davidsons and their big road bikes. They parked outside and walked in, full of nonsense. Young guys, young bucks in their leathers, tattoos on both arms, and just looking for a fight. The old man, who had obviously come of age many years before, just sat there quietly minding his own business, speaking to his wife on the telephone and eating his supper.

They walked up and said, "How's it going, old man?" The first thing they did was ruffle up his hair. One of them was smoking and he took his cigarette and stuck it right in the old man's food. Another one spilt his coffee all over him. They all just generally pushed him around. That was the end of his supper, so he quietly got up, went to the counter, paid for his supper. The lady was so embarrassed, so sorry, but there was nothing she could do. She could see these young men were out to cause trouble. They were laughing at the old man and saying, "What's wrong with you? Are you chicken? Can't you stand up for yourself? Don't you want to fight?" He never said a word. He took his change, put it in his pocket, switched off his cellphone, said goodnight to the attendant at the counter and slowly walked out of the diner.

All the young chaps were inside, laughing their heads off, causing trouble, drinking, shouting, playing snooker. Suddenly they heard the huge engine of a massive truck start up outside. They looked at each other and went to the window to have a look. The driver put his big truck into gear and drove over all of the very expensive motorcycles and crunched them into a tangled mess. With that, he gave a good hoot and drove out, up the driveway and back onto the highway.

I suppose I have to repent of it, but I must say that I could see the funny side of that story.

A true story I heard a while back was of a very wealthy old man with a massive Mercedes-Benz sedan, who was driving very quietly on his own down the Marine Parade in Durban, just trying to find a parking place where he could park his car and look out at the beautiful ocean that God created. As he was driving along he saw a parking place looking right onto the sea. He put on his indicator, and just as he was about to turn in, a bunch of youngsters in their late teens in a beach buggy nipped in, in front of the old man, and parked their car. They all jumped out laughing. One of them came up to the window and said, "It must be tough getting old! Sorry about that, old man." With that, they all laughed and walked off down the pavement.

About a minute later they heard the most almighty crash and bang. They looked back and saw that their beach buggy had been pushed right out of the parking place, over the pavement, onto the sea sand, and was totally messed up. The huge Mercedes-Benz motor vehicle reversed and carried on driving down the road. As the old man went past them, he said, "Yah, it's pretty tough being rich as well. Cheerio." And off he drove.

I can't help smiling when I hear these stories but that's not coming of age. What it does do, however, is make you realize that there are limitations. You might not be able to drive a beach buggy or a Harley Davidson, or mix it with the best, but God has a way of maturing us. I believe that as we get older He gives us other abilities that we never had when we were young. He makes us more patient, more understanding and wiser.

To the senior gentlemen reading this book: please don't try that last trick! I don't think the Lord would appreciate it, and I don't think the young men would either. Rather lead by example.

Growing up teaches you to be a good judge of character. My late Dad was a blacksmith, born and bred in Scotland. He came out to Africa at the age of eighteen with five pounds in his back pocket and a small little suitcase, to make his fortune. He got a job as a blacksmith in Pilgrim's Rest, a famous tourist attraction on the east side of Mpumalanga, where the early gold prospectors used to find gold.

He'd only been there a few years when the Second World War broke out. He couldn't get back to Scotland because, with the German U-boats on the go, there were no passages and no ships, so he joined up with the First Battalion of the Transvaal Scottish in Johannesburg. The regiment was all volunteers. He went up into North Africa, to fight for freedom and liberty. He was taken prisoner of war in Tobruk and spent three and a half years in prisoner-of-war camps in Germany and Italy. At the end of the war, when he was repatriated, they sent the young men back to their countries of origin, so he was first sent back to Scotland.

Why am I telling you all this? Because he'd been through much character-building stuff! He had walked past the Belsen concentration camp, where he could smell human flesh being burned in the huge incinerators. He had worked, stripped to the waist, alongside men and women in the salt mines. He said the men and women in there were so thin that you could not tell who was a man and who was a woman. He had seen things that very few people today have seen.

But, through all of that, my Dad was a very good judge of character. After he came to the farm to retire, many a time he would sit on the verandah of his little house, which was directly behind mine, and see people come to visit me. He would never say much, he would just watch them.

Sometimes a man of the cloth, a minister, would come and visit me. Every afternoon I used to go up and sit on the verandah and have a cup of tea or a Coke with Dad, while he drank his beer. He would say to me, "Watch out for that man. There's something I don't like about him."

I would reply, "What are you talking about, Dad? That man is a man of God."

"I don't care what he says he is. Just watch out for him."

As sure as anything, that man would turn out to be an impostor or would let the show down.

On the other hand, sometimes a man would come along who would be as rough as they come: hard-drinking, hard-living, hard-swearing.

My Dad would say, "I like that man."

I'd say, "Yah, but he's a rough character, Dad."

"Yah, maybe he is, but he's a man you can rely on."

Sure as anything, he would be dead on line. That man would be a hard-working chap who kept his word and kept his side of the deal.

I don't think being a good judge of character is a gift, but I think that when one has been around the block a few times, eaten a few bags of salt, and walked this road of life, one becomes very wise to these things.

One of the most humiliating moments in my life was

when, as a young man of nineteen, I had gone over to Scotland to do my agricultural training at the North of Scotland College of Agriculture. Before being accepted, I had to do some practical work, especially coming from Zambia, Central Africa. One of my tasks was to work on a pig farm just outside Aberdeen in the north east of Scotland.

The first thing I had to contend with was the severe winters which they had over there, sometimes working in snow up to a metre deep. Coming from tropical Africa, working outside was quite a challenge at the start. One of my jobs was to drive a small tractor right up onto a mountaintop every day to feed the dry sows (the sows that had been put to the boar and were now starting to put on condition and get ready for farrowing down). They had been left up on the top of the mountain in a paddock in a huge area, and every day I had to go up with this small tractor and trailer and bags of high-protein pellets, and feed them.

One morning I got right up onto the top of the mountain. It was freezing cold. I'd fed the pigs and was about to come down the mountain when I got stuck in a muddy patch. I could not get that tractor out. I need to remind you that I come from a background where I grew up in a town. My father was a blacksmith and we were living in a mining town, so I had no practical experience whatsoever with machinery or tractor driving, unlike my sons who I spoke about earlier on. All I had was my driving licence and I had only got that a year before I went overseas. This farmer could make no plans! I had to walk all the way down the mountain, back to the main homestead, which took me a good hour plus. It was drizzling and I was freezing and wet.

When I got down to the main homestead, the farmer had just arrived in his short-wheelbase Land Rover. He was a man probably in his mid-sixties at that time. In his broad Scottish accent, he asked me what was wrong.

I said, "The tractor got stuck up on top of the mountain."

He said, "Well, it shouldn't have got stuck, because we haven't had that much rain."

Of course, I got quite angry with him. I said, "Well, it is stuck, and I need some help!"

He said, "Don't worry; jump in the Land Rover. I've got a winch on the front of the Land Rover, and I'll winch you out of the mud."

When we got right up the mountain and I showed him where the tractor was, he stopped the Land Rover. I'll never forget this as long as I live.

I said, "Aren't you going to attach the winch?"

He said, "No."

He got onto the tractor, started up the engine, engaged the diff lock (which I didn't even know existed) and just quietly drove it straight out the mud patch; parked it on the dry piece of land, all without saying a word, got in his Land Rover and drove back to the farmhouse.

Needless to say, my face was as red as a beetroot and I never lived that story down for the whole time I worked on that farm. The Bible says in Proverbs 3:13–14: "Happy is the man who finds wisdom, and the man who gains understanding; For her proceeds are better than the profits of silver, and her gain than fine gold." I can honestly say to you that there's no agricultural college that could have taught me some of the principles of life that that old man taught me in that one exercise.

I've been studying the book of Joshua. We hear about the Joshua generation – and praise God for them – for young people who are dynamic and on fire for God and who are going to do great things for God (and they are, by the way, all over the world!). I love mixing with young people, because they are always optimistic, always adventurous and always looking ahead, but we must remember that in order for us to become more useful for God we have to come of age.

Joshua, when he took over from Moses, was not a young man. He was a man who had come of age. In fact, Joshua must have been of the same age group as Caleb, and Caleb was over eighty years old when Joshua gave him his inheritance. Bear in mind that when Moses was up Mount Sinai, hearing from God, Joshua was at the foot of the mountain. He never left Moses. When all of the children of Israel, including Aaron, were busy building a golden statue of a calf to worship, Joshua was waiting for Moses to come down the mountain with the Ten Commandments. No way was he a teenager at that time! After that, the Israelites wandered in the desert and learned hard lessons for forty years.

Right at the very end of his life, when Moses was a hundred and twenty years old, he disobeyed the Lord. And what a hard lesson it was. What a tremendous price he paid for that!

I've often had talks with the Lord and said, "Well, I thought that was so hard," only to realize that our God is a holy God. If we don't obey Him, we unfortunately have to live with the consequences. God allowed Moses to look across the Jordan River into the land of milk and honey, but he was not allowed to go in. It was Joshua who took the children of Israel across into the Promised Land. I was there myself, last year, and can tell you it's a hard country, the Negev Desert, very harsh.

Joshua would have been taught many lessons when he was a young man. When God passed the baton from Moses to him, you can rest assured that he was not an inexperienced young man. He was a man who had come of age, fully mature in every way. Of course his lifestyle matched up to his responsibility – and Joshua is known as one of God's greatest generals.

We look at our precious Lord and Saviour, Jesus Christ; indeed our greatest example of one who has come of age. Even as a young boy of twelve, thirteen years old, he was confounding the high priests at the great temple in Jerusalem when His mother and father couldn't find Him. Yet, at home, He was just Joseph the carpenter's son, and Mary's son. He served His apprenticeship as a carpenter. He helped Joseph in the carpenter's shop. He lived with Joseph and Mary for thirty years before He started His ministry, the greatest ministry that has ever taken place in the world.

Jesus was full of humility. He was not a braggart; He was not one who was always telling everybody what He could do. Jesus led by example. He raised the dead; He healed the sick; He set the captives free; He preached the acceptable Word of the Lord. He took over from where John the Baptist left off, and He set us free.

If Jesus, who is God made man, had to wait for thirty years before He came of age, how much more you or I? Like never before – especially in the technical age in which we live, where we hear of young men who have invented programs on the computer like Facebook, and who have become multibillionaires before they reach the age of twenty-five – much maturity is needed, otherwise things will go very badly wrong.

We need foundations and we need roots. We need to be accountable. There's nowhere in the Bible where you hear of Joshua calling Moses "my mate" or "my china". It was with great respect that Joshua waited on Moses. It was with great respect that Elisha served his master Elijah. He served him faithfully in order to receive the mantle. The disciples themselves walked and ate and slept and lived with Jesus for three solid years, night and day, before they were allowed to go through, first of all, the baptism of fire, which made them salty; and then to be baptized with the Holy Spirit, which gave them the courage and the wisdom to go into all the world and to preach the Gospel. It didn't just happen.

Even at this last Mighty Men Conference, some people would indicate that "you've been so lucky to have been able to organize and to speak at such an occasion." What they don't realize is that it took thirty years of blood, sweat and tears to get to this stage – and we're still not there.

Remember the old story when the young golf professional came up to Gary Player, one of South Africa's great sporting sons and ambassadors, and said, "You know, you're so lucky that you play such a good game."

He said, "Yes, son, it's funny, the harder I practise, the luckier I seem to get!"

To come of age is not just a coincidence or something that one stumbles upon. It takes a lifetime. And even then, we are still very far from the standard which the Lord Jesus Christ wants us to reach.

We all know the story of the eagle and the eaglet only too well. There comes a time when the young eagle has to fly, and its mother starts slowly but surely taking away all the down and the comfort of the nest, and only the sticks are left. Then she takes away the sticks and there's nothing left. Eventually, she literally pushes her young off the edge of the cliff face and the little eagle has to stretch his wings and fly. But she never leaves him. If he falls and falls and doesn't fly, she'll catch him on her wings and take him right back up to those craggy heights again, and do the same thing again, until eventually he flies.

So it is with you and me when the Lord brings us to maturity. Sometimes it's not a pleasant experience. But it's necessary. I've often watched a cow and her calf. After six months, that calf is weaned by its mother. Usually the farmer does it. But even in the natural, a cow will eventually wean the calf herself because she has another calf in her womb, and it's getting ready to be born. She will sometimes treat that calf very severely, kicking him so that he does not drink until she dries off.

Coming of age can be a very painful lesson to learn. It's like the scales fall from your eyes and suddenly you can see. That's exactly what happened to John Wesley. He had a Master of Arts degree in theology but after travelling halfway around the world preaching the Gospel, he still had not met the Man from Galilee. It took a trip back from America on a ship that was caught in a storm and was about to sink. John Wesley saw some Moravian believers, men, women and children, singing praises to God while the waves were breaking over the deck of the ship, which was about to sink. They were ready to go home and to meet with Jesus – and he realized at that point that he was not even saved.

He had to come all the way back to Aldersgate in London. He had to humble himself in a small Bible study. That's where Almighty God met him. He said, "Scales fell from my eyes. My heart was strangely warm." I believe he was baptized in the Holy Spirit. After that experience, he went out and literally turned the world upside down. But it cost him severely. God had to put him through many tests before He released him into his worldwide ministry.

We need to have everything stripped from us in order to realize what's important in this life. Then God can set us free to take on the world for Jesus Christ, just like He did with John Wesley who used to say, "I spend time with God, He lights me up, then I go out and preach and people watch me burn." That can only happen when you have come of age.

Chapter 3
Who will be at your graveside?

Many years ago we were holding a campaign in Swaziland. We had quite a large team, maybe thirty or forty people, and we were camping at Mbabane, the capital of Swaziland, where we were holding a one-week camp at the Somhlolo stadium. We were having a chat after supper and a brother who was a member of the team said to me, "Angus, how much time are you spending with the people who will be standing around your grave when you die?" I was a comparatively young man in those days, almost twenty years ago. It stuck in my mind and I've never forgotten it. It's a question that maybe we can all think about, irrespective of whether we're twenty-five or sixty-five. How much time are you spending with those who will be standing around your grave at your funeral? Quite a sobering thought.

I have had the privilege of speaking to dignitaries, kings, prime ministers, leaders, international sportsmen, politicians, and thousands and thousands of people. But God has brought to mind: How much time am I spending with those who will be standing around my grave on the day of my funeral? If you really think about it, there probably won't be very many.

I believe that when the great evangelist Billy Graham was at the graveside of his wife Ruth, he specifically wanted a small funeral service. Apparently two caskets were made by some lifers (prisoners serving a life sentence) in prison. They were made out of simple plywood. His wife was buried in the grave and evidently he is going to be buried right next to her. He is over ninety years old and apparently he said to that select number around her grave that he hopes it won't be too long before he joins her.

Ask yourself the question, as I am doing now, who will be at your graveside? It will be your spouse, your children, close friends, your grandchildren, if you're old enough to have them, and that will be about it. The rest will be sympathizers, people who knew you from a distance, just coming to pay their respects. When the funeral finishes, they will be the first ones to leave, because they've got to get on with their lives. Those who are nearest and dearest to you will stay on a bit longer, just to try and be as close to the memories they have of you as possible.

In my own life I've come to the conclusion that I'm going to make a determined, conscious effort to spend more time with my best friend, my helpmeet, my wife – whom I love more today than the day that I met her almost forty years ago – and my children.

My younger son loves horses so much, and he said to me the other day that he's looking forward to the day when he can go on an outride with his son and father, the three generations together. Behind our farm we've got some beautiful outrides into forests. We can literally ride for six hours without seeing another human being. It's a very special time that we share together. We fill our saddlebags with breakfast, hot tea and coffee, breakfast sandwiches and fruit, and then we ride for hours. My son doesn't speak readily, but when he does speak it's worth listening to. Sometimes I literally have to wait until he starts speaking, listen to him, and respond. Those times have been very precious to me. He now has his own family and I don't see him as often as I used to. I just thank God for those days. We are still very close to one another and still ride together.

As I'm writing this chapter, I'm looking out of the window of my prayer room, straight across to the place where my late Dad used to live. It's a park home, a small cottage, and he used to sit on that verandah, especially after my mother went home to be with Jesus. He stayed alone in that house. He was very happy there but I think he used to get very lonely. He used to wait for me. Every single afternoon I'd go up and sit on that verandah. Sometimes for ten minutes, sometimes for half an hour, normally never longer than about forty-five minutes to an hour. I just thank the Lord that I did it.

I would say to young men who have fathers who are still alive: Don't waste time on trivial things. You can fix the tractor tomorrow morning. You can complete that particular job on the farm next week. If your Dad's available, go and spend time with him. I would give a million rand to be able to sit and have a cup of tea with my Dad, but I have to wait until I see him one day in heaven.

On that point, I just thank God that I will see him in heaven, because I had the privilege of praying the sinner's prayer with him when he was still alive. If you have a parent, a loved one, who's old and does not know Jesus as Lord and Saviour, please do not waste time, but rather go and tell them about your blessed Saviour, so that you'll know that you'll meet together again in heaven.

Chapter 4

The marriage feast

Recently I returned from England, where I had the most incredible experience. We addressed a Mighty Men Conference in Worcester, in the midlands of England, a very, very fertile and beautiful part of the British Isles. Our dear friends, David and Di Harper of Top Barn Farm, just outside Worcester, hosted the event. They invited us over as speakers. They literally put out the red carpet. They bought a huge marquee tent which could seat two and a half thousand people. By the grace of God, it was filled to capacity from the beginning to the end.

I was so touched because a large contingent of South Africans who paid for their own airfares came across with us. There were some from Namibia and others from South Africa. What wonderful support! That was the first time that's happened in my life.

God did a special work there. When I look back, I can understand why the devil did not want me to go to England. Like never before, he tried everything that he could to stop me. We were told at the eleventh hour that in order to be admitted into the UK we had to get a visa stamped inside our South African passports. It's a new law that has recently come out. We made the application and two days before we were due to leave, my son-in-law Greg, who was going with me, received his passport with the visa stamped inside. No problem – but mine was refused. We had to get into the car and drive six hours to get to the British Embassy first thing in the morning of the day before we were due to leave.

Already there was pressure. When we got there, they said that the reason they did not give me a visa is because I'm of British descent and therefore not eligible to have a visa. I said, "But I have a South African passport!" Anyway, there were lots of complications. By three o'clock that afternoon we were able to get a special visa, which a very kind lady, the assistant consul to the British Embassy, gave me. We then drove all the way back to get ready to fly out the next day.

We got onto the aeroplane in Pietermaritzburg and were flying towards Johannesburg when the pilot said he was terribly sorry but there was a problem in the engine. The generator was faulty and he had to turn back, not to Pietermaritzburg but to Durban, which is another two hours in the wrong direction from Johannesburg. We landed in Durban, very concerned that we would miss our connecting flight to Great Britain. They tried to put us on another plane but there wasn't one. By this time I realized the ploy of the devil. There was something very exciting going to happen up front. I didn't know what it was, but I knew one thing: The devil did not want us to go to Britain.

Miraculously, they managed to fix the aeroplane. They put us back on board and the pilot, a lovely man, made application to fly to Johannesburg via the quickest route possible. It was granted and he flew us straight to Johannesburg. The air hostesses were waiting for us as the plane landed and we, the team, literally ran through the departure gate to the plane, which was on the verge of departing for England when we got there. We managed to get on, literally at the last minute. With all the stressful pressure that was going on I was actually very excited, because I knew that God was going to do something awesome in Britain.

We got to Worcester – which is about an hour south of Birmingham in the English countryside – on a beautiful summer's day. Everybody was really excited, obviously always anxious, because there's no guarantee of anybody coming. I've walked that road so many times before and I'm still walking it!

However, after having a good shower and getting dressed and ready, once again the Lord was faithful. The men started to arrive. The tent was full. The first night was amazing. We had lots of first-time commitments, many healings took place, and from there it just progressed. As the weekend went on, there were more "Amens" and more tears shed.

I always remember that great old revivalist Charles Finney, who said, "Where there is no Mr Amen, and no Mr Wet Eyes, there is no revival in the meeting." Well, there were plenty of "Amens" and wet eyes everywhere. In fact, it was a continuation of the Mighty Men Conference we had had at Shalom just a short while before. Of the two and a half thousand men who were there, approximately eight hundred of them were South Africans. I was so proud of them!

As the weekend came to a close, on the Sunday morning, as always, the women and the children came to join their menfolk. At the end of the service (and I wasn't even preaching about marriage – always about the family, obviously, but not about marriage) an amazing thing happened. Five couples came up onto the platform and said that they wanted me to marry them immediately, right there and then. Five couples! I was absolutely blown away.

Well, we had to. I didn't have my book, which has all the

prayers written out in order and the marriage vows, etc., so I just had to ask the Holy Spirit to show me. I believe He did. We were looking for rings all over the place. The men were on their knees, because I asked them to kneel and propose to their brides on the platform.

Then I married them. I told them that the next day they had to go to the local registry office and have the marriage legally bound, but they could go home as man and wife. That's what they wanted. That's what really touched my heart. We are talking about redeeming the time.

I heard a saying once: The road to hell is paved with good intentions. People are always saying:

"We must do it. We must do it."

"I must give my life to the Lord one of these days."

"I must get married one of these days."

"I must have my child dedicated to Jesus one of these days."

But time runs away. There is no time to waste. We need to do what God tells us to do. That's all part and parcel of coming of age.

I came off the platform absolutely exhilarated. Everybody was laughing, clapping and weeping. It was an amazing event.

Another two couples came up and said that they'd been married in the registry office but they'd never had God's blessing on their marriage. We were able to go through those vows again and ask God to bless them.

One man I will never forget. I'm sure he was a professional boxer. He had close-set eyes, a broken nose, was in superb condition, very, very, well-muscled, but I just saw a softness and a brokenness in his face as we prayed for him and his new wife.

We then said goodbye to everybody with much joy and thanksgiving. Praise God for the team at Top Barn who hosted that amazing event. Just one couple, Richard and Karen Nicol, did such a sterling job rallying all the people, not just from England but from Scotland, Ireland, Wales, and all over. I met a potato farmer who had come all the way from Hungary just to hear the Word of God.

We got on a high-speed train – and when I say high-speed, I mean high-speed. I don't think I've ever been in a train that fast in my life. We sped down to London and were there for the evening service of the *SA Gemeente*, the South African congregation of the *Nederduitse Gereformeerde* (Dutch Reformed) church, which met at London's City Temple. They'd obviously done their homework with their advertising, because the church was packed to capacity. The balcony was full to overflowing. Downstairs was full; the overflow room with an overhead screen up, so that the whole service could be transmitted to them, was full. The minister, Dominee Dawie van Vuuren, is a lovely man of God, who put us up in his own house for the evening before we flew out to South Africa the next day. His own children gave up their bedrooms for us. I was deeply impressed by that.

The service started with some beautiful music. After that, I preached a message on faith. When I'd finished, I made the altar call and everybody stood to their feet to make a recommitment to Jesus, which was wonderful. After I had prayed just one prayer for commitment and for healing, many acknowledged that they had made first-time commitments. The dominee and I closed the service together.

We were leaving the church, which was already just

about three-quarters empty, and people were greeting me, when a young man with a beautiful young lady holding his hand ran up to me. She was tall, with blonde hair, a Croatian. His name was Johan. He was weeping. I can only think that he'd been at the Mighty Men Conference up in Worcester.

He said, "*Oom* Angus, please you cannot leave yet."

He got hold of and was holding me by one arm, and my son-in-law Greg – who had been given strict instructions by his mother-in-law: "As soon as the service is over, you get Dad out of the meeting so that he can rest!" – was pulling me by the other arm. I told Greg just to hold on a bit when I saw the tears in this young man's eyes.

I asked, "What is the problem?"

He said, "Before you leave here tonight, I want you to marry us."

I was deeply touched and said to Greg, "Just hang on a minute."

We went back to the pulpit, to the platform. I turned on the mike and told the people that this couple wanted to get married immediately. The church started filling again and the whole bottom section was full. I asked him to get on his knees and, with tears running down his face, and his dear wife-to-be totally overwhelmed – remember that none of this had been rehearsed or arranged, they were just in ordinary casual clothes – he asked her to be his wife. She, in turn, with tears running down her face, said she would gladly accept.

I asked her, "Why do you want to be married so quickly?"

She said, "Because I love Jesus Christ."

That was enough. There were tears everywhere. With

that, another four couples came onto the platform and asked if they also could be married. We didn't have enough rings. Some young ladies sitting in the bottom section just ran up. In no time at all I had a handful of beautiful, special rings, which were obviously returned later on, because we didn't need them all.

By this time there were couples all over the platform. They were weeping, they were rejoicing, they were laughing and crying. Noses were running; mascara was streaking their faces. You know something? They were totally oblivious to it all. They had come and met with God. They had been convicted by the Holy Spirit that they needed to get married and they really couldn't care who was watching or who wasn't.

All the young people came out from the pews and sat on the floor around the base of the altar area. They were looking starry-eyed at these young couples as the young men were proposing; almost like young people watching a film of *Romeo and Juliet*. I said, "This is like a replica of *Seven Brides for Seven Brothers*," that famous old movie.

There was much rejoicing. Dominee Dawie was running around with marriage contracts. There was a senior couple in the front row. They were experts in marriage counselling and in preparing people for marriage.

The Dominee said, "Would you be prepared to come back on Wednesday night at seven o'clock?"

They all said, "Yes."

Dominee Dawie phoned me a week later and I asked him how the marriages were going. He said that they all came back on the Wednesday night and had counselling. They were in love and were going full-out for the Lord.

When God starts to move, things start happening.

People's lifestyles change. People start getting values. People start putting important things first. That's exactly what happened with those young couples. All in all, that day I married twelve couples.

I came home and shared the story with the people at our little church in Greytown and another couple got married after that service. I spoke at a conference a week later down in Amanzimtoti. At the end of that service, another couple got married. Fourteen couples married within the space of probably about two weeks. It was one of the most special times I've had in my Christian walk. I've been preaching for many years now, just over thirty years, and I've never ever experienced this before in my life.

I said to the young folk, "If your parents phone from overseas," (because the young people who were getting married in central London, very close to St Paul's Cathedral, came from all over the world), "and they ask you why you couldn't wait, tell them: 'Because you don't want to live one day longer out of God's will.' Now you're free to go back to wherever you stay as husband and wife."

People were clapping. Joe Niemand, that young son of mine in the Lord, who goes with me and sings at all the campaigns, came up onto the platform, got a barstool, sat on it and started singing beautiful Christian marriage love songs.

It was the perfect wedding. I could almost smell the fragrance of fresh flowers in that church. There was such a joy, such openness, such a cleansing; such purity. After they had taken their vows and promised to honour God and each other "... until death do us part, in sickness and in health, in riches or in poverty," they were so caught up that I battled to get their attention.

I've married many, many couples since I've been preaching the Gospel; in fact, I took the marriage services of two of my own daughters. But I've never experienced marriage services like those that took place on that Sunday, first of all in Worcester in the tent, and then in that huge nonconformist church that the *SA Gemeente* are hiring in the heart of the city of London.

People were talking about it. The newspapers in South Africa wrote about it. It was also reported in the magazines. Why? Because it was an event, a happening, that's why! Those people have a very unique marriage story to tell their children one day. I'd really like to say that I believe that the marriages of those seven couples will go the full distance, simply because they've come of age and realized about priorities in their lives.

The Bible is so clear about the fact that it's for this reason that a man shall leave his mother and father and be joined to his wife, and the two shall become one flesh. That's what happened on that eventful Sunday in Great Britain. I praise God for those young people who are leading from the front. What an example to all the other young folk who were watching that day!

It's time for us to come of age.

Chapter 5

Time

"There is not a single moment in life that we can afford to lose," said Edward M Goulburn. One area in my own life where I can honestly say I've come of age is that I've started to value time, the urgency of the hour. "Do not say there are yet four months, and then the harvest," Jesus says, "but lift up your eyes, and look, the fields are white unto harvest" (John 4:35, paraphrase). We don't have a moment to waste. We cannot say that we will sort out the problem in our family tomorrow, because tomorrow may never come.

A friend we knew has since gone to be with the Lord and we believe that she is reunited with her husband. He was a wonderful man but unfortunately he had a drinking problem and every now and then he would fall off the wagon, as they say. One night he came home absolutely drunk as a coot in the early hours of the morning, and fell into bed next to his wife. She was so angry with him, she said, "I wish you'd die!" With that, she went to sleep.

She woke up in the morning to find that he was still lying next to her but there was no movement coming from him. She shook him, to find that he'd died during the night. She was absolutely devastated by this. She spoke to Jill and me about it. We had to reassure her and tell her that God understands. She prayed a prayer asking for forgiveness and then she had to press on with her life. She never had the opportunity in this life to say sorry to her husband, that she didn't really mean what she'd said.

Time is an urgent commodity. The author of a book I have recently read says, "Time is urgency." We need to use it wisely, not waste it, and take every opportunity that comes to rectify areas, attitudes, and unforgiveness, because we don't know if we've got that time tomorrow. We must not waste a single moment. In James 4:14, the Lord says: "What is your life? It is even a vapour that appears for a little time and then vanishes away."

Job says: "O, remember that my life is a breath." I want to tell you, when I was lying on the lawn having a heart attack, as the paramedic said I'd had, I realized how valuable and how precious time is. We're one breath away, literally, from eternity all the time, and yet the way some people live you'd never think it. Wasting valuable time, saying things they don't really mean, and then not having the opportunity to rectify them. Rather than waste the time saying things you don't really mean, don't say anything.

I remember my brother once telling me of an old gentleman who was in the sporting industry, importing golf equipment, golf balls and clubs. My brother was a golf professional at that time. He went down to this Indian gentleman's huge warehouse. It was full of expensive equipment. The old man sat in his office.

My brother went in and said, "You've done so well in life. You've made so much money. You've been so successful. Well done!"

The old man looked up at him and said, "It's cost me my health to make this wealth. Now I'm spending my wealth to try and get my health back, and it's not working."

It's so important to use our time wisely. I have very few regrets in my life. The Lord has been so good to me. I have had such an exciting life, but if I did have one regret in life, it would be that it took me so long to start serving the Lord with earnestness and urgency. I was thirty-two years old when I gave my life to Jesus in a sincere and honest way. God has redeemed the time for me. However, I often think of those lost years that I could have used so profitably when I was younger. But we need to press on and use the time that we have left and not cry over spilled milk.

The great English evangelist John Wesley turned the world upside down once he'd met Jesus Christ and was baptized with the Holy Spirit at Aldersgate. He stood five foot six (1.65 m) tall. He rode over three hundred and sixty thousand kilometres on horseback and preached forty thousand sermons in his life. Right up to the time he died at the age of about eighty-nine, his first sermon was always preached at five o'clock in the morning. He said, "I am not careful for what may be a hundred years hence. He who governed the world before I was born shall take care of it likewise when I am dead. My part is to improve the present moment."

That is what we've got to do. We've got to live for the now. Yesterday's gone, tomorrow's not ours, but we can live for today. Even as you read this book, you are blessed to still be able to make a difference in somebody's life by using your time profitably. You might be reading this book and saying, "Well, I've messed up in my life, and I've run out of time and options." No, there's always time enough.

I think of Mother Teresa, a small little lady who stood about five foot two (1.55 m). She was a nun who decided to start taking care of the untouchables, the ones that no one in society would go near with a bargepole, the people lying in the gutter, literally rotting, being eaten alive by maggots, lying lost and forsaken in open sewers. She went to Calcutta and started to take these people out of their miry pit, to wash them, to clean them. She gave them hope.

Some of them would even tell her not to touch them because they were so grossly infected, and their body covered in maggots. They were rotting. But she always touched them, just as Jesus touched the sick, the poor, the lepers and the least in this world. She washed them, cleaned them and put them in a clean bed between two clean sheets, and let them die with dignity. That's all she did.

There is something that every one of us can do. They say that the road to hell is paved with good intentions. Let us not fall into that trap of saying: "Tomorrow. Tomorrow I'm going to do this and that." It never happens. Start today and say:

"I'm going to write that letter to that loved one and ask forgiveness today."

"I'm going to settle that debt today."

"I'm going to visit the man I owe money to and tell him I can't pay him immediately, but I'm going to pay him as soon as I can."

You'll see the difference it'll make in your relationship. Tell your loved ones today that you love them.

You say, "Well, I want him (or her) to suffer a little first..."

Don't do that! Don't make that mistake, because you don't have time to wait. Make that phone call today. In fact, put the book down and go and make the phone call, make that resolution, and then chase it up, follow it through.

There's a famous Scripture in Matthew 6: 33: "Seek first the kingdom of God and His righteousness and [then] all these [other] things shall be added to you." If you put God first, and His principles and commandments first in your life, you'll find that everything else will start lining up and falling into place.

St Francis of Assisi was a very well-loved man of God, who is reputed to have said, "Preach the Gospel at all costs, and only if necessary, use words." I've studied all the great men and women of God. That's my passion. Very rarely will you hear about the fancy sermons that they preached. It is rather more about what they did that made the difference. They used what they had, not what they didn't have.

I think of Mary Slessor, a very famous woman of God. There's a book, *The Expendable Mary Slessor*, written about her by James Buchan. I don't know if he's a distant relative of mine or not, but he wrote her life story. She came from a very poor background in Aberdeen, Scotland, where my forebears come from.

That poor little red-haired Scottish lass went out to Nigeria in early 1876 to preach the Gospel of Jesus Christ. She arrived in one of the most unattractive places on earth, with miles and miles of swamps and millions of insects. Fevers were rife. In those days, according to the local belief, if twins were born, one of them had to be killed. She was responsible for saving the lives of countless children, as she would always rush in and take away one twin and raise it herself. She raised many, many children.

In his biography, Buchan says that the Africans badly needed the help of those rare and precious people, the builders of bridges between conflicting sections of the human race, and Mary Slessor was one of these. The British described her as a tornado but the Africans called her quite simply, *Eka Kpukpro Owo*, which means "Mother of all the peoples". In the front of the book there is a photograph of Queen Elizabeth II, the queen of England, laying a wreath at her grave during her visit to Nigeria in 1956.

What a wonderful honour and privilege to be known by the largest African nation on the continent of Africa! Yet Mary Slessor grew up in a one-roomed apartment with her parents and family. Her father was an alcoholic. She had a terrible upbringing but she redeemed the time. She took the Gospel to where very few men were prepared to venture.

She died at the age of sixty-seven and left a tremendous legacy behind her. There's another photograph in that book of one of the children who she saved: Daniel Slessor, with his two beautiful daughters. Mary Slessor has redeemed the time and left a legacy. She is seated in heaven now, waiting for her children to return.

My dear friend, please don't waste valuable time. "Look at the fields, for they are already white for harvest" (John 4:35). We don't know how much time we have left on this earth before we go home. The secret is not in how long you are going to try and live on this earth, but rather in how much you are going to do with the time that God has given to you.

Chapter 6
Revelation

There's a very well-known verse in the Bible found in Proverbs 29:18, which says in the King James Version: "Where there is no vision, the people perish." In the New King James Version, which is the version that I understand and appreciate more, it says: "Where there is no revelation, the people cast off restraint." The word "revelation" means prophetic vision. In other words, where there is no prophetic vision, the Christians perish.

How is your vision today? Do you have a vision? It's the revelation that God gives to you that gets you up in the morning and enables you to go to work. We have a saying: If you aim at nothing, you're sure to hit it. We need revelation. I'm realizing that more than ever.

When I was a young boy, I remember reading a story from the magazine *VSO (Voluntary Service Overseas)*. It spoke about a young man going into the jungle somewhere in the Far East, in the steamy jungles of the Philippines, cutting out a settlement for the poor people, building a dam, getting a generator going, starting a school. It absolutely enthralled me and I wrote off to them to volunteer my services. I was about fourteen, fifteen years old at the time, with very little education, and no qualifications. That was the revelation, the vision that I had.

That vision was very soon trounced, stamped into the ground, and it died. Whose fault was that? Only my own! I've realized now that the only difference between a person who succeeds in life and one who doesn't, is that the one has a revelation, a prophetic vision, and the other doesn't.

It's absolutely amazing to me to see the types of servants that the Lord Jesus Christ uses to propagate His Gospel throughout the world. He never uses the men and women that you and I would use.

Remember Mother Teresa, the small little Roman Catholic woman, who had a revelation to help the poor? That's all her ministry consisted of: Taking the poor and giving them some dignity before they died. Yet, in modern times, I don't know of another woman in this world who is better known, more famous, more successful if you like, than Mother Teresa. She has been hailed as an example of what God can do through a human being whose heart is yielded to Him. Hers is an amazing testimony of a woman who had a prophetic vision from God and saw it through. That's not to say that she didn't have opposition or make lots of mistakes along the way. But, at the end of her life, she was content with what she had done.

Think of Albert Schweitzer, a doctor who started the huge Lambarene mission hospital in West Africa. He was a very accomplished classical musician and every time he needed funds for his mission hospital, he would go back to Europe, go on a tour and do shows all over Europe to raise money to take back with him to the mission station.

He was dearly loved by the people but he was also criticized because chickens would come walking into the operating theatre when he was operating! He was an animal lover. He didn't even want to kill an ant. People would question him on his hygiene, etc., but that didn't deter him at all. He was a man who did what he believed God called him to do, and he lived a life of total fulfilment.

We need prophetic vision. Habakkuk 2:2–3 says that you must write the vision down; you must make it plain, so that others can run with it. But first of all, you must have a burden for the revelation that God has given to you. If you don't have a burden, a desire, it will never come to pass. Look at Habakkuk 1:1. It says: "And the burden which the prophet Habakkuk saw..." That burden is translated as vision.

At Shalom we have a burden for young children who have no families. That burden, that vision, that dream, has become a reality. We now have a children's home and our first children are actually graduating from school. We are so proud of them! Our eldest boy is an accomplished musician and a composer. Another of our boys has won his provincial colours for rugby. There is another boy who I believe is possibly going to give Usain Bolt, the fastest man in the world, a good run for his money one day. This young boy is just barely a teenager but is beating everybody at the high school in running. And so it goes on.

You must remember one thing which is very important. You need to get your prophetic vision, your revelation, from God, not from man. At Shalom we have a saying: A good idea is not always a God-idea and a need does not justify a call. In other words, we must hear from God and do only what He has told us to do. Then it will come to pass.

It doesn't matter how big those mountains are that stand between you and the fulfilment of your vision. Remember, God put the mountains in place. He is the One who built the mountains and He will make a way for you to climb straight over that mountain. So that mountain is never too big for you, because God will never allow you to attempt something that you can't handle with His help. But you must have a clear Word from Him.

You can rest assured that many Job's comforters – those who come and tell you that you've made a mistake, and come with a "word from the Lord" to say that you've made a mistake when you haven't – will be the very ones who, when you succeed, will think that you're the greatest thing that's ever happened. Don't listen to man. Listen to God.

Don't cast your pearls before swine, Jesus said. You don't tell people about this revelation, this prophetic vision, for them to come and mess it up, and walk all over it, and walk it into the mud. Keep it very close to your heart and don't allow just anybody to share in it, until it's come to pass.

The perfect example of that was a talented young man by the name of Mike Tyson. He let people come in and take his dream, his vision, his revelation, and literally trash it – and him. Mike Tyson was one of the most prominent and promising heavyweight boxers of all time. He was in a reform school and was already well developed by the age of twelve.

He was taken to some boxing promoters, who put him in a boxing ring with an up-and-coming professional boxer. The youngster managed to go a full two rounds with the up-and-coming professional, which very, very few men would ever be able to do. We're talking heavyweight division. These men all weigh over two hundred pounds (91 kg). They saw his potential. An Italian–American senior gentleman took Mike under his wing, not only as a potential boxer, but as a son. I think he even grew up in his home.

This youngster was amazing. By the age of nineteen, he had had something like twenty-three first-class boxing tournaments with the best in the world and he had not lost one match. In fact, twenty-one of them were by knockouts, some of them in the first round. Two went the distance. He was all set to be the heavyweight champion of the world, undoubtedly the youngest ever.

Then tragedy hit. The old trainer got cancer and died. The young man was without a father, and without a boxing promoter, and he started going downhill fast. His adopted father had said that he would become the greatest heavyweight boxer ever, if he just kept the vision. I don't think he was even twenty years old when he became the world heavyweight boxing champion. That's when the scavengers of this world moved in and took him over. The boxing promoters used and abused him, and allowed him to sacrifice his hard, disciplined training for wine, women and song.

In no time at all, this great prospect in the sport of boxing was history. He ended up biting off part of a boxer's ear, he started getting beaten, which was unheard of before that, and then he was accused of taking advantage of a young woman and landed up in jail with a sentence. He has gradually just gone down and down until today he's not even a boxer any more. It's a very sad story.

In order to see the revelation that God has given you come to pass, you need to be disciplined. I think it was Jack Dempsey, an amazing heavyweight boxer during the Great Depression of the 1920s, who said, "When you're sleeping on a concrete floor in a freezing winter, it's very easy to get up at four o'clock in the morning and go for a eight-kilometre training run, but once you become champion of the world, and you have silk pajamas on and you're sleeping in a beautiful four-poster bed with a comfortable mattress and lots of blankets, it's not so easy to get up in the morning and go for that run." That's why it is so absolutely important to write your vision down, to make it plain, and then to share it with those who are nearest and dearest to you.

That's exactly what happened to me with the Seed Sower, our big yellow Mercedes-Benz truck. God gave me a clear vision. I waited for that vision for six months. Every morning, from four o'clock until twelve o'clock, I remained in my prayer room and God gave me a clear picture that He wanted the Gospel to be preached and Gospel material, in the form of tracts and Christian books, to be handed out from Cape Town to Jerusalem, going up the east side of Africa, and following in the footsteps of the intercessors who had gone before.

I had five hundred rand in my back pocket and I had a revelation, a prophetic vision. I've never had the privilege of hearing God speak to me audibly. There are not many people who have, and have lived to tell the tale. He spoke to me through the Word, through dreams, visions, fellow men, and by opening and closing doors. I got the make of the truck, Mercedes-Benz, the only make that we know of that you can get spare parts for from Cape Town to Jerusalem. The colour was bright, bright, canary yellow. I found out later from a remedial teacher that when a child has a reading problem they put a thin yellow Perspex sheet over the writing and the child can see it so much more easily. He told me the right type of lighting plant and the specifications of the truck. He gave me the exact details.

So far we've got as far as Kampala, Uganda, and we're going to finish this work in 2011. We will be in Jerusalem, by the grace of God, going through the Sudan, Egypt, and into Israel. We'll take a team of drivers with us. There's a platform on the side of the truck, which comes down with a winch. There's a huge lighting plant that will literally light up a small town; speakers, so that the Gospel can be preached; and we have thousands and thousands of John's Gospel booklets in different languages, that we'll hand out as we go.

That vision has increased my faith tenfold. I thought I had faith when I started that project but I soon realized that my faith wasn't big enough. I was continually praying and asking God to give me more strength; fasting and spending time in my prayer room as the accounts started coming in. We value that truck at just on a million rand now, complete with the sound system, the extra diesel tanks, the trailer and the spares, and we had five hundred rand when we started. God saw us through but we were tested to the absolute uttermost. That was for our own good, because through that we've grown.

If you're going to walk on water for Jesus it's best not to speak to the swimmers, because Jesus wants us to walk on the water, not swim through it. It is so important to have the right men around you, men of the same heart, men who are also wanting to walk on the water for Christ, men who are also wanting to attempt great things for God and are expecting great things from God, men who want to lift up the name of Jesus Christ and allow Him to work signs and wonders and miracles through the spoken Word.

You must be in the right state of mind, spirit and soul when you take on a prophetic vision, a revelation, for God. I read the other day that it's so important to have a heart of thanksgiving when one starts to attempt the impossible for God. Lazarus had been dead for four days and they said his body was already decaying in that heat in Israel. And yet, if you read in John 11:41, Jesus was already thanking His

Father before Lazarus came out of the tomb. He didn't wait for Lazarus to come out of the tomb and then thank His Father. No, He thanked His Father before Lazarus came out. It is vital with that vision to give thanks to God before it actually happens.

As I mentioned, just a few months ago, when we were waiting for two hundred thousand men to arrive at Shalom, there was no guarantee of anybody coming. That was the time that I was up the mountain, literally. In fact, I was in a pine plantation just on the border of our farm Shalom, and I was sweating blood. I was in the olive press and being squeezed like I'd never been squeezed before. The devil was already laughing at me and telling me quite clearly that this time it was over. Yet Jesus Christ came through for me, like He always does. But I had to have a heart of thanksgiving. I was thanking Him in advance for what He was going to do, just as the Master did, even though I couldn't see any evidence of it happening.

We must just do what He says and our vision will come to pass. That's exactly what Jesus' mother, Mary, said to the ushers at the marriage feast in Cana. They came to Mary and said that Jesus had done a most outlandish thing – He'd told them to fill all the jars with water. She said, "Just do what He tells you to do." They did, and the water was changed into the sweetest wine that they'd ever drunk.

A heart of thanksgiving makes you express in advance what is on its way. The Israelite army would sing the victory songs before they went into battle. It's like a farmer singing harvest songs when he's planting his crop. It sounds ridiculous to the world. But, you see, the way you build up your faith is by keeping your eyes fixed on Jesus, and not on the circumstances.

I read an article by John Henry Jowett and Henry W Frost, who say that praise is the most vital preparation for the working of miracles, because miracles are performed through spiritual power and our spiritual power is always in proportion to our faith. Therefore, our faith changes things!

Nothing pleases God more than praise as part of our prayer life. God also loves to hear His people praising Him. Although I could see nothing with my naked eye while I was waiting for the finances to come in for the Seed Sower, I started to praise God for what He was going to do. As I write this book, we owe nothing on that Seed Sower.

Because it's a 4x4 lorry, custom-made in Germany, we've been able to have numerous campaigns into Central Africa, right into the bush, where no conventional vehicle will go. It's very, very remote. Just to see that truck coming into a village in these remote northern areas of Zambia, where the borders of Zambia are flanked by the Congo on the left and by Tanzania on the right... They knew we were coming. They carried banners up. We thought it was a huge army coming towards us. We didn't know what was happening. They were coming to welcome us to their district. It was absolutely amazing!

To come of age means that we've actually got to become childlike, not childish, in our faith. When one of my sons was a little boy, if I told him that the moon was made out of cheddar cheese, he didn't doubt it. Neil Armstrong, who walked on the moon, could have told him: "Son, I've been there. It's just full of dust." He would have said: "No, my Dad said it's made of cheddar cheese." That would have settled it. That's the kind of childlike faith that the Lord can work through. The danger is that, when we come of age, we start not living as recklessly as we did when we were younger. God forbid that that happens. We must become more reckless for Christ, who can do all things through those who choose to walk by faith.

Henry W Frost says that once when he was in China, he'd had bad news from home. "The deep shadows of darkness," he said, "seemed to cover my soul. I prayed, but the darkness remained. I forced myself to endure but the shadows only deepened. Then suddenly one day, as I entered a missionary's home at an inland station in China, I saw these words on the wall: 'Try giving thanks'. So I did, and in a moment every shadow was gone, never to return. Yes, the psalmist was right. He says in Psalm 92:1: 'It is good to praise the Lord.'"

We have a favourite saying at Shalom: Good people don't go to heaven, believers go to heaven. The only way that we can please God is to believe on His Son, our Lord Jesus Christ. All the good works in the world will never get us to heaven. The Bible is very clear about this. Jesus says in John 14:6: "I am the way, and the truth and the life; no one comes to the Father but through Me" (NASB). That's very straightforward. Even a three-year-old child will tell you what that means, yet people try to explain it away.

We're not talking about trying to earn our way into heaven. We can't do that, but we are saying that we want to use our faith in a practical way. The book of James says: "You show me your faith; I'll show you my faith by my action" (James 2:18). If you love Jesus Christ, and He has done something very special in your life, you'll never be content again until you are walking on the water.

The power of the tongue is so vital when you are attempting to realize your God-given vision. What you say, is what you get. Like never before, once you're walking on the water, you've got to keep your eyes firmly fixed on Jesus. To take your eyes off Jesus and look at your circumstances is suicide. I'm talking from pure, undiluted, experience. Whatever the challenge might be, when you speak, especially when you're encouraging your team, you need to be speaking God's Holy Word at all times. Not man's opinion and not even what you see with your carnal eyes, especially if you're the leader. You have the vision. You have got to be constantly confident that Christ is going to come through for you, otherwise don't even start it.

When you begin to have a negative attitude and to speak negative things, you are tying God's hands and Jesus can't move. You've got to start seeing those things just like Elisha the prophet's servant, who came out of his hut early in the morning. He looked up at the hills and he saw the enemy gathering together. He was petrified. He went back into the hut and called God's prophet out. The man of God came out and he prayed a prayer: "Lord, let my servant have eyes of faith." When the servant looked up again and he saw the legions of angels from heaven and the chariots of fire, he could only say: "There're more of us than there are of them." It changed the whole situation.

There's nothing worse, nothing more disconcerting or offputting than when you've got men and women around you who start losing faith and start on the numbers game. When I say the numbers game, I mean get the pocket calculator out and work out that we don't have the money, we don't have the finance; we can't do it, we don't have the manpower. As soon as that happens, death begins to come over your vision. You need to stop it right there and then and rebuke it, and get back to the Word. That's why it's so important with a revelation to have a Word from God, because when the going gets tough it's the Word that will pull you through.

God has given me a clear Word to preach the Gospel. I made a vow to God many years ago when the farming was tough. We were going through a tremendous drought and I said, "Lord, if You see me through this drought, I make a vow that I will preach the Gospel until I die." That's what I'm doing at the moment, and I'm doing it joyfully and gladly. You know something? Our farms are going better than they've ever gone before.

God is a gentleman. He will always honour His promise, but make sure that you honour yours! That happens by speaking life and not death over the situation. Even when you don't feel like it, even though you can't see it with your naked eye, you need to know that, come what may, that revelation that God gave to you, that prophetic vision, will come to pass.

The consoling and exciting thing for me is that the Lord seems to have a beautiful habit of choosing men and women who, in the eyes of the world, are complete failures. Of course we know that is because He does not like to share His glory with any man, so He persists in taking the uneducated, the unqualified, those who can't speak properly, those who have no formal training, those who have no formal education, but always those who have a heart for God. In fact, there's a Scripture in 2 Chronicles 16:9 that says: "The eyes of the Lord run to and fro throughout the whole earth to show Himself strong on behalf of those whose heart is loyal to Him." God will use any man, any woman, any boy, or any girl, who is totally consecrated to Him.

That's the opposite of how it works in life. I have

a beautiful photograph before me of the rugby world champions in 2007. Every single one of these men is a magnificent sportsman. They worked so hard to get to the top of their game. There's absolutely nothing wrong with that. They deserve it. Many of them are Christians, too, by the way. However, when I look at this, I realize that in the world it's the biggest, the best, the fastest, the most intelligent, the better looking, etc., that the world chooses. In God's mathematics, though, He uses a person who's normally scared, but is prepared to trust Him and to hear Him; often the "off-scouring of the earth", as the apostle Paul regarded himself.

I'm looking at another picture in this same room. It's of three young men in front of a rodeo chute, with their heads bowed. They're holding Stetsons in their hands, and they've got their riding chaps on. These are cowboys. Inside that chute is a bull that probably weighs just over a ton. He comes out of that chute with one thing in mind: to throw that rider off and possibly even to kill him. These three young men have their knees bowed and they are praying sincerely. The photographer caught them in that act. They know that, without God, they're not going to win; they might not even come out alive, and God is very real to them.

One thing about revelation: If it doesn't scare you, it's not big enough. Why does it have to be so big? Because, when it works, people must know that you and I had nothing to do with it, we were merely vessels. It was all God. He must get the glory. So it's with much excitement and expectation that we come of age and begin to trust God and not our circumstances. Don't be afraid to start trusting God for small things first. As you see them come to pass your faith will grow, and you'll start to trust Him for bigger things.

How big is God? He's as big as you allow Him to be. My dear friend, God does not want any favours. We've got to stop trusting in our own ability and our own finances, and we've got to start trusting in the Man from Galilee, Jesus Christ. He will never let you down and He will never fail you.

Chapter 7
Times of testing

This afternoon, as I'm writing a new chapter for this book, I've just had to say goodbye to my youngest daughter, who is going into hospital to have her baby. It's with mixed emotions that I said goodbye to her. Tomorrow I'm going to be the proud grandfather of yet another grandchild, my seventh, but she's the youngest, she's the baby as it were, of the family. I could see that she and her husband were just a little bit anxious – excited but anxious – because it's another new frontier that they're going through, as are my wife and I.

Even as I write this, I'm so convinced, yet again, that the growing-up period in a person's life has nothing to do with their age. If you remember, there was a very famous song: "He ain't heavy, he's my brother". The song was written by an American, who was walking late one dark night in the East End of London. He saw a young street boy carrying his lame brother on his back. His brother was almost the same size as he was and he was really struggling. This songwriter wanted to help.

He said, "Can I help you, son?"

The boy replied, "No sir, he ain't heavy, he's my brother."

This was a statement made by a youngster, probably not even twelve years old and yet fully come of age. It's definitely the hardships and the trials of this life that mature us.

I know that this time tomorrow, by the grace of God, I'm

going to be rejoicing. My daughter will be well and rested; she'll have another little baby. This will be her second child. The family will be rejoicing but, at this moment, we are in a state of uncertainty. We know that everything's okay, but we also realize that anything can happen. It's only by the grace of God that we can be confident. It is definitely maturing stuff.

I have yet to read the biography or life story of any man or woman of God who's impressed me, who has not been through times of testing. It's not something one can learn at Bible College, or even at university. It comes from the school of life, the school of hard knocks. That's why Paul can say that he rejoices in his tribulation, because "tribulation worketh patience; And patience, experience; and experience, hope" (Romans 5:3–4, KJV). So every time we ask God to mature us, He allows us to go through times of testing. Every time we ask God to refine us, we go through the fire. Every time we ask God to make us more appreciative of the things of this life, we go through times of testing. There is no other way.

My late Dad came from a poor country family in the north-east of Scotland. He was the oldest of seven; he had five brothers and a sister. His sister was the youngest. When he finished his schooling he got a bursary to go to college, but he cashed in the bursary and gave it to his mother to help with bringing up the children, because my grandfather was a farm worker and money was very short and scarce.

He taught us at a very early age to appreciate food, simply because he never had a lot when he was young. We were never allowed to leave any food on our plates when we were small. The golden rule in our house was quite simply: You can take as much food as you like, but make sure you eat all of it. I'm talking about when I was a young boy of five or six years of age. Because he never had much food, he really encouraged us to eat well; simple, basic food that my mother cooked. But nothing was allowed to be left behind. If it was, we were taken into the bathroom and disciplined. Then we would still have to eat it.

My Dad went through great hardships during those terrible winters in the north-east of Scotland, when food was scarce. Often the country folk would resort to taking a few salmon out of the laird's river, taking a few pheasant out of the laird's trees at night, taking a few rabbits from the laird's estate at night. That was how they managed to stay alive in those days. It was literally a matter of survival.

When my Dad came out to South Africa to make his fortune at the age of eighteen, carrying a little suitcase probably not much bigger than a child's school suitcase, and a couple of pounds in his back pocket, he had come of age. When the Second World War broke out and he joined up in the First Battalion of the Transvaal Scottish, it was the closest thing he could get to Scotland. They wore kilts, but I think he was one of the very few Scotsmen in that very noble battalion.

He got caught in North Africa by that wonderful German general, Field Marshall Rommel. He then proceeded to spend three and a half years in prisoner-of-war camps, first in Germany and then in Italy. Many of his fellow prisoners never completed the journey when they had to do that horrific fifteen-hundred kilometre march, in winter, as they retreated with the German soldiers from the advancing Russian army. They died of exposure, of hunger, on the road.

These men had not been subjected to that type of lifestyle before. They'd come from Africa where it was warm, where food was plentiful. They would sell their boots for a loaf of bread. They would smother their feet in grease and try to get hessian sacks, wrap their feet in the sacks and try to walk. Needless to say, within a couple of days they would succumb to frostbite, and these grown men would have to sit on the side of the road and literally die, because they couldn't walk any more, and their friends couldn't carry them for fifteen hundred kilometres.

My Dad and a couple of others made a plan. Somehow, they got a bucket. Using a pole, they would sling it between themselves. They'd get a little fire going underneath, inside that bucket. As they walked along the road they would find a potato here, a turnip there, an old cabbage, and they'd put it in the "pot" and keep cooking. They force-fed themselves and they kept their boots. They kept walking.

At night, instead of lying down in the snow and dying through suffocation, they would tie themselves to trees with a piece of rope and sleep that way, so that they would not succumb to the gentle snow that could lull them into the sleep of death. If my Dad had not been subjected as a young boy to the hardships of survival and looking after himself, he would not have survived that terrible death march that claimed so many prisoners of war. As a result, he had an absolute phobia about the wastage of food.

I remember as a young man in what was then Northern Rhodesia, now called Zambia, playing rugby. I was a wild young colonial boy, probably about twenty-three years old. We had a stag party (a young man was getting married) which was held at the rugby club. It was a great occasion and everybody was excited because he was one of our friends and he was getting married the next day. The beer was flowing, the party was going and the music was loud.

All the men were happy. Then, of course, the alcohol started to go to their heads and they started getting rough. By this time, everybody had eaten enough and drunk too much.

There was a beautiful buffet of cold meats, boiled eggs, sandwiches and food. One young man picked up a boiled egg, threw it across the room and hit someone else on back of the head. Everybody laughed. Except one man. I'll never forget him. His name was John Thompson. He came from Fife in Scotland and had, I'm sure, the same background as my late Dad. He was a blacksmith and an extremely powerfully-built man.

I just heard this voice with the broad Scottish accent shout out, "Who threw that egg?" The music stopped, the room went quiet, and everybody just sat there, literally petrified. He said it a second time, "Who threw that egg?" No one owned up. Eventually the party got under way again and the young man who had thrown the egg walked quietly over to John and said, "It was me." John said to him, "Don't ever, ever do that again in my presence because, where I grew up, we would have given our eye teeth to have a boiled egg. We just never had one." I've never forgotten that.

I think my Dad has handed on that legacy to me, because I cannot stand the wastage of food. The other day I had to restrain a laugh because my second-eldest grandchild, a little girl, Jaimee, came to have some breakfast with Granny and Granddad and brought a few of her friends. She sat at the table and made a loud statement: "Granddad says we can have anythink we like, but we must eat it all." It was nice and loud and clear, so that all her friends could hear it. There are so many hungry people in the world and yet no one will appreciate food until they haven't had any.

No one will really appreciate a loved one either until they

don't have that loved one any more. I've said many times to young men, "Spend time with your Dads while you've still got them. As I said, I'd give a million rand just to have a cup of tea and a chat with my old Dad again.

Our foreman Simeon Bhengu received a beautiful pick-up as a gift from my sons because of all his hard work and service. He polishes that vehicle daily. He can't read or write and he doesn't have a driver's licence but he has just driven past my house right now. Obviously his grandson is driving the pick-up – I couldn't see who was inside it – and he must be driving in first gear at about three or four kilometres an hour.

He is so proud of that vehicle! He has built a special garage for it and no one, but no one else is allowed to drive that vehicle, except a couple of his relatives who have licences, and he sits right next to them. I've never seen a man look after a piece of machinery as well as Simeon is looking after this pick-up. You see, it's more than a vehicle to him. It's a status symbol as well, because he's the only man in our district who has a vehicle of that quality. It is as new and as spick-and-span as the day that we bought it for him. All of his life his mode of transport has been a bicycle, or walking, and now he has a one-ton pick-up, with a canopy on it, that can take him, his wife, his children and his grandchildren to town together in his Sunday best, and not only be respectable, but be looked up to. That's because he appreciates what he's got. The only reason that he appreciates it is because he's had to work for it all his life. Only when you haven't got it, do you really realize what this life is all about.

As my daughter and son drove out of the yard a short while ago, and my wife and I were in the wood store collecting firewood for our fire tonight (it's the middle of winter as I write this), I noticed that my wife got a little bit quiet. I put my hand on her shoulder and she looked up, tears filling her eyes. We know it's going to be fine – but we love our daughter, our son, and our little grandson so much – and we appreciate her so much. They live just up the road from us and she phones her mother every single morning.

Whenever your children are going through a time of testing, it seems to almost be more painful for you than for them. It's another chapter in coming of age. Something you never get used to.

Chapter 8
Long-range planning

I remember fondly a man who played an important role in my life as a brand-new Christian. When I got saved in the Methodist Church, I was required by the authorities to sit what they called a lay preacher's exam. An established lay preacher, who became a very good friend of mine and whom I respected and esteemed greatly, followed me up and told the authorities, "If you force Angus to do a lay preacher's exam, it'll spoil him as a speaker." At that time I had very little time of my own, as I was a full-time farmer developing a brand-new farm and my wife and I had a very young family of five children. I barely had time to preach, let alone to study, and I don't know if I had the ability either!

The authorities agreed to allow me to continue to preach without writing the exams and I was given the title of exhorter, which is probably the only title I've ever had. It's an office that was started in the Methodist Church by John Wesley, and in those days the exhorter used to stand on the street corners and encourage the people; challenge the people to press on and to run the race and finish strong.

This lay preacher had come from a stormy past. God had set him free from alcohol and given him a brand-new start. When he preached, this man always reminded me of a Wild West preacher. He looked like a real western cowboy and I really enjoyed his company.

He died a few years ago. He loved his family intensely and the thing that saddened me so much when he died was that he had done no long-range planning. He left his wife with all kinds of unfinished business, not to mention the fact that she was deeply in debt. There was no proper will put in place, and as a result his children had to gather around and help their mother try and stop the creditors from taking her house away from her. That really affected me, and I realized that we can be so diligent in serving others and helping other people by going into far-off lands and preaching the Gospel – going up into darkest Africa as it were; going across the sea to India and China – and yet, back home at the ranch, as they say, things are not done in a godly and orderly manner. That brings no glory to God whatsoever.

We need to do long-range planning. I find the best example of that in the Bible in 1 Chronicles 22. It's the account of David preparing to build the temple of God. We know that David loved the Lord with great intensity, like few men have ever loved God. He spent most of his youth serenading the Lord with his harp, writing psalms, sharing his heart. The Bible says that David was the apple of God's eye. He was a man after God's own heart. He had such fervour for God and a love relationship that most of us can only envy.

He wanted to build a temple to worship his God. He wanted a temple so grand, so beautiful, that nothing like it had ever been built before, a temple, a worship centre, that people would come from all over the world just to see. The sad news was that God told him clearly that he would not build that temple, because his hands were stained with other men's blood. David had become a warrior king. He had established the children of Israel as no other king ever had before.

I was in Israel just a short while ago and I went into the place where his tomb is. Anybody can go into that sanctuary, because David said that his Father's house would be a house for all nations. So Muslims, Christians, Hindus and Buddhists can go in and pay their respects and worship at the tomb in which David's body is laid, but you do have to wear a head covering and men and women are not allowed to go into the same place. The women go into one area, which is separated by a small little wall, a curtained area, from the men on the other side. But I want to tell you that King David – the warrior king – is revered by the Jewish people like none other.

God said to David that he would not build the temple. He showed him that his son Solomon, the wisest man on earth, would build the temple. But the beautiful thing about David was that he had such a heart for God that he wasn't concerned about his own reputation, or even about who would get the glory for building the temple.

Because Solomon was such a righteous man, God said to him: "Anything you want, I'll give you."

Solomon said: "I want wisdom to govern my people."

God said to him: "Because you ask so correctly, not only will I give you wisdom to govern your people, but I will give you untold riches and blessings."

So, although Solomon actually built the temple, before David died he organized all the raw materials. He got all the silver and the gold and the bronze and the iron together. He got the cedars of Lebanon, almost holy trees; trees planted by God, as they say, felled and moved down into the Mediterranean Sea and pulled along by ship to Joppa, the oldest recorded seaport in the world. From there, they pulled those logs all the way up to Jerusalem, right up to the top of the mountain. He put everything in place.

In Israel, if you stand at the Wailing Wall, you can still see the foundation blocks of granite that were put in place for this great and amazing structure that was built to the glory of God. Even though David never built the temple himself, he ensured that everything was in place for his son Solomon to build it to the glory of God, which Solomon did.

As I've had time to contemplate over the last months since the last Mighty Men Conference, God has asked me, "What have you put in place for the future generation?" Jesus says that we must live for today, because tomorrow will have enough problems of its own. And that's quite true, but I heard one wise old saying: We must live expecting Jesus to come today, and we must plan as if He's coming in a thousand years. We must live our day-to-day lives as if the Lord is coming back today and make sure that there are no unsettled accounts in our life and that we have no unforgiveness in our hearts towards one another, but then plan for the future as if He won't return for another thousand years.

It's so sad sometimes to hear of farmers whose sons literally have to wait for their fathers to die before they can inherit the land which should have been theirs a long time ago. I know a number of cases where farmers live to a ripe old age, sometimes into their nineties, because of the wonderful outdoor lifestyle they have and the good food they eat. When the farmer dies and the farm is eventually handed over to the son, the son is middle-aged himself. He has no more fight left in him because he hasn't been allowed to make decisions, or to take the initiative, and so the farm normally degenerates and just exists. By the time the third generation comes along, there's no farm left. It's been sold off. Poor long-term planning!

I've been told by the Lord, and have obeyed Him, to hand over our farms to our sons, to hand over the title deeds (and the debt!), when they're still young. My older son received his when he was in his middle-thirties, my younger son in his middle-twenties. Yes, as the saying goes, it is expensive to go to school, because there are school fees that have to be paid. But when are they ever going to learn if we don't give them the opportunity? One thing I want to tell you which enthrals me about a young man is that he's got so much vitality, so much energy, so many dreams and passions and plans. They do things differently from men of my age.

My older son is running a huge strawberry export operation, something I would never have dreamed of and didn't even think was agriculture, but he's proved me wrong. He employs more staff than anybody in our district at harvest time. He's doing extremely well financially. He is able to use a lot of his finances to benefit the kingdom of God.

The other son, who has a flair for livestock, can ride a horse and has an eye for a beast like I've never had. That comes from allowing them to take the helm, take the reins and run with it. Of course I'm always there to help where I can, but they come to me rather than me go to them. They ask advice and I give them whatever I can. Not that I can give too much these days, because of the speed with which agriculture is changing.

We have a church on our farm which has a five hundred-seater auditorium. Another spiritual son of mine (we have been together since he was sixteen years old) has also taken the helm. He is running the church. Nothing gives me greater pleasure than to attend church on a Sunday morning when I'm not away from home preaching elsewhere, and to sit as one of the congregation, not on the platform in a big armchair or some kind of spiritual place of office, but just to sit as a member of the congregation and to hear the Gospel of Jesus Christ preached to me, and for me to allow God to minister to me through him. It can be humbling, especially at the outset, but it's wonderful to see how God is using him and his family to bring in souls for Christ.

It also brings a tremendous bonding between yourself and your loved ones, just as it must have with David and Solomon as David began to prepare for his son to take over. That's how God meant us to be. The whole godly plan for mankind is for a father to bring up his son in the fear of God, and then to release him and let him carry on. That's exactly what Jesus did with the disciples. When the disciples met Jesus, they walked with and watched Jesus. Then, after He had taught them, Jesus walked with them and watched them. Then they went out and they did it.

That's exactly how we are supposed to bring up our sons and daughters. First they walk with us, then we walk with them, and then they walk on their own. A father who is worth his salt should always ensure that his son exceeds him in whatever he's taught him to do. It's so sad to see a father jealous because his son is excelling. I'll be honest with you, I cannot understand how that works. My sons ride horses better than I can ever ride a horse, they are better farmers than I've ever been, and I'm believing that my spiritual sons are going to be better preachers than I've ever been. They're going to step out of the boat and walk on water like I've never done before, because that's what long-range planning is about. There is an urgency in these days that is more critical than it was when I gave my life to Christ.

I have just returned from Great Britain, where I saw good people far from God. Edmund Burke, an 18th-century Irish philosopher, once said, "In order for lawlessness and violence to prevail, all that good men have to do is nothing." That's basically what I saw in Britain. Good people, who were far from God. Not anti-God, just not even aware of God. There is such a sense of urgency for lost souls to come to Christ. To see young men who have been gloriously saved preach and live a life for God that is full of purpose and sincerity, is really very warming to my heart.

What God is showing me is contained in one word that sums up this whole chapter. That is "release". We have to release everything that we have if we are going to succeed in our long-range planning. We have to release our gifts. We have to release our responsibilities. We have to release our vision. We have to give it out, sow that seed, so that many others can pick up the torch and run with it.

I think of the great patriarchs who have gone before us: the John Wesleys, the George Müllers, the William Careys, and I see men who, when they died, left nothing. They didn't leave an empire. When John Wesley died, I think he left six silver teaspoons and six pounds in his account. I think he said one pound should go to each pallbearer, those men who carried his coffin, and he basically left very little else.

George Müller was a man through whose hands millions and millions of pounds sterling had passed. He brought up about a hundred and twenty thousand children in his lifetime. You can imagine how much money he must have had available in order to do that. When he died, I think he left a table, a chair, a desk, a bed and a few pounds in the bank. He owed nothing to anybody.

William Carey translated the Bible into many different languages. When he died, there was also very little left in the bank. It's so sad to hear of a man of God who, when he dies, leaves millions of rand in his account in the bank. You have to ask yourself the question: What was he preaching about?

People often ask me who's going to take over what we are doing here when I die. First of all, I don't really know what there is to take over. Secondly, as I write this book, I have spiritual sons all over this world. I have sixty-five, in fact. I write them a spiritual letter every month. I pray for them every day. I try to meet with them at least once a year, because some of them are living in far-off countries like the USA, New Zealand, Australia, Great Britain, Zambia, and all over. I try to impart to them what God's telling me. I know that when I die – because some of them are doing it already – they will continue to preach the Gospel of Jesus Christ. That is all that I can leave them. They'll preach it in their own style, with their own flavour, in their own language, because many of them don't speak English as their first language.

There's one thing I've realized with my own children: They will never do what you tell them to do. They'll do what you do. I've seen that, to my own detriment, many times. It's not even so much what you say, but who you are, that will determine whether that long-range planning will be successful. I don't think we have time left on this earth to write out reams of commandments like Magna Carta. I don't think young people have the time these days to read such documents. But one thing they can do, they can emulate you and me, and they do, for better or for worse.

Our responsibility is to get our house in order. Our responsibility is to show the younger generation, by example, what God expects of us. If you get up at four o'clock in the morning to have your quiet time, your son will do it. He might not do it right away, but he'll remember. Many men have come to me and told me of their fathers who were godly men who used to rise in the wee hours of the morning and pray and read their Bible, even by candlelight sometimes, yet they themselves have gone off at a tangent to the far country, only to come back and to remember what their fathers did.

I've just been reading again about one of my role models, Dr David Livingstone, who was a man who didn't leave an organization behind him. He didn't found any great Christian missionary association. He was a single man. He came from very, very poor and lowly beginnings. He was just an ordinary worker in the mills in Scotland. He had an absolute hunger and desire to learn and educate himself. While he was working at the age of ten or twelve, he used to take a book with him and he began to educate himself. Eventually, he became a medical doctor.

By the leading and unction of the Holy Spirit, he went to Africa, where he started not even so much to preach, as to live the Christian life. I come from Central Africa myself and have visited the place at Chief Chitambo's village, which is in the area of the Lala tribe, right in the heart of present Zambia – a very quiet place, right next to a vlei (a wetland) – where his heart was taken out of his body when he died and buried under a tree, because the people loved him so much. They said, "We'll embalm his body. We'll send it back to Great Britain, so that they will know we did not murder him but that he died. But his heart shall remain here."

He was a man who knew about long-range planning because he had an absolute passion to see the abolition of that horrific trade of human flesh called slavery. His title in Africa is "the good man". He and men like William Wilberforce, and many others, were instrumental in stopping slavery in Africa.

He's the only white man that I know of whose names have still been left prominent in Africa. The town of Livingstone on the banks of the Zambezi River at the Victoria Falls still stays intact. Blantyre, Scotland, is a little town of about two thousand inhabitants where David Livingstone grew up. Blantyre in Malawi is, I think, the second-biggest city in Malawi. The mission station right up by Lake Malawi, called Livingstonia, is still standing.

My brother spoke to the principal of a little school in Zimbabwe a few years ago. The school was called the Livingstone School.

My brother pointed out the name to the principal because of our Scottish roots. In fact, my own mother's family was called Livingstone. The principal said, "That man was a man who had vision." "The good man" was a selfless man, a man who loved everybody equally.

David Livingstone was trying to find the source of the Nile. Not to make money, but to try and get commerce and industry into the heart of Africa, which he believed would alleviate the trafficking in human flesh. Long-range planning! To this very day that is still being done by missionaries who probably don't even know much about David Livingstone. He left a legacy through God. Just like his namesake, King David of Israel, who had a vision that that temple would glorify God, David Livingstone had a vision that Africa would be a Christian nation.

As I said, I went back to Britain a couple of months ago to speak at a men's conference on a farm called Top Barn Farm in Holt Heath, near Worcester. There are two beautiful Christian farmers there, David and Di Harper. We saw the fire of God come down like I haven't often seen. Out of a crowd of two thousand five hundred men, which is an amazing feat in Britain today, eight hundred were from Africa. I also had the privilege of preaching in the City Temple, a large Nonconformist church right in the heart of London, just down the road from St Paul's Cathedral. The church was packed with Africans too, people who have a heart for God.

I believe that that long-range planning of Dr David Livingstone is bearing much fruit. There are missionaries going from Africa to Europe to take the Gospel to a people that are lost, a people who are so caught up with technology and intellect, that they have forgotten the simplicity of life. God is using ordinary men and women – who have received and embraced the Gospel that was taken there centuries ago by the forefathers of the people who are living in a godless society at the moment – to take it back and preach to them. I believe that one of the biggest churches in the Ukraine is shepherded by a black man from Nigeria. That is absolutely amazing and encourages me no end.

Please be sure that you do your long-range planning correctly. What does that mean? It means sitting your son, your daughter, on your knee when they're small and reading them Bible stories. Talk about the things of God. Break bread; take Holy Communion in your home. Speak about your expectations and your visions for your business, your farm, your ministry, your college, your school, your university. Speak about them to your children. Let them sit and listen, and they will automatically inherit your heart, the heart of God. I'm sure that King David didn't have to sit down and speak to Solomon. Solomon knew exactly what David expected with the building of the temple, because all the specifications had been given to David and to Solomon by God Himself.

If ever we've had to listen to God, it's at this time. David's vision and passion extended beyond his own lifetime. That's what long-range planning is about. My vision and my passion must extend beyond my life. That's why the 2009 Mighty Men Conference meant so much to me, because the Lord saw fit to allow me to be removed from the biggest conference we'd ever staged – close on two hundred thousand men – and yet my sons and spiritual sons continued with that conference as if I were still there. In fact, they exceeded what I would have done if I had been there. God was then gracious to bring me back to conclude the conference the very next morning.

Chapter 9

No regrets

For me one of the sweetest Scriptures in the Bible is 1 Timothy 6:6: "Godliness with contentment is great gain." I might have some areas in my life that if I had to live this life again I wouldn't do in the same way, especially before I met Jesus Christ as my Lord and Saviour, but I have no regrets at all. I think it's a very important thing for us to come to grips with, especially early on in life.

Failures are inevitable, because no man is perfect. The Bible says: "All have sinned and fall short of the glory of God." We need to put the failures behind us and press on. It's like paying school fees. I can remember as a young farmer planting new crops for the first time. Very rarely will you make any money out of it. You have to work through it, perfect it, and then eventually you start to make money and a success of the crop. Whether it is livestock, arable farming, timber farming, or raising chickens, it's something that needs to be mastered. The farmer that keeps changing to different farming methods, going from one farming method to another, is a man who will not make it and will invariably go bankrupt.

We need to understand that every single one of us makes mistakes. It's almost as if God uses those who really mess up. That's why I love Jesus so much. Think of St Augustine, a most amazing man of God, who was born in the north of Africa. He was an absolute playboy of note: a womanizer; hard-drinking; hard-playing. And then he came to meet

Jesus. His books are still favourites, even today. He is a man who is revered before other men, a genuine saint. Even though he'd been through so much in his early days, he was a man who was content at the end of his life, because he'd met Jesus Christ.

Look at Saul, who later became Paul the apostle. He was an absolute tyrant, a religious junkie as we'd call him today, a man who was bent on hunting down Christians and making sure that they were flogged and put in jail, if not killed. God met him on the Damascus Road and changed his life forever. He wrote two-thirds of the New Testament under the inspiration of the Holy Spirit.

That story goes on and on. My own life: God took me from one extreme to the other. I love to hear the phrase, "That guy is over the top" or, "He's a radical Christian." I don't think there's such a thing as a radical Christian. I think he's just a normal Christian. How can you not be radical when you fall in love with the Prince of Peace?

Godliness with contentment is great gain. My heart is saddened when I see some of the men who have done it all. They've got the colours, the blazer; they've represented their country in sports. They've made millions and millions of dollars. They're famous – and they're empty – because they realize that they've been chasing up the wrong road. It's so tragic.

We need to find out what it is that God wants us to do. Many people have asked if they can come and join me in the work that I'm doing for the Lord at Shalom. Many have come. In my younger years, I opened my arms and accepted them gratefully, believing that they'd been sent by God. Maybe they had, just for a season. Then there are others who are still with me to this day, through thick and thin, through the ups and downs, putting up with my idiosyncrasies and my attitudes. God has just used them. Remember, I'm also at school! I'm still in Grade 1.

If you have an earnest desire to do something constructive with your life and you're waiting for that big moment when the flash of lightning's going to flash across the sky and a ticker-tape message is going to come from God, I want to tell you that will never happen, because God wants you to walk by faith. If He speaks to you like that, you don't need faith. Without faith you can't glorify Him. I want to exhort you to start exactly where you are.

George Müller probably still holds the record for having looked after the biggest number of children in his lifetime, with no money. He never asked for a cent, yet God supplied every one of his needs. What a testimony! He started off with a boarding house and half a dozen children.

Billy Graham is rated as probably the greatest modern-day evangelist of all time. He has mentored nine US presidents, preached live to millions and millions of people, and countless millions via television, radio and books. I remember him saying in his memoirs that the first time he ever preached in his life was to six prisoners in a jail. One was picking his teeth, another one was looking out of the window, and a third one wasn't interested. That's how he started. But the most important thing is that he started. That's the key. If you want to be content in life, you need to be following your dream. You need to dream big, but start small.

It's the same with farming. As I write this book, I'm looking over the three farms that God has given to us, which my sons are running. I came here with a dream, a vision. That vision was to get a deposit down on a five-acre plot, so that we could just stay in the country. By God's grace, and maybe God's divine hand upon us, we had the opportunity of taking over a piece of overgrown wattle bush – not even a forest, just bush – totally unkempt, that fires go through every year, and the bush just gets thicker and thicker. There are parts of this farm where the bush is so thick that even the reedbuck could not pass through there.

My wife and I built a little house within three weeks of arriving on the farm. We had probably the most terrible labour force I've ever worked with in my life. They were all the drunkards, the thieves, and the wasters who couldn't get work anywhere else. I couldn't speak the local language. But you know what? We started. Thirty-two years later, we can thank God that we have established farms.

The Lord told Jill and me right from the outset to make a place for His Holy Spirit to move. A few months ago, we completed a men's conference where we accommodated between a hundred and fifty- and two hundred thousand men for over a week. I can assure you that the Holy Spirit moved like I've never, ever experienced Him before. That's the miracle-working power of Jesus Christ.

The only regret that you'll ever have when you come of age is that you didn't take all the opportunities that were given to you. I've so often said to my children: "What's the worst that can happen? You can fail, but at least you tried." My young son Fergie said that to me once, I think when we hired a stadium for the first time.

I asked, "What if it doesn't work out?"

He answered, "Dad, at least you've tried."

Peter got out of the boat and started walking on the water. He took his eyes off the Master just for a second, looked at the size of the waves around him, the storm, and started to sink because his faith wavered. Jesus caught him. We say that Peter was a man of little faith. But look at the boat and see the other eleven disciples sitting inside the boat, hanging on for dear life. Then we can say: "Peter, but at least you tried."

The Lord is not interested in your ability. He's only interested in your availability. When I came to South Africa from Zambia and we bought this piece of overgrown bush, I truly thought that when I got farming again, I would be content. How mistaken I was. I worked eighteen hours a day, I worked myself to the bone, my wife never saw me, my children never saw me and I kept saying it was for their sake. It wasn't. A lot of it was for my own ego. But we made it. We paid for the farm, paid back our debt and were settled farmers, but there was no peace, no satisfaction, no contentment in my life, because I was chasing the wrong dream. I was on the wrong road. I was going the wrong way.

On 18 February 1979, my life was transformed when I met Jesus Christ as my Lord and Saviour. Then I really had a reason for living. I was speaking to my elder son just the other day, talking about areas in our lives, in my life in particular, where I'd messed up. He said, "But, Dad, that's why it's working. People can identify with you, because they know that you're just an ordinary person."

We must be real with one another. We must be honest with ourselves, first and foremost, and then with one another. I have had more problems, more testings, more fires, more droughts, more floods, and more heartache since I came to know Christ than before I knew Him. The difference is that I had no regrets. I was at peace and I knew that Jesus Christ was at the helm of my ship.

A man once used a beautiful illustration. He said, "I'd

rather be in a rowing boat, a small little dinghy, with Jesus at the helm, going around Cape Horn (South America) in a huge storm with enormous waves, than be without Him on the *Queen Mary* ocean liner, on a lake, on a calm day with not one breath of air."

That's exactly what's happened to me. Because I know that I'm in God's perfect will, I know that ultimately, at the end of the day, all things will work together for my good, because I'm doing what He asked me to do. That's where contentment comes in. There's nothing else I'd rather be doing than what I'm doing at the moment; preaching the Gospel of Jesus Christ to lost souls.

It's enough to keep me preaching for the rest of my life when I get an e-mail from a Christian worker somewhere in the Sudan telling us that he watches us preaching every Saturday morning at seven o'clock and it's keeping him going. He's living in a mud hut with a grass roof, obviously with a battery and access to the internet and satellite TV, and he's working for an organization which is taking care of the poor, the needy and the hungry.

When a lady writes to me and says that her husband was going down for the last time through alcohol and drugs, had totally lost self-respect and all sense of responsibility for his family, and came back from a conference a completely changed, reformed man, that is what keeps me going.

You see, my friend, there's a difference between a hireling and a son or a daughter. A hireling works for his wage. A son or daughter works for their inheritance. That's the difference. I'm a son. The work I do, I do because I love Jesus Christ, not for any personal gain whatsoever. I don't want my reward here on earth. I'd rather receive it in heaven.

A few years ago there was a song called "Thank You" that was sung by a great Gospel singer, Ray Boltz. The song is about a man who dreamed that he died and went to heaven. He was standing on the seashore and people came to him, one after the other, shaking his hand and saying, "Thank you. Because of you, I'm in heaven today."

He replied, "But I've never met you. I never knew you."

Then a man explained, "A missionary came to the church, showed a film, made you cry, and you put money in towards that mission. As a result, I'm here today." Storing up riches in heaven, where rust and moth cannot destroy them...

When I think hard about it, there's only one regret that I do have in life, and that is that it took me so long to truly accept Jesus Christ as Lord and Saviour, and that I took so long doing things in my own strength, trying to find purpose in life, trying to find satisfaction. If I'd only come to Christ earlier, I wouldn't have had to suffer half the trials and tribulations that I've been through, and I would have been a lot more effective for Him in the kingdom. That's my only regret. Apart from that, there are none.

On that point, I might add that many people have come to me for prayer and help with some really heart-wrenching stories of trials and tribulations. I'd say that about eighty per cent of those people have brought that affliction on themselves by doing things their own way and not seeking the face of God. I can only speak, obviously, from my own experience but I think that applies to many of us. Many of these afflictions and problems that we encounter in life come about from a spirit of pride. The Bible says that pride always goes before a fall. In fact, in 1 Peter 5:5, the Lord says very clearly: "God resists the proud but gives grace to the humble."

Just a short while ago, I was in a large rugby stadium speaking about the fact that we have to learn to say sorry to one another. It's such a small little word but it takes a lot of humility to implement. Sometimes we need to say sorry, even when we think it's not our fault. When we humble ourselves, people are always so quick to help.

I remember arriving at Shalom farm thirty-two years ago. I had nothing. I couldn't speak the Zulu language, I didn't know when it rained here, I didn't know what kind of diseases the farmers had to combat in this area, I didn't know what time of year to plant my crops, or what crops to plant, for that matter. I took my hat off my head, held it in my hands, humbled myself, went to my neighbours and asked for help. You know, they were falling over each other to try and help us.

I remember that we had no water at that time. One day a farmer just arrived with his tractor and trailer and deposited a thousand litres of water in a water tanker, right on our doorstep. Farmers would come over and help me calibrate my planting machine and teach me about the different spray programmes that they used to combat disease and insect damage, etc..

If I'd come down from Zambia and said: "I come from Central Africa, which is known as the breadbasket of Africa. Where I come from, we get up to seven and a half tons of yield per hectare of maize, without any effort. The cattle flourish there. We do this and that and the next thing," the farmers would probably have said: "Well, what are you doing here? If it was such a wonderful place, why didn't you stay there?" They did eventually ask me what it was like in Zambia, but it's almost a form of pride when you start talking about how great it is where you've come from, what you did and what you achieved. It actually puts people off from helping you.

The people asked Martin Luther what the three greatest virtues of a mighty man or woman of God are. He said, "Number one, humility; Number two, humility; Number three, humility." That's true. There's nothing more refreshing than to see a man or woman who is being greatly used by God, whether it be in the sporting field, in business, in politics, or whatever, displaying a spirit of humility. It's a wonderful thing to see.

A man whose life story has impacted me tremendously – I never had the privilege of meeting him because he's gone to be with the Lord – is William Duma. He was born in KwaZulu-Natal, in the Umkomaas valley in the southern part of the country. He grew up herding his father's cattle. He used to wear a *beshu* (the Zulu word for a kilt). He was very small in stature, had a slight squint in one eye, and was nothing to look at physically, but he became a mighty, mighty warrior for Jesus Christ. He was used tremendously to win many souls for the Lord and was used particularly in the area of divine healing. God really anointed him in that area.

The story goes that he was invited up to Zambia by a traditional Baptist Church to preach the Gospel. On the Sunday morning the congregants were all sitting waiting for this mighty man of God from South Africa to arrive. Apparently the church was packed full. There were no seats available. In the traditional Baptist church the entrance is at the back. You walk up the steps, into the back of the church and down the aisle until you reach the altar. Then, of course, you walk around the altar and into the pulpit.

A minister was standing at the altar rail. It was nine o'clock and there was no sign of the preacher. The minister was waiting, looking at his watch. Everybody was starting to shuffle and fidget, and he wondered where this man was. Then he heard a very faint little knock at the back of the church, behind the pulpit, where the vestry and the kitchen and scullery were. He walked quietly round the back, through the curtain, through the back of the church, opened the back door and there was the mighty man of God waiting at the servant's entrance. Now we know why God used him so powerfully.

On another occasion three men, two white men and a black man, were given a tremendous gift of a trip to Israel, the Promised Land, because of services they had rendered. They'd really served God faithfully and mightily. The black man was William Duma. When this organization asked the men if they'd like to go, the two white men automatically, like I'm sure I would have done as well, jumped at the opportunity, "Thank you so much. It's very kind. When do we go?" Suitcases were packed and ready.

They asked William Duma. He replied, "Can I come back to you tomorrow? I need to get permission from my Lord first as to whether I can come or not." He did actually go but would not agree to it until he'd had permission from God. Those are the type of people – and the heart – that God desires in you and me in order to move powerfully.

One thing I've learned in my walk with God is that He's no respecter of persons. He will use any man, any woman, any boy, or any girl, whose heart is totally surrendered to Him. He will bring about revival, and He has before, in the most unusual ways. Often we expect the power of God – the fire of God – to come down in a certain church group or in a certain way and God uses a totally different way altogether.

I wear a band around my arm that stays with me night and day. It has one word on it, "Africa," plus the very well-known Scripture, 2 Chronicles 7:14 (NIV): "If My people, who are called by My name, will humble themselves..." Whose people? God's people! Who are God's people? They are those who believe that Jesus Christ is the Son of God. If they will humble themselves, God says, He will heal the land.

Humility must start with the believer. If we are proud – and we can be very proud – then God bypasses us. The hardest time to be humble is when God is using us. It's very easy to be humble when no one's noticing you, when you're not making any impact and nothing's happening. But when you preach the Word of God, for example, and the harvest comes in, it's so hard to remain lowly and give God all the glory when He starts to use you, and to prosper you.

A very good example of that is found in 1 Samuel 25, in the Old Testament. It's the story of Nabal and Abigail. There we see an example of pride coming before a fall. We see that if the man had remained humble, he would have continued to prosper. But he became self-contained and he started to think that he was actually something. That was the end of his life.

Nabal was an extremely rich farmer. He was married to a very, very beautiful, very intelligent woman, Abigail. The Bible says that he had three thousand sheep and one thousand goats. It was shearing time in Israel and he was busy shearing his sheep in Carmel.

David was fleeing with his six hundred men from Saul. They were camping a couple of miles away and had been protecting Nabal's shepherds in the hills while they were looking after the sheep. They had not lost one of the sheep and they kept all the wild animals away. David heard that Nabal was shearing his sheep and they were going to have a feast. He was going to kill some sheep and feed them to his shepherds and they were going to have a party. David sent a contingent of his young men to ask if he could just have some meat for his men because he'd protected Nabal's shepherds and he had to look after his own young men.

Nabal was anything but humble, obviously a self-made man. Once you become self-made, don't forget that it's only by the grace of God that you've got as far as you have. I was also a self-made man. I want to say to you that this is sometimes a dangerous thing. It makes one very arrogant and proud, because you actually start to believe that you did it yourself. You become very impatient with other people and very dictatorial. That causes a lot of trouble.

Nabal was absolutely rude to the young men. The Bible says that they turned on their heels, went back to David and said that Nabal had refused them any food and had rebuked them. David was so angry. Straight away they strapped their swords to their sides and they were on their way to put an end to Nabal, his family, and indeed all the shepherds and the whole community. They were going to kill them all.

One of the shearers had been listening to Nabal's conversation with David's representatives. He ran to Nabal's wife Abigail, and said that David had sent messengers from the wilderness to greet his master, Nabal, and he had reviled (scorned, or scolded) them. They'd gone back and he was very afraid that David would come and destroy the whole village.

Quietly, on her own, Abigail got hold of a few donkeys

and took two hundred loaves of bread, two skins of wine, five sheep already dressed, five seahs of roasted grain, one hundred clusters of raisins, and two hundred cakes of figs and loaded them onto the donkeys. She and her servants then quietly, without Nabal knowing, took off down the road to meet David's enraged men coming towards their farm.

This is so important. When she saw David coming, Abigail got off her donkey, fell on her face before David and bowed to the ground. When she fell at his feet she asked forgiveness for her husband. "Please," she said, "don't let the behaviour of this scoundrel [son of the devil] Nabal anger you." She called him a scoundrel because no one could actually speak to him or get any sense out of him. David was so impressed by her humility and her attitude that he actually forgave Nabal. He turned around with his men, took all the gifts and was very thankful for them, and went back to where he was camped.

When Abigail got home, Nabal and his shearers were all having a party. They were very drunk by this time. She never even spoke to him. The next morning, when the wine had left Nabal, she told him what had happened. The Bible says that his heart died within him and he became like a stone. It happened that after about ten days the Lord struck Nabal and he died.

The end of the story is that David eventually married Abigail, Nabal's widow. All that that foolish farmer had to do was just humble himself and part with a small bit of his wealth, and he would have more than saved the day. Thank God for our wives, who so often come in at the last moment and help us!

The word "minister" directly translated actually means

servant. Yet many of us, and I'm talking about my colleagues and myself, think that when the word "minister" is spoken it's supposed to represent some kind of an office. When we preach and we serve, we are supposed to be on our knees, like Jesus was when He washed His disciples' feet on the night that they had the Last Supper, and not prancing around like some kind of lord, having people bowing before you. We've got it the wrong way around.

Sometimes it takes years before the penny drops and one realizes the true order in the church of God. The Lord Jesus Christ says that in heaven the first shall be last and the greatest the least. We need to understand that. Many people talk about the crowns they're going to receive in heaven. I can honestly say, like David, that for me to be a doorkeeper in the house of the Lord is all I desire – if I can even get that far – just to be able to sit and look at the beauty and majesty of Jesus Christ every day.

Talking about pride, that mighty ship the *Titanic* was built in Great Britain. I don't know what the weight of the ship was. It was rated as the greatest ship that had ever been built. The steel plate that was used for the cladding of the sides of that mighty ship was especially thick. It was a gigantic ship with huge motors and special extra boilers for extra steam. It took literally thousands of passengers. It was said to be totally indestructible.

It's a scary thing, as soon as we start to talk like that it's almost as though God gets offended, because nothing is indestructible to God. Nothing is bigger than God and nothing is more popular than God.

The *Titanic*, on its maiden voyage, never even reached its destination, the United States of America. One night it was travelling full steam ahead. The crew and captain knew full well that there were huge icebergs in the sea, but because they were so confident, and maybe just a little bit proud that nothing would hold up the *Titanic*, they hit a huge iceberg. That iceberg opened up the side of the ship just like a can opener opens a tin of beans. In no time at all, this mighty, mighty work of man sank to the bottom of the ocean like a stone. We've heard it before: How the mighty hath fallen! Maybe that ship would never have sunk if a little bit more humility and a little more faith in God had been exercised.

Often I've had to try and give counsel to couples with broken marriages. When I speak to the couple and ask them what went wrong, very often they say that there was no third party in the breakdown. There was no other person, no unfaithfulness; it was just a lack of communication. That is so tragic. All they needed to do was say sorry. Such a little word: Sorry. That would have been the beginning of healing, but when pride comes in: "I'm not going to say sorry. It's not my fault. I'm tired of this," straight away there's a breakdown coming. You will never force someone to say sorry, or anyone to repent, because it just doesn't happen.

I have a very special horse, Big Stuff. He's become more popular on our *Grassroots* programmes than I am. He's a wonderful Quarterhorse X Thoroughbred, but he's also got a mind of his own. I can take him down to the water but I cannot make him drink. We cannot force our loved ones to love us or respect us and we cannot demand anything. We must earn it. God has orchestrated life just like that, to keep us humble.

In the Middle East the shepherds lead their sheep, while we in the West drive our sheep with sheepdogs. The shepherds in the East know their sheep by name. They whistle, they call, and the sheep come because they love their shepherds. It's not a demanding relationship, it's a love relationship. That's what we should have in our marriages and in our homes, in our businesses, on our farms, and in our sports teams. It should be done through love and humility, leading from the front.

It's so sad to demand something when you haven't earned the right. I remember riding around the farm a few years ago with a young man who was very much the gentleman farmer. He stopped the land cruiser that we were driving in and started shouting at his tractor driver because he said the driver wasn't ploughing correctly or deep enough. The driver was obviously quite tired, weary and dusty. He stopped the tractor and said, "Well, come and show me how to do it." Of course, the man's face went red, because he didn't even know how to plough. He just shouted a bit more and drove on. You will never earn respect that way.

When I went off to agricultural college in Scotland as a young man, the way I was taught was that I had to do everything myself, starting with a pick and shovel and then working my way up. A much nicer way would have been for that young farmer to stop the pick-up and when the driver came to the headland, just to ask him to stop the tractor, excuse himself from his visitor and take five minutes to say to the driver, without raising his voice: "If you don't mind, I'd like you to plough in this gear. I'd like you to close your top link a little bit, so that the front shoe will go in a bit deeper. This is how you do it," and then put the tractor in gear and plough for twenty, thirty metres. The driver would quite happily have said: "Thank you, sir. I see what you want." We would have then gone home. That's what God is looking for. Unfortunately we have to go through the hard knocks in life to learn these things.

Thinking about those shepherds again, I really don't believe that it's right to drive the sheep from behind. You can get so much more done and become so much more successful just by humbling yourself.

If you go to the average farm in South Africa, the workers have usually been on that farm for generations. They know the land, the seasons, they know how animals prosper and do well, and they also know the pitfalls. All the farmer has to do is ask them. That's something I learned the hard way, because if you don't ask, nobody will tell you.

I tried myself to build up a rapport with my farm workers. We would sit down as a group. We wouldn't talk about "my"farm; we'd talk about "our" farm. I would discuss things with them and they began to have the confidence to share what they felt, what was on their heart. Ninety per cent of the time they were dead right.

I would ask, "Do you feel that we should put our extra top dressing of fertilizer on our maize now?"

"Yes, I think you should. Because I feel that in about a week's time it's going to rain. I can just feel it."

"How do you know?"

They wouldn't be able to explain it, they just know. As sure as anything, it would rain. The fertilizer would be taken up inside the plant and we'd end up with a bumper crop.

Or they would suggest that it was maybe time to wean the cattle, or maybe just hang on a bit. "There's a cold front coming up and the calves are going to need a bit more of mother's milk."

Small little principles! It would make them feel so good when it came to pass. To encourage people is such a wonderful thing; just a right word in the right season. These are not great profound truths, these are facts of life. Unfortunately for many of us, we only learn them when we come of age.

I know a farmer in this district who has a combined labour force of over nine hundred workers in his sawmill, forest and farm. He is a consultant and has many managers in place, working for him. When he goes to work in the morning, it is purely on a consultancy basis. They tell me he knows the name of every single employee. He will greet every person by their first name. Whether the woman is a sweeper in the factory, whether the man is making the tea, whether he's a truck driver, or whether he's an under-manager or an artisan, he will be greeted with respect. They'll do anything for him and they regard him with respect because he notices them.

That's how Jesus operated. Remember when He walked into Cana, where He performed His first miracle at the wedding, when He turned the water into wine? He came into Cana and saw a man standing underneath the tree and recognized him. Because God, of course, knows everything! He said, "Your name is Nathanael, a man in whose mouth is found no guile [deceit]."

That greeting so influenced Nathanael that he knew that Jesus Christ was the Son of God. I don't believe it was just because he was so astonished that the Lord knew his name, especially since He'd never seen him before. I think it was the humility with which God greeted him. Just like the disciples, when Jesus proceeded to wash their feet during the Last Supper on the last night before He was crucified. That silenced all of them. That taught them exactly what God requires of you and me. If you want to be the greatest in the kingdom of God, you must be prepared to be the servant of all.

St Teresa of Avila said: "Christ has no body on earth but yours, no hands but yours, no feet but yours. Yours are the eyes through which Christ's compassion for the world is to look out; yours are the feet with which He is to go about doing good; and yours are the hands with which He is to bless us now." That's exactly what God is expecting from you and me. My dear friend, it's not the big things in life that make the difference, it's the little things. Unfortunately, some of us take a long time before we realize just exactly what God requires of us.

I've just been given a book written by Richard Stearns, the president of World Vision. He quotes a man by the name of Frederick W Faber: "Kindness has converted more sinners than zeal, eloquence, or learning." When trying to influence people, even your own family, your children or your spouse, it's really not so much what you say but who you are, and what you do, that makes the difference. Opening that car door for your girlfriend or fiancée or wife speaks volumes. You don't have to tell her that you love her when you do something like that. Making sure that she's well seated at a table at a restaurant, making sure that she gets the menu first are supposedly small little things. But they aren't. They're telling her in loud, capital letters that you love her and respect her. Ladies, making that beautiful hot meal for your husband when he comes home from work means so much to him. Having your children nicely bathed, clean and smelling nice and sweet, ready for Dad to come home, is such a blessing for any father who's been working hard all day.

Kindness is what it's all about; preferring others to

yourself, instead of always trying to stick up for your own rights. That's what saddens me so much in today's society, where all the different groups are standing up for their rights: Women, standing up for women's rights; men, for their rights; children, for their rights. When you come to Christ and accept Him as your Lord and Saviour, you no longer have any rights. You give all your rights to Him, because you die to self and you start to live for Him. I can honestly tell you that it was only when I gave up my rights for God's rights in my life that I started to live life to the full.

Remember, your children will not do what you tell them to. They will do what you do. If you lose your temper, if you're arrogant, conceited, if you keep thumping the table because you want your rights, they'll do exactly the same. If you humble yourself in the presence of other people, they'll do exactly the same. You see if you are unfaithful to your wife, your children will know that. The tragedy is that they will be unfaithful to their wives, even though they despise you for it. If you beat up your wife, they will beat up their wives, because they will do exactly what you do, even though they despise you for it. That's why it's so vitally important to live life with a servant's heart.

When we say sorry to someone who is younger than us or who is lower in stature than us, or has a more minor role when it comes to authority than we do, then people sit up and take notice. I think of the time when I was actively farming. I had a crisis on the farm. I was growing seed maize at the time and it was right in the heat of summer on our farm. It would have been about January or February. Sometimes the heat is very, very uncomfortable. As a result we would start work at a quarter to five in the morning and try to knock off at about two o'clock, when it became unbearable.

This particular day we couldn't stop. We were pulling the flowers out of the maize plants, because we were growing seed maize for a company. There is a certain breed of maize where the flower has to be extracted before it sheds its pollen, because we were trying to cross-pollinate our maize. The company had said that they would not tolerate any of the pollen flying around in the fields; otherwise they would condemn the crop. Obviously it was an absolutely critical time in the crop. That particular day the wind had been blowing. At about two o'clock, the women who were helping me pull the flowers out of acres and acres of maize, which is very tall, sometimes over six feet (1.8 m) tall, were exhausted. You walk around, up and down the lines, with your arms up in the air all day. It's very, very tiring. Some of these women were old enough to be my mother, never mind being my age.

We sat down on the contour bank at the end of the field and were resting, just getting our stuff together before we went home, when the seed inspectors from the company arrived. They had done a quick cross-section of another field and they said that the flowers had all been shaken out by the wind, and were about to start shedding pollen. They would come back in an hour's time. If there was any flower shedding pollen, they would unfortunately have to condemn the crop. That would mean a complete crop failure and bankruptcy and, ultimately, the end of the farm. It was as dramatic as that. They were terribly sorry about it, but... Off they drove.

I was shattered, because I was tired as well. I said to the women, "We've got to get back into that field and pull those

138

flowers out now." I must be honest with you, I was tired, I was irritable, and I didn't ask them – I told them. I was quite short with them.

The leader of the women turned around in front of all the Zulu women and said, "We're not going back in."

I immediately got angry and demanded that they go back in, and that they would do it immediately.

They said, "We're not doing it. We've worked our full day. We've worked out our task and we are now going home." They picked up all their stuff and started walking off the job.

I was devastated. I didn't know what to do. I was a Christian at that time and I felt the Holy Spirit say to me, "You've gone about it totally the wrong way. You've done it back to front. You need to humble yourself in their presence."

I was trying to argue with God and saying, "But, Lord, they work for me."

The Lord was saying, "But they've worked their task. They're exhausted. You know that, because you're just as tired as they are and you're half their age."

So I shouted out to them, "Just wait, please."

They stopped and turned around when they heard the change in the tone of my voice. I walked up to them and said, "I want to first of all apologize for the way in which I've spoken to you. You've worked very well today. You've done more than your fair share of work and you don't have to come back. You quite rightly have said that you've worked your hours. I would like to appeal to you to please help me." (Totally different attitude, you see.) "The inspectors have told me that if those flowers are not pulled out of the plants within an hour, they're coming back to condemn the crop. If they condemn the crop that means that we've lost the crop, there's no more work for you and I've lost the farm. Please, I'm appealing to you to please help me. I will compensate you with money and time later on."

They looked at each other and – because of my attitude, not because I was going to compensate them with extra money or time – I think they actually felt terribly sorry for me, because I must have looked quite forlorn. They said, "We will."

They came back, put their stuff down, got stuck into that field and worked an extra hour. Sure as anything, within an hour the inspectors were back. They checked out the field, found it was totally clean, wrote a nice report and passed the crop. I thanked the women quite profusely from the bottom of my heart. Yes, you can take a horse to water but you can't make it drink.

The same thing applies to your children. Sometimes you need to humble yourself and speak to your children in a decent manner. They will do anything for you. It's the same with your spouse: if you've made a mistake, ask forgiveness. It doesn't matter whether it's your fault or not. That heart attitude will defuse a potential bomb in your home. The Bible tells us clearly that a gentle answer will turn away wrath. That happens so often.

Sometimes the best thing to say is nothing. The Bible says that "in the multitude of words sin is not lacking, but he who restrains his lips is wise" (Proverbs 10:19). That's probably the hardest job I have – to shut up sometimes. I get myself into trouble sometimes by speaking too much and too soon. These things are not learned at any school. They are learned through the school of life.

Many a time when I visit a different farming town and ask the farmers how many of them start their work in the morning with prayer, Scripture reading, and possibly even the singing of a couple of hymns with their people, they look at me blankly. They have said to me on occasion, "But we don't have any Christians on our farm, so how do we start?" I'm always quick to say, "You'd be surprised," because I was very surprised when I implemented this for the first time. I was convicted by the Holy Spirit to start doing things correctly, so I said, "We will start work every morning," (in my time, not their time – that's the difference), "by reading the Bible, praying and by singing." I was a fairly new Christian myself.

Do you know that out of the crowd came forth upstanding Christian men, who took the Bible, read Scriptures, led the people in singing a couple of hymns, and also a time of prayer. That touched me deeply, because I didn't really think there were any Christians on our staff. When I've told that story to farmers, they do the same thing. We now have groups of farmers, praise be to God, all over the nation, in fact, all over the world that are starting work every morning with prayer, thanksgiving and Scripture reading.

You know something? It sometimes defuses tension. It also makes an opportunity for people to talk to each other, for employees to come to their employers and speak their heart instead of talking behind their backs, because they feel that they can approach their employers. Employers go the extra mile and understand the plight and the problem that the employee might encounter, simply because they have a common denominator. His name is Jesus Christ. It's the love of Christ that covers a multitude of sins in this world.

I heard a story once about the Gordon Highlanders, a crack Highland regiment. One of the young soldiers, a

Christian man, was doing his national service. The first night he was there, he walked into the barracks and got on his knees beside his bed to pray. He was heckled and humiliated by all the other soldiers. The old sergeant major had just come back from the pub and was pretty well drunk. However, he knew exactly what he was doing, because he did it every day of his life. He was a professional soldier, with scars on his face and a foul mouth. He saw the young man at the end of his bed, praying. He sat down, pulled off his hobnail boots and threw them as hard as he could at the soldier, hitting him on the back of the head. His head was cut and it started bleeding. He said, "You sissy. When are you going to grow up?" With that, he fell back in his bed, totally drunk, and passed out.

The next morning at four o'clock he was wide awake. That was sheer discipline and habit. He swung his feet out of bed, remembered what he'd done with his boots the night before, and thought he'd better go and try and find them. As he swung his legs out of his bed, he looked down in front of him. There were his boots, placed neatly side by side, and shining from a spit and polish. The young soldier had gone the extra mile. That tough old soldier broke down and started weeping. He went over to the youngster's bed and said, "Laddie, tell me about your Jesus." Kindness speaks louder than words.

Chapter 10

The fear of God

There are two characters in the Bible that I really admire, look up to and use as my role models. The one is Elijah the Tishbite and the other is John the Baptist, of whom the Lord said, "There has never been a man born from the womb of a woman who is greater on this earth than John the Baptist."

Neither of these men had any fear whatsoever of the authorities. They feared only God. As a result, they had tremendous impact in the area in which they were working. Elijah the Tishbite was known as "the hairy man with the leather belt". I can just visualize him coming out of the wilderness, where he'd been spending time with God. King Ahab was a soft, unpredictable, unstable, gutless man who was totally dominated by his wife, Jezebel. He looked and saw Elijah coming from way off and said, "O Troubler of Israel, what do you want from us?" Although they didn't particularly like Elijah, they had a tremendous respect for him, because they knew he was a man of God. He was the prophet who just stopped the rain for three and a half years and then told his king, "You'd better gird up your loins, get in your chariot and get cracking because the rain's coming." Of course the rain came.

One thing I have realized in my life is that you cannot serve two masters. Jesus said that very clearly in Matthew 12:30: "He who is not for Me is against Me, and he who does not gather with Me, scatters abroad." It's impossible to serve two masters. When you try, you can please no one. People don't have to like us as believers but they must respect us, and the best way to earn respect is to be a man of your word. That's exactly what Elijah was. Whatever he said, he did.

The other man who had the same Spirit, which was to prepare the way of the Lord and to turn the hearts of the fathers to the children, and those of the children to their fathers, was John the Baptist. He came out of the wilderness and accused Herod, the authority of the time who had the power of life over death, of being an adulterer. He said, "You took your brother's wife." Yet the Bible says that Herod respected and admired John the Baptist. I've seen it so many times. Whether you like them or not, when you see righteousness and truth and God's Word prevailing through a man or a woman's life, you have to admire and respect them. That's what happened with Herod. The only reason that Herod killed John the Baptist by beheading him was because of pressure from his wife, who was humiliated by the man of God's charges.

They say that Mary, Queen of Scots, feared the prayers of John Knox more than a legion of soldiers. She feared him because she knew that he was hearing from God and he was walking in God's ways. That is what God expects from us today. We cannot dabble in other things if we are going to be effective for God. We need to keep focused on God.

You can't dabble in politics and in religion. Either you're going to be an ambassador for Jesus Christ, or you're going to be an ambassador for the party that you represent. I'm not saying for a minute that there's no room for Christians in politics. Not at all! William Wilberforce was a politician and he was used very powerfully. That was where he specialized, and that's where he spent his time. His arena, his field, was parliament. God gave him tremendous victories through his debates in parliament where, through the power of the Holy Spirit, he and David Livingstone, and many others, were instrumental in abolishing that horrific, open abscess in the heart of Africa called the slave trade. He was used to heal it once and for all.

I've realized that you cannot be totally effective if you don't concentrate on one area. It's like a sportsman. He can be a good all-rounder, but if he really wants to excel in one sport, he's got to choose. Many of our sportsmen in South Africa have had to do that. I know the late Hansie Cronje was one of the greatest cricketers of all time. When he was at Grey College I think he was captain of the rugby team as well. He had to make a choice. Either he was going to play rugby or he was going to play cricket, but he couldn't do both.

One of his predecessors, a mighty man of God by the name of C T Studd, who was the most eligible bachelor in Great Britain of his time, came from a very wealthy family. He used to ride horses in winter and play cricket in summer. He had to make a choice whether he was going to continue being a professional cricketer, or whether he was going to preach the Gospel. He chose the Gospel. Hence that wonderful organization called *WEC* (*Worldwide Evangelisation for Christ*) which was started by C T Studd. He died in the Congo and was buried there. He was a man who made a choice and stuck to it.

Chapter 11
Punishment vs chastening

When we are young and starting out in life, it's amazing how many times we will seem to find a reason for something going wrong. It'll never be our fault, by the way; it's always somebody else's. Then we come of age and we realize that it's actually our own doing. We cannot continue to blame our parents or our superiors or our teachers for something that's going wrong in our lives. There must come a time when we have to take responsibility ourselves. Parents, once your children have grown up and left home, all you can do is to pray for them. They have to take responsibility for any bad decisions or mishaps that take place in their lives.

A young farmer came to visit me just a few days ago. He's actually a spiritual son of mine and I love him very much. He sat down and we spoke at length about agriculture and farming. We were really enjoying our time together but I could see there was something bothering him. It was only after we'd been chatting for some time that he mentioned the hardships that he's been going through.

He is a very successful farmer but, as happens to most farmers, he has been going through some severe times of testing. One thing I've realized about farming is that it teaches you patience. If it's not the crop, then it's the price of the crop. If it's not the price of the crop, then it's the drought. If it's not the drought, it's the flood.

I said, "You know, nothing that has come upon you is

strange. The Bible talks about that. There's nothing new under the sun about these trials and tribulations that we go through as believers that the early Christians didn't also go through. One of the greatest of all who suffered was Paul. He went through shipwrecks, he was stoned, and he was whipped, thirty-nine times. On a couple of occasions, he was beaten up. When we are in God's army, we're subject to the battles but we must always remember that the war has been won. The battles are mere skirmishes. Jesus has already won the war."

He asked me, "Why do you think God is punishing me so much?" I asked him how he came to that conclusion and he said, "Well, it's in the Bible about the Lord chastising His children."

We looked it up in Hebrews 12:5–11. Of course, the Bible does say that the Lord chastises His own, just like a good father chastens and chastises his son so that he will grow up to be a responsible, qualified citizen. If he doesn't chasten him, he doesn't love him. That was a tremendous revelation to both of us, but the word "chastisement" is not punishment. It's translated as discipline. The Lord disciplines those whom He loves.

I got the picture of a blacksmith working at a forge, putting a piece of iron into the fire with his tongs and letting it get absolutely white-hot, then taking the steel out with the tongs and banging it into shape with a huge hammer. After cooling it down he puts it back into the fire and then beats it again. But he's not punishing the iron, he is tempering it so that it's ready for the job that he requires it to do. Then he forms it into a spring, a tool, a ploughshare, or maybe even some agricultural equipment.

So it is with the Lord. He's not punishing us, because

Jesus Christ took all of the punishment for all of our sins on the Cross of Calvary. When He died, He said: "It is finished." He meant it. He has paid the ultimate price for all our sin. He tells us to go and sin no more, for our sins are forgiven. However, when we do come short and we slip up, the Bible tells us: "If we confess our sins, He is faithful and just to forgive us our sins and to cleanse us from all unrighteousness" (1 John 1:9).

The Bible says very clearly that there is no condemnation for those who are in Christ Jesus (Romans 8:1). The Lord never, ever condemns people; only the devil condemns people. The Lord convicts people. Once He convicts us, we have to deal with that sin in our life, repent of it – which means stop doing it – and move on. When we can realize that, all of a sudden we start seeing the big picture and we can cope when things maybe go wrong for a season. We don't feel condemned.

As for myself, I know that I can face anything if I know that I'm still on the right road, if I'm still fighting the good fight, still running the race. I can take it on if I know that I'm going the right way. When condemnation comes up against me and I start to feel that God has forsaken me, or that God is punishing me, then I can assure you that I'd give up very fast.

This young farmer is such a sincere man. He's been continually questioning God and asking Him for answers. The last thing that we talked about was that as a believer it's not always advisable to keep asking questions. I'm sure it sometimes hurts the Lord. It's like the little boy who asked his Dad, "Are we going to have supper tonight, Dad? Will we have food to eat?" Yet he's never, ever gone to bed without a full tummy. If anything, it would not only hurt his father, but probably anger him.

I told him that I remembered reading an account in Corrie ten Boom's book, *The Hiding Place*. Corrie and her beautiful sister Betsie were interned in a concentration camp during World War II. Corrie was sitting on the ground with Betsie in her lap. The Gestapo had severely hurt them and Betsie was actually dying. Corrie was holding her tight. She looked up and cried out to God, "Lord, why are You allowing this to happen?" Betsie whispered to her, "Corrie, if you know Him, you don't have to ask why."

That is such a profound statement. I've never forgotten that. If you know the Lord, you don't have to ask why. To keep asking questions of the Lord: "Why? Why's this happening? Why's that happening? Why did that happen?" is actually an insult, in a way, to God. I told this young man that if you know the Lord, and that comes by spending time in the Word, you don't have to ask "Why?" because Jesus is so gentle, the Bible says, that He will not break a bent reed, or extinguish a smouldering flax. There's no chance that He will hurt you or punish you because you haven't done something right.

When we'd finished discussing the difference between punishment and discipline, it was like a light switch went on for that young farmer. I could see his face just light up. It was as if a fifty-kilogram bag of cement fell off his shoulders. He could realize that God wasn't working against him, God was working with him. Through his hardship, through all his trials and tribulations, God was teaching him about the rules of life, about the hard knocks of life, and preparing him for the tests that were coming up front before him. Instead of thinking that God was trying to punish him, he realized that God is actually his ally.

This young man left my prayer room rejoicing. His brother is a former international athletics trainer. I said to him, "Go and ask your brother: When he used to discipline his athletes, was he punishing them? He will tell you, no, not at all. He was tempering them, getting them ready for the big occasion, for the Olympic Games, for the world championships. As part of the discipline, they had to get up early in the morning; they had to run; they had to do pressups; they had to do star jumps; they had to swim. They had to eat correctly; they had to rest properly, so that they were ready for the main event. That's exactly what the Lord Jesus Christ is doing for me and for you. He is tempering us for the big occasion."

Romans 8:31 says that if God is for us, there is no man that will stand against us. We need to keep on persevering and eventually we will reach our target if we do not lose hope. Galatians 6:9 lines up with that; it says that we should not grow weary in doing good, for in due season we shall reap, if we do not lose heart.

Going back to my Scottish roots, there's a wonderful story spoken about Robert the Bruce, the famous Scottish king who was apparently looking into the face of defeat when the English invaded Scotland during the 1300s. He was holed up in a cave high up in the mountains of Scotland. His soldiers were all in disarray, and to all intents and purposes he was defeated. While he, a broken king, a defeated man, was sitting in that cave, he looked across the cave. On the side there was a little spider that was trying to swing via its web from one side of the cave to the other. It swung once, and didn't quite make it. Twice, three times, four times. It just kept swinging until eventually, on the ninth attempt, it made it. Robert the Bruce realized that if he persevered, he could make it. He went out and collected his troops together and they defeated the English.

Through perseverance and keeping on, we will eventually have the victory. Young people – I'm thinking particularly of myself in my earlier years – will try once, twice, and, if it doesn't work, they give up. I really believe that as we get older we realize that Rome was not built in one day. There's something about being consistent, about being faithful, which eventually brings the victory.

Just the other day I read in a beautiful daily devotional reading: "If you want more faith, I will introduce you to the school of sorrows." That's how faith comes. It is so sad for me to hear of my colleagues, fellow preachers, who teach that if you're in debt, or if you're going through a time of economic hardship on your farm or in your business, it's because you have no faith. If you are sick in your body, it's because you have no faith and you haven't trusted God, because God's people don't get sick and they are never in want. That is a lie from the pit of hell!

I have studied many of the great men of God; it's my passion. I'm talking about William Booth, founder of The Salvation Army; James Hudson Taylor, founder of the China Inland Mission; William Carey, the missionary to India who translated the Bible into so many languages; and David Livingstone, who pioneered missionary work in Africa and is still a revered man of God in Africa. I'm talking about men who have shaken the world, like D L Moody, C H Spurgeon, and many others.

If you read their life stories, you'll see that every one of these men went through extreme hardships. They were familiar with hardships, with blood, sweat and tears, but they were overcomers, every one of them. William Carey said, "Attempt great things for God and expect great things from God." Every one of them succeeded and did amazing things for Christ. The early Christians were fed to the lions – and the Lord took them home from there.

I know for a fact that, without faith, it's impossible to please God, especially on the road that I've walked in agriculture. But God has never, ever forsaken me or let me down. I've been through a few skirmishes but I've never lost the war, because the war has already been won. But to say that a man is getting punished by God because of his lack of faith, or because he cannot trust God, is a sin indeed. The Lord doesn't work like that. He encourages and loves us and He chastises those He loves so that they become better, stronger, more mature Christians to fight the fight and to run the race.

God is sovereign. We live in an imperfect world. The Bible tells us that the devil goes around like a roaring lion seeking whom he may devour, so we need to understand that. We need to keep our guard up, we need to be diligent, but at the same time we need to remember that God, in the form of His Son Jesus Christ, through the power of the Holy Spirit, is not against us. He is for us. He's on our side.

John Newton, the writer of the beautiful hymn "Amazing Grace" was a captain of a slave ship. You can imagine that he must have had some tremendous battles within himself after he'd been converted, because of the horrific things that he'd allowed to happen on those slave ships. He lived well into his eighties and he wrote many, many famous hymns. He was also a preacher. When he was lying dying on his deathbed, he was so weak he could hardly speak. The man who was attending him heard him trying to say something. He put his ear right to John Newton's mouth. John Newton whispered, "What a great sinner I am." Then with his last breath he said, "But what a great Saviour Jesus is!"

That is the bottom line. Jesus has saved us from eternal death and damnation. That is one of the most important things in coming of age – to realize that God is not fighting against us, He's fighting with us. In fact, He says very clearly: "The battle is mine. Stand. Be strong in the Lord" (Ephesians 6). Paul even says, "Rejoice in your tribulation because tribulation worketh patience; patience, character; and character, hope." I've never yet met a man worth his salt that has not been through some kind of trial or tribulation. The people I meet who are interesting – men of character – are men who have been through fiery trials. That's why Paul could say that he rejoices in the tribulations. That's the steel again, being tempered, ready for the big test.

Sometimes the safest place to be is on your knees, because you can't fall any further. Often the most dangerous place to be is on top of a pedestal. People have a habit of putting you on a pedestal and then knocking the pedestal over. I've learned to treat criticism and flattery as the same enemy.

Just a week ago, I was at a huge rugby stadium. I've had the privilege of speaking at many, many stadiums in the last few years. Every single time God has sent the people. The stadiums have either been packed to overflowing, or very full. Once again, doubt crept into my heart. I was waiting in the downstairs room. I couldn't see out, so I didn't know what to expect. Things appeared to be quiet outside but that was just because the room was very well sealed off. Doubt started to creep into my heart. "Lord, will they come?" Will they come? Maybe it's a question every evangelist asks: "Will the people arrive?" When I walked out and got onto the platform, and saw the stadium full of eager souls waiting to hear God's Word, I started to weep. I wept out of shame because, once again, I had doubted the faithfulness of my God.

I think the biggest disappointment to our Lord is when we cannot believe that He will honour His promises. So, as we mature as Christians, let us stop asking so many questions and let's start believing. Let's stop walking by natural sight and start walking by faith. The Lord always honours faith. St Augustine said, "Faith is to believe what you cannot see but the reward of that faith is to see what you believe."

Chapter 12

Comrades

One of the most important things that God has shown me as I have come of age is that He never, ever meant us to live independently of each other. He designed us to live in community. He designed us to live with one another and to live for one another.

Isn't it amazing that the world system is directly opposed to that? Right from when we were small children, we were taught to stand up for ourselves, to be self-starters, not to depend on other people, to be self-employed, to be totally independent of everybody else. Sometimes people get that part of it right and it's disastrous. Often when I go to a hotel I will see a wealthy old person who's living independently of everybody else because they have money or means, and they're absolutely desperately lonely.

Then I go to an old-age home, where people don't have much money, but they've got each other. They seem to be doing so much better. In the middle of the night, when you can't sleep and you need company, or you need someone to help you, there are people there for you. All the money in the world won't help you if you're lonely and in pain and scared. There's nothing worse. That's why the Lord Jesus says: "What does it profit a man if he gains the whole world and forfeits himself?" (Luke 9:25, RSV).

The older I become, the more I realize the importance of friendship and relationship; obviously always firstly with God, then with God's creation – meaning my brothers and sisters in Christ – and then everything that He's made for us. I really love my Quarterhorse X Thoroughbred horse called Big Stuff. He's very special to me and has become more than a horse; he's become a good friend. I also have two white English bull terriers that drive my wife crazy because they tear up everything that's in sight, but I've really grown to love them so much. I live on a most beautiful farm and I've learned to appreciate the trees, the pasture lands, the hills, the valleys and the seasons.

At the moment I'm enjoying life to the full. But it wasn't always like that. Before I came to know the Lord Jesus Christ as my personal Lord and Saviour, I was always so busy trying to make ends meet, trying to make money, trying to pay for the farm, and so on, that there was no joy left. I was on that proverbial treadmill, going nowhere fast.

The main reason why I'm writing this chapter now is that I've just had a week off. My wife and I have been staying at home, relaxing. My younger son went to buy some cattle. He wants to start a herd of beef cattle and he needed some good foundation stock. He asked me to go along with him. It was such an honour and privilege. With the type of life that we're living at present, it's very hard to spend time with my children because I'm away so much. When I come home, I'm so tired I spend most of my time resting. When he asked me to go with him to buy cattle (livestock is definitely my first love as a farmer), I was deeply honoured.

We left early in the morning. He had a substantial amount of money that he wanted to invest in cattle, so there was much excitement, definitely on my part. Maybe on his part more apprehension and a bit of fear as well! There's nothing wrong with godly fear, by the way. We got to the farmer's shed near Golden Gate in the Free State, a most beautiful part of Africa, with sandstone cliffs and hills and lovely valleys.

The organization was outstanding. I really want to say that our being Christians gives us no licence to be slack and disorganized. It brings so much glory to God to see things done in a constructive manner. That's exactly what happened. It was very cold when we arrived; the temperatures were in single figures. The farmer had huge gas heaters in his big open shed where the bullring was and the sale was going to take place. There was hot coffee and tea laid out, even hot bean soup and sandwiches. I thought: Nothing but the best for the Lord. We put our names down, got our buyer's number, which we have to flash up when we make a purchase, and started to meet the people. The camaraderie was really excellent.

I'm not farming the land any more, I'm farming for souls. My sons have taken over the farms. I want to suggest to any senior farmer reading this book that maybe you need to pray about handing your farm over to your son before you get too old, so that you can enjoy it with him and enjoy being part of what he's doing. Remember, when you give him the farm, you give him the chequebook as well and, indeed, the debt. We met old people, young people, part-time farmers, full-time farmers, big farmers, small farmers, women farmers... It was amazing.

The hospitality was superb. I cannot describe it. Lunch was brought around on a tray for us while we were still bidding for the cattle. We were offered soft drinks every half hour, on the half hour. Before the auctioneer started, there was a minister – obviously invited by the farmer – to open the sale with prayer and Scripture reading. Then the bidding started. My son was sitting right next to me with the calculator. I was doing the bidding. He was trying to keep my arm down most of the time! But we had such excellent fellowship together. We spoke about the sale all the way there and all the way back. Together, with God's providence, we've got the nucleus of a beautiful herd of beef cattle. Two days later, we went to a bull sale and purchased two beautiful bulls.

The wonderful thing for me was just being able to relax, to talk about the weather, the animals, the beef prices and then to start talking about the things of God. One man came up to me and actually started weeping. His friend's life was completely changed at the last Mighty Men Conference. He told me his friend had been a playboy of note, a married man with children, yet he had three or four girlfriends. After the Mighty Men Conference, he'd come back, put all his cards on the table, got his family around, repented, wept, and had broken off all those relationships. He's going for God now.

This man was able to tell me that at the sale yards, while looking at the cattle in their different lots. That, my dear friend, is surely where Jesus operated the best. I can just imagine Him being at that sale. Well, He was anyway, but two thousand years ago, moving amongst the farmers, amongst the fishermen (they must have had fish auctions as well), wishing them all the best and saying:

"That's a lovely parcel you've bought there."

"That's a good price you got for that one..."

Then the man asking if Jesus could just step aside, and sharing his heart with Him, and Jesus praying for him and healing him.

At the sale there was a group of black emerging farmers, lovely men, who had bid on a particular parcel of about ten animals, only to be turned down afterwards by the bank, because they didn't have their paperwork in order. The animals had to be brought back onto the sale. It was a bit embarrassing. We were the last bidders before these men bid higher than us. The auctioneer was very apologetic and said, "Well, unfortunately the animals have got to be sold again." He asked us whether we'd be prepared to take them at the price these men had bid. We said, "Yes, of course," and as a result we got the cattle.

Those men called me aside afterwards and asked me to please pray for them and for their farming. We made a couple of jokes that we'd have to give them the calves of these animals, and so on, but there was such a natural building of friendships and relationships. I came back from those couple of days feeling like a completely new man.

It's so important to develop friendships. To have friends, you have to be a friend. This is something very important that God shared with me. Sometimes you'll go to an old-age home and see an elderly lady or gentleman sitting all by themselves in the corner – and often you can see that they are very bitter and twisted old folk. People get so upset with their family, because they'll be told that no one ever comes to see them. I don't say that it's justifiable, but when you read between the lines and get the full story, you'll see that there's a reason. You'll often find that when they were young they were very selfish, and maybe didn't want to have any children anyway, because it was going to interfere with their social lives. Or maybe they had children and just did not give them any time, because they were so busy with their own programme.

Being a farmer, I can tell you honestly that you will reap what you sow – every time. If you do not sow love,

159

you will not reap love. You'll be all by yourself. If you sow selfishness, that's exactly what you'll reap; if you are self-centred, you'll end up on your own. But if you've sown into other people's lives, you'll be inundated with friends, relationships and family. That's what I love so much about the poorer communities.

If you go deep into Zululand you'll find no children's homes or old-age homes there. The old people and the children are absorbed into the social structure of the community, because they just don't have any money to send their loved ones away. So they take care of them. You'll find no mental asylums in those rural areas. If there's a man or woman who's simple and has the mind of a child, that person will just wander from village to village and sleep in anybody's house. They'll be given food to eat and clothes to wear. I'm sure that's the way it was meant to be.

Jesus was once sitting talking to a group of men and women. They came to the door and said, "Your mother and Your brothers are here to see You." Jesus said, "Who are My mother and My brothers, but those who obey the Word of God?"

As believers we have the extremely wonderful bonus of belonging to a very extensive family. Wherever I travel – I might be right down in the southernmost part of New Zealand, or up in the northern part of Africa, or in a built-up area in the middle of London – within five minutes of speaking to my fellow believers there, I'll feel that I've known them all my life. That never happened to me before I became a Christian. Before I became a Christian, I could be friends with a man for twenty years and still not know him, because of that independent spirit:

"Thus far, no more..."

"Don't share any personal problems with me, because I've got enough problems of my own."

Have a casual talk... "Let's talk about the weather, but nothing deeper than that..."

But with believers you can open your heart, and within half an hour you can be weeping on each other's shoulders, encouraging one another and praying for one another. That is the beauty of being a comrade-in-arms with the Lord Jesus Christ.

My "running career" was very short-lived. I prayed for a young lady who was paralysed. Many others also prayed for her, that God would heal her. God did, and she was restored.

Trying to build up her faith level, I asked her if she believed in miracles.

She said, "Yes."

I said, "Do you believe I can run the Comrades Marathon?" That's about ninety-odd kilometres. It's two standard marathons back-to-back: 42.2 km plus 42.2 km, and another five on top, just for good measure. It's a killer. I've never been a runner. I was in the heavyweight division. I've done weightlifting, power-lifting and I've played rugby. I ride horses. But I've never been a runner.

She said, "Yes."

I said, "You're on!"

I challenged her. With less than six months training, which is ridiculous, I managed by the skin of my teeth to qualify to run the Comrades by doing one standard marathon (42.2 km) and literally squeezing in with a couple of minutes to go. I qualified. Then I ran the Comrades Marathon with my future son-in-law, who has now become my son.

I will never forget that race as long as I live. I did not

finish the race. I need to be honest with you. After running from Pietermaritzburg, I was just coming into Durban when I collapsed and passed out, fourteen kilometres before the finish. I was totally dehydrated. I did everything back to front. I ran too fast in the beginning, didn't take in any electrolytes, or eat any food; I drank very little, and basically dehydrated myself completely. One of my dear old ladies who prayed for me said to me that Jesus put the lights out.

Lance Armstrong, the great cyclist, seven-time winner of the Tour de France, said, "Pain lasts for a day but to quit lasts forever." I can honestly tell you that I did not quit. I passed out. During that race I experienced fellowship and friendship like I've very rarely experienced before or since. It wasn't at the front of the race, where all the gold and silver medallists were running. It was right at the back of the race, where people were struggling just to try and finish within the time frame.

At one stage I remember running and a lady in front of me tripped over. She'd kicked one of the catseyes in the middle of the road. She was extremely tired and she fell over and took the skin off her knees and elbows on the tarmac. She let out some terrible words of blasphemy. I was barely able to keep myself going at that time but I saw young men run up, pick her up, dust her off and help her keep running.

I saw groups of people, obviously from the same club, running together. When one or two members of the club started hitting the wall, as they say, and giving up, they'd come alongside them on either side, talk to them and encourage them just to run to the next light pole, then the next pole, then the next pole... and eventually they would get their stamina back, and their courage, and start running again. Amazing camaraderie, hence the name, the Comrades. I believe the race started after a group of soldiers from the First World War got together just to talk about old times and to encourage one another. Now there's something like twenty thousand runners running it every year.

Basically, I believe God is saying that we need each other. The disciples needed each other, especially when Jesus went home to heaven to be with His Father. You and I need each other. Not just in the hard times; we need each other even in the good times. Sometimes it's so sad to achieve something, accomplish something, be part of something and have no one to share it with.

I remember many years ago – thirty years ago – I went over to Scotland with my oldest daughter. Jill was at home with the rest of the children, who were all very young and at school at that stage. I preached there for three months. It was very hard for me, because we're a very close family. Those three months became like three years for me. I missed my wife, my best friend, so much.

But I remember one autumn afternoon. I was staying in a beautiful castle down in the southern part of Scotland outside a lovely city by the name of Dumfries. It was about four o'clock in the afternoon. The sun was starting to go down pretty quickly, as winter was beginning to move in. The trees were the most amazing colours. I'm talking about oak trees, birch trees, all those trees that grow in Europe. They were all changing colour, from yellows, to oranges, to bronzes, to blood-reds. They were the most beautiful sight I'd ever seen. I walked over a little stone bridge, like those that you see in the movie *Brigadoon*, a sparkling, clear stream running under the bridge. I heard the deer rutting (the owner had six hundred red deer), getting ready for the breeding season. I could hear the antlers banging as they were getting themselves into condition. Beautiful pheasant were running across the road. All I wanted to do was to share this amazing sight with my wife Jill. But she wasn't there. It took away everything from me. It became not even worthwhile, really. I was just so disappointed that I couldn't share it with her and I realized again: What's the point of having it, if you can't share it with anyone?

As I'm writing now, I'm sitting in the car looking over the strawberry fields which belong to my older son, Andrew. I can see him in the distance. He's just given instructions to his workers. The sun's beating down. Spring is in the air and there's one huge bumper crop of strawberries going to be lifted in the next three to four weeks. I haven't had anything to do with it, so I can't take any glory or anything, but it's so wonderful to know that he's doing the thing he loves the most. In a small way, I can be a part of that. My other son is on the other farm. He's waiting for his first batch of beef cattle to arrive, the ones that we bought at the sale together just a few days ago.

We've preached one thing only from the Mighty Men Conferences to the stadiums, to the city halls, to the indoor arenas, to the huge churches: A country will only be as strong as the family unit in that country. If there is no family structure, there is nothing else to hold it together.

An old gentleman came to visit me yesterday. He was in tears, because he has a fine young son who's been going out with a young lady for many years but they have just not got married. They are talking about having children. He said to me, "It's not right. They can't have children if they're not married." I saw the pain in his eyes. He said, "Before I die, I want my son to be married and I want to be able to nurse those grandchildren on my lap, so to speak."

The importance of being dependent on one another! That's why many people will not get married. They see such disaster on the home front. They see the divorce rate climbing all the time and they're not prepared to take the risk. The old gentleman just wants to see his son married to this woman. His son loves her but just doesn't seem to have the courage at this point in time to ask for her hand in marriage. We've prayed about it. I believe that they will get married very soon.

I remember a pop singer, way back, many, many years ago, by the name of Janis Joplin, who sang in one of her songs: "Freedom's just another word for nothing left to lose." Isn't that so tragic? She died of a drug overdose. If we don't expose ourselves and open ourselves up to one another, we become a burden to no one, but we actually become of no consequence.

Jesus exposed Himself to us. He didn't have to, but He wanted to. He showed us the way to live. He humbled Himself. Remember, He served the disciples with the basin, the towel, the water, and washing His disciples' feet. He chose to get involved. He chose to be a part of mankind, because that's how He ordained it to be from the beginning.

The first family that ever existed was the Father, the Son and the Holy Spirit. That is why the family is so important to God. That is why the devil is trying his absolute damnedest to destroy the family, because he knows that once he's destroyed the family, there's nothing left. The strength lies in us depending upon each other.

Marriage is about covenant. It's about depending on one

another. It's about sharing what you've got. It's not a case of fifty-fifty; it's about one hundred per cent from both sides. You cannot be part of a marriage if you're a selfish person. Marriage is all about giving. But you cannot out-give God. That's one thing I've realized in my life. The more you give to God, the more God gives back to you. How? Many different ways! Through children and grandchildren, through brethren in the body of Christ... It's the most wonderful, wonderful experience to be part of the family of God.

When I was a single man, I went over to Australia and worked on a beef stud farm. I had enough money and could have booked into a hotel. I could have lived there quite comfortably but I was lonely. I went to probably the poorest family in town. The man worked in the Roads Department, the woman was a waitress in the evenings. They had three or four children. They made very little money. I paid them a small amount for board and lodging. They didn't ask for much.

I was put in a room with the two boys. There were three bunks and I had to slide into the middle one. The food was absolutely minimal. In fact, I used to sneak around to the pub afterwards and get myself a mixed grill just about every day. But that family included me in everything they did. Whatever they were doing, they would take me out with them. They were very special to me. When I eventually left there, I remember giving them my week's salary because they were really struggling, yet they'd made me feel so welcome and I felt so at home with them.

At the moment I'm listening to a CD called *American Five* by the late Johnny Cash, "The Man in Black", one of my favourite singers. He was a man who had a very hard past. He was involved with drugs and alcohol and he landed up in jail for a short while, but one thing I appreciated about him was that he always sang from his heart and he spoke the truth. The CD I'm listening to was given to me for my birthday. I believe it was the last one Johnny Cash made before he died. You can hear by the way he's singing that he's short of breath and he's just about to meet His Saviour, but the words are very stirring for me.

My youngest daughter listened to it. She said it was very sad for her to listen to. But the man is singing from his heart about the real issues in life. Basically he's making the same point; that we can't walk this road, we can't live this life on our own. Unfortunately, for many of us – and maybe even like Johnny Cash – it takes a while before the penny drops and we realize that we need each other. Johnny Cash is now with his precious Lord Jesus because he was a believer. He didn't always get things right but he acknowledged Jesus Christ as his risen Lord and Saviour. He will never be lonely again.

I think of that very famous English First Division soccer team, Liverpool. Their theme song for the team and the crowd is "You'll Never Walk Alone". Those are words from a famous hymn. I'm sure that thousands and thousands of those fans are not even aware of that fact: That if Jesus Christ is your Lord and Saviour, you will never walk alone. Isn't it amazing that a man can be sitting at a soccer match on a Saturday afternoon singing a famous hymn about our Lord Jesus Christ, and be totally oblivious as to where it comes from, yet still know that we are not meant to operate on our own?

Personally, my favourite soccer team is Manchester United, which is managed by Sir Alex Ferguson. The thing which impresses me most of all about Ferguson's ability is that his team always seems to either win the soccer league every year, or at least be runner-up. He is very consistent and his team operates as one body. He seems to have an amazing ability to get the players to work together, not as individuals.

There are other soccer teams in the world which have much more illustrious individual players, but to get them to play together as a team is another story. Any team sport requires that the players depend on each other in order to be successful. Once again, that camaraderie is absolutely vital if we are going to succeed in anything that we are attempting to do in this life, whether it be in sport, or business, but most of all, of course, in serving God.

I reflect back to when we had the 2009 Mighty Men Conference, where we had approximately two hundred thousand men come together for a weekend, some of them having arrived here three or four days beforehand. It's quite something to try and comprehend with your finite mind. The success of that amazing event was due to teamwork. I thank God for my sons and many, many spiritual sons who put their backs into the preparation of that men's conference for a solid year before it actually took place. I had the easy job. It took me one weekend out of my preaching schedule but it could never have happened if I'd had to organize it myself. It would have just been impossible.

Chapter 13

Sufferance

I never thought that sufferance could be a blessing. I look back at the years of my youth. I was extremely self-confident and totally fearless. The reason for that, I realize, is because I'd never suffered. I would tackle anything: Ride problem horses and delight in the challenge, take on any challenge that came my way, purely because I had no idea of what the consequences would be if I failed. It's only when you've suffered that you start to realize that there's a lot more that could go wrong in life – and indeed that there are consequences that affect other people which result from impulsive decisions.

People often say that they wish that they could have more faith. The first thing we do is introduce them to the school of sorrows. That's how faith comes. There is no need for you to have faith if you are not being tested. I'm not saying tempted, I'm saying tested. God does test us. That's for our own sake, not for His sake. He allows us to go through fiery trials so that we'll come through on the other side with hearts that are soft and full of compassion and understanding. As the old saying goes: No pain, no gain! That, indeed, is what the school of life is all about.

When you're young, you think you know the answer for everything. All those quick formulas... I remember my own Dad, whom I love so much. As I'm getting older, and I look back on his life, I respect and love him even more. He was an uneducated man but he'd been to the school of life, the school of hard knocks. When I was a youngster in my teens, I didn't think my Dad knew too much. When I got into my mid-twenties, I started thinking that my Dad had a few points. Of course, when I got into my mid-forties and right up till now, I think my Dad was a genius. That only comes through life experience. That's why most of the prominent leaders in the world are senior men when they take up their positions. They're not too quick to make instant decisions because of the consequences that might follow.

President Abraham Lincoln comes to mind as an example. That man had such a hard life as a youngster. He had very little formal education; he was self-educated. Yet he became one of the greatest presidents that America has ever had, because he spoke from his heart and he spoke from experience.

One of the greatest men of God to have ever impacted our fair continent of Africa is Dr David Livingstone. He was definitely the most loved. Why? Because he was a man who suffered greatly for the nation! He loved the black people with an absolute passion. He gave them everything.

He came from very meagre roots, a self-educated boy working in the cotton mills in Blantyre, Scotland. He put himself through university, studying medicine. He became a qualified medical doctor, then an astronomer. Being able to read the stars, he was able to map out large tracts of Africa, which up till then had never been mapped. He was a botanist; he identified many plants for the first time. He was a linguist. He made it his business to learn the languages of the black people.

But most of all, he was a man of God, an ambassador for Jesus Christ, a man whom the black people loved with an absolute passion. But it cost him severely. It cost him his life. He died at the age of sixty, having given his all and spent his all for the sake of the Gospel of Jesus Christ.

There's a price for everything in this life. Livingstone paid the price of helping to abolish the horrific slave trade by simply laying down his own life and also that of his family. His wife died in Africa as well. Her body was buried underneath a baobab tree at the mouth of the mighty Zambezi River. His children hardly knew him. The Scripture in John 15:13 comes to mind: "Greater love hath no man than this, that a man lay down his life for his friends" (KJV). That's exactly what David Livingstone did.

By the way, he wasn't the greatest of preachers. In fact, from the reports I've read, he was a very average to below-average preacher, but he had more impact than any evangelist who has ever lived, save the apostle Paul and, of course, the Master Himself.

Often young men have come to me and asked if they can go with me to preach the Gospel. I love having young men going out with me to preach the Gospel. Most of them are much better preachers than I'll ever be. But there's a question: "Are you prepared to drink of the cup?" Not the cup of prosperity, not the cup of blessing, but the cup of suffering.

That's the question that the Lord asked me on my way into the town of Ladysmith when I went to book the town hall for my first ever evangelistic outreach. He asked me three questions:

"Are you prepared to be a fool for me?"

I said, "Lord, that's not a problem. I'm a fool anyway."

Second question: "Are you prepared for people to say all manner of evil about you for My name's sake?"

I said, "Lord, that's not a problem", although after

171

all these years I'm now starting to understand what that means.

Thirdly: "Are you prepared to see less of your family for My name's sake?"

Even in those early days I believe I shed a few tears, not knowing the full extent of what that meant. I said, "Lord, by Your grace. By Your grace, I can." That is the cup of suffering for me.

I've found in my life that the harder it's gone with regard to campaigns, outreaches, trips into Africa, or overseas, the more successful they've been. There's always got to be a price to pay for everything in life. Nothing comes for free. People say the Gospel's free. It's not. It's very costly. It's costly in time; it's costly in relationships, in family time, in money. Huge costs, if you're going to do it properly. The men's conference that we had a few months ago cost us literally millions, in fact we emptied the kitty to do it. But look at the benefits: Thousands and thousands of households being changed forever, because men's lives have been touched.

Missionary Jim Elliot said with regard to preaching the Gospel, "It is no fool who gives what he cannot keep in order to gain what he cannot lose." There is always a tremendous price to pay for serving God. But you know something? I wouldn't change it for anything in the world. If I had to live my life over again, I would do the exact same thing and do it gladly, simply because the Word of God says so. And if you really think about it, this life here on earth is just a mere moment in time in comparison with eternity, where we'll be with our Lord Jesus and with our fellow believers forever.

Many people have role models in their lives – great sportsmen, businessmen, agriculturists, etc.. But my role model is the Lord Jesus Christ Himself. He is my greatest example. He is the One I want to emulate, no one else, at the end of the day. There is no one that I know of who has suffered anything like the Lord Jesus Christ suffered.

When things go tough and get hard, I'm learning not to keep saying, "Lord, why is it always me?" but to rejoice in my tribulation, knowing that it is working good in me. So, the further along life's road that I walk, the more I realize that in order to be effective for God, I must allow Him to increase in my life and I must decrease. Then it does appear that I have more impact in what I'm doing. The Lord really comforts me with the fact that He has promised me (and you) that He will never allow us to be tested or to suffer more than we are able to bear. Sometimes we think: "Lord, I can't take it any more." He reassures us that we can. He says: "My grace is sufficient for you. My strength is made perfect through weakness."

As we continue to come of age, we understand that we have to grow up in order to come of age. The only way we can grow up is to go through the school of hard knocks, as they say. It makes us wise, it makes us more tempered; it gives us more understanding, more patience, more love. We don't judge so quickly. We definitely don't point fingers. We have more mercy for those who have fallen or slipped by the way. That also makes us more holy people. Remember, holiness is the end product of obedience.

I want to close this chapter with a poem written by David Volmer after he returned from MMC 09. It is printed here with his permission.

I choose You

Lord Jesus

I am no longer afraid of persecution,
Nor concerned with worldly retribution,
Lord, I choose You.

Even if I must leave these things behind,
Possibly become estranged from mankind,
Lord, I still choose You.

You said I must follow without condition,
To live my life in complete submission,
Lord, still, I choose You.

To love You above all else is expected,
For this I will perhaps be rejected,
Lord, I choose You.

I may be asked to make a sacrifice,
Perhaps with less I must suffice,
Lord, I still choose You.

Total surrender is what You ask,
Complete dedication to this task,
Lord, still, I choose you.

To carry this burden is light,
The weight of this cross my delight.
Because on the cross that one day,
True love was put on display,
When You chose me.

I choose You, Lord.
Amen.

Chapter 14
Poverty

Isn't it amazing: When you are young, perhaps a school leaver, your idea of success is to make lots of money, to be famous, to be at the top of your league. Yet, so often, that's actually the last thing that you really should be focusing on.

In order to have success in this life, in order to live a life which is fulfilled, one must have a vision and be focused on that vision. A mighty man of God said, "A man's purpose on earth is to love the Lord and to enjoy Him forever." There is so much unhappiness in the world, because the very things that we think will bring us peace and contentment and fulfilment in life are the things that will bring us into extreme poverty. It's with great sadness that we look at some of the "icons" of this world. Michael Jackson had one of the saddest lives that I've ever heard of. Elvis Presley was another one. These were pop stars that shook the world. They had everything that money could buy. They had fame and wealth, but no peace and no joy.

Some men that I know who have made it big in the eyes of the world, head up huge corporations, and are extremely wealthy, but have nothing to show for it at the end of their lives. Their families have rejected them; they are physically sick and some of them are mentally ill as well. Again that Scripture comes to mind: "What does it profit a man if he gains the whole world and he loses his soul?" In this world there are many "poor" rich people who possibly need more help than those who don't own anything in this life.

Many years ago, when we were just starting farming – and were living in our small wattle-and-mud house that I had had to build in three weeks when Jill and I arrived with our truck and trailer from Zambia – an extremely rich man, a lovely man, came to visit us and have a cup of tea with us. As he was leaving, Jill gave him a pocket of potatoes, just as a small gift. He was so overwhelmed. He couldn't believe it. He was, in fact, quite emotional. The reason for this was that no one ever offered him anything, because they all thought that he had so much money he didn't need anything. But that pocket of potatoes spoke loudly to him that we appreciated him and his visit to us, and we wanted to give him something back in return.

Unfortunately, poverty has a stigma attached to it. At the moment I'm reading a book called *The Hole in Our Gospel* written by Richard Stearns, the president of World Vision. He talks about the fact that poor people are often despised and looked down upon, regarded as foolish, lazy, not able to achieve, because they are poor. I've seen it myself. A poor man's motorcar will break down at the side of the road. People will drive past and despise him and say, "That man can't even look after his motorcar correctly!" not realizing that he just does not have the finance, or the wherewithal to run that car properly. But he needs it, because that's how he's earning his keep, using it as a taxi.

Poverty often has nothing to do with a man's intelligence or ability to work hard. In fact, says Richard Stearns, most poor people work harder than wealthy people. They have to, in order to eat. If we took a good look at our circumstances, at where we've come from, we'd realize how privileged we are to have had a good education; maybe to have been brought up in a godly home; to have been motivated from an early age to become an achiever and given the opportunity to study further and have a good tertiary education. Then we would understand why we have been successful to a measure.

If we'd been born in the Third World – where there's not enough food to eat; where we'd have to fetch and carry water in order to wash and get ready for work; and then, once we've got to work, feel tired because we've had nothing to eat, so our minds are not working too clearly and our bodies are weary because physically they're lacking nourishment – we would realize that poverty has got nothing to do with an individual person. It's to do with the circumstances in which he has been brought up.

When you see that man leaning on his shovel for a couple of hours, perhaps he's trying to regain strength to finish his task? And you think he's lazy... Or when that person cannot get that sum – that is so simple – right at school, you may start to have a bit more patience and understanding when you realize that he's battling to think straight. He's just short of energy, because he's had no food that morning.

I'll never forget an incident that took place in the northern reaches of Mozambique. We'd been up there, preaching, with the Seed Sower and away from home for quite some time. The going was very tough. A pastor had invited us to his village to preach the Gospel. Needless to say, there was no running water, no lights, or anything. We pitched our tents that we camped in. There was a forty-four-gallon (210-litre) drum full of water that was given to us by the pastor to use for drinking, for washing, and so on. Being typical westerners, the team used the whole drum before the night was out, washing, brushing our teeth and cooking. As a result, the drum was empty.

My little bell tent was placed right next to that forty-four-gallon drum. I'm a very light sleeper. At about three o'clock in the morning, I heard someone very light-footed walk past my tent. They obviously weren't wearing shoes. About half an hour later, I heard water pouring into the drum. Then the gentle feet walked past my tent again. Half an hour later, more water was poured into the drum. This went on until about five o'clock in the morning.

I got up out of bed and was having my quiet time. When I heard the water being poured in for the last time (by this time the drum was overflowing), I peeped out of my tent and saw the pastor's wife with a twenty-litre bucket on her head. She'd been carting water for us from three o'clock in the morning. It was a walk of about half a kilometre from the drum down to the river, where she had collected the water. I was so humbled by that act of faith, of serving, of humility, because, when everybody got out of bed, the drum was waiting, full of water, for us to be able to bathe and to wash ourselves, to make tea in the morning – and we had not even seen her. True humility, like you will never see in an affluent society, unfortunately.

Poverty teaches us perseverance. It builds character into us, and it teaches us immense patience. In the rural areas of Africa, I've seen people sit at a hospital and wait all day just to have an appointment with the doctor. Yet, when it comes to those who live in a prosperous society, I find patience a virtue that is terribly lacking.

There's a beautiful prayer that St Francis of Assisi wrote:

Lord, make me an instrument of Your peace.
Where there is hatred, let me sow love;
where there is injury, pardon;
where there is doubt, faith;
where there is despair, hope;
where there is darkness, light;
where there is sadness, joy.

O Divine Master, grant that I may not so much seek
to be consoled, as to console;
to be understood, as to understand;
to be loved, as to love.
For it is in giving that we receive;
it is in pardoning that we are pardoned;
it is in dying that we are born to Eternal Life. Amen.

These are the qualities that the Lord is looking for in His people. These are the qualities that bring fulfilment in life. Yet the world teaches us the absolute opposite. The world teaches us that we must stand on everybody to get to the top. The world teaches us that the more arrogant and independent we can become the stronger and the more successful we'll be. That's the absolute opposite to what God teaches us to be.

I remember watching a video that was given to me by a friend and sent over from America. The video showed your regular family from the First World nations. I think they came from New York, USA. The family unit consisted of a father, a mother, a teenage daughter and, I think, two boys. I don't think they were Christians. They went out to Africa, to Kenya, to live amongst a rural tribe. The children had just about lived on fast foods. They had their Walkmans plugged into their ears most of the time. They were totally switched off when it came to the things of life.

When they arrived with their electric toothbrushes and all their fancy gimmicks and gadgets, they faced a very rude awakening. The tribe picked them up at the airport in a truck. That was their first shock; riding in the back of an open truck. They took them right out into the bush, where there was no running water, no electricity. They had to start right back at the beginning.

The first ten days were absolutely horrific. I think the young teenage girl almost had a nervous breakdown, especially when she had to be part of some ceremony where they slaughtered a goat, cut its throat while it was still alive, and the blood was poured out into a container. The goat was then skinned and the carcass hung up in a tree to be cooked with all the entrails, which had been washed.

The young boy took a liking to one of the dogs and started feeding it. The dog's bowl was a bit dirty, so he washed it in a drum of drinking water. As a result, none of the family could drink any water and it was an absolute disaster. They had to take another drum and drive twenty, thirty kilometres to find drinking water. Yet the head of the home, a black man from the tribe, showed extreme compassion towards this young boy when he broke down and wept having realized the terrible mess he had made. Slowly but surely, a bond started to build between this headman of the village and the young boy. He began to teach him how to hunt, how to make a bow and arrow, and started teaching him about the different plants, the bird life and the animals.

The mother from New York had to do all her washing by hand. She began to see what this African mother had to do when it came to work and things like personal hygiene.

She began to understand some of the rigours and the tremendous pressure that people live through because of poverty.

The young teenage girl had by this time found that her Walkman was of no more effect or importance to her, and was totally useless. All her fancy cosmetics became irrelevant to her. She started to appreciate the more real things in life, like taking care of the little babies, like sitting and talking. That was something else that the youngsters of the American family had forgotten how to do – how to sit around the fire at night and talk, sing and laugh, because there was no TV, no iPods, no Walkmans, just each other. They began to come out of themselves, to develop and to form a love for one another, to talk about day-to-day things.

Slowly but surely, they started to grow. I think they were only there for a few weeks. When the time arrived for them to return to the US, the children were heartbroken and wept. They didn't want to leave their newfound friends. The parents themselves were not looking forward to returning to "successful living".

There is nothing wrong with being successful. In fact, the money which God has given us, and the ability to generate it, can be ploughed back and used in the kingdom of God. But it has to be used in the right context. If you just keep taking food to hungry people and not teaching them how to grow their own food, all you're doing is making them dependent upon you. The only person who will benefit from that is you, because it'll make you feel good, but it won't help the person at all. You've heard the old cliché: Instead of feeding the man a fish, give him a hook and teach him how to fish for himself.

Life can be very complex because, as Richard Stearns says, you can educate somebody, you can teach them skills, you can even set them up in business but if, for example, the economy of the country is in a mess and the man cannot sell his produce at the market, or he graduates from school with top marks but cannot find a job, none of that helps very much.

The Bible says that godliness with contentment is great gain (1 Timothy 6:6). Some of the most discontented people I've ever met in my life are people who have much. They're never satisfied with what they've got. They always want more. Some of the most contented people I've ever seen are those who have little, but appreciate everything they have.

In this day and age in which we live I think it's so important for us to get back to basics. It's the blue-collar worker who is in demand today, not the white-collar worker. University degrees are a dime a dozen. I have nothing against education. My children are all educated. However, to have a man who can use his hands: A plumber; a blacksmith (like my late father was); an electrician; a carpenter (like my Saviour was); a farmer (like many of the greatest prophets in the Bible were), is something that society is looking for today, especially when you go on missions into Africa or into underprivileged Third World countries. They are looking for practical help, not theory. Some of the finest preachers I've ever heard in my life are men from Third World nations. They are not looking for preachers. God forbid. They have enough. They are looking for people who can teach them how to repair a motor, or an engine, when it breaks down.

One of the finest documentaries I've ever seen in my life was a *National Geographic* documentary about the San people (the Bushmen). This one was about a small little tribe, a clan, who lived off the land in the Kalahari Desert. They had one borehole and a small little borehole pump that supplied all the water for their goats, sheep, and all their needs. The little single-cylinder diesel engine that drove the borehole, that pumped out the water, broke down. It was in the middle of their driest season. Eventually, in order to exist, the people had to move off and try and find water elsewhere.

A man – I'm not sure if he was a Christian or not – came out from overseas to visit them. He found that there was nothing left. Everything was deserted and they were gone. He tracked them down and found them two hundred and fifty kilometres away. They were really suffering, almost to the point of death. They had one poor old horse that they tried to keep fed, because they thought they could use the horse to hunt down an animal. They used to collect all the wild cucumbers that you find in the desert and mash them up together just to get enough moisture to feed this horse. One of the younger men eventually rode the horse and tried to kill an antelope to feed them.

This man, their visitor, called them back. He was obviously a diesel mechanic by trade, not a professor of anthropology, or anything like that. Within half a day, he had repaired their little diesel engine. The pump started and the water started flowing. There was absolute pandemonium. There was rejoicing. It was like heaven had come down to earth. It was unbelievable. All because one man fixed a little single-cylinder diesel engine and brought joy to a whole clan of Bushmen people.

I saw a cartoon once in a Christian magazine that really saddened me. It was a photograph of a preacher, a huge man with a really fat belly. He had a big black Bible and was pointing down to a little boy, preaching to him. The little boy had a begging bowl. He also had a fat belly, but it wasn't because of lots of food, it was because of malnutrition. The little insert at the bottom of the cartoon was: "Tell me, preacher, will there be food in heaven?" The only way that we can deal with poverty is in a practical manner, not in a theoretical way. People need practical help.

People need hope, too. Without hope, there is no future. Many years ago, my wife and I were invited to a mid-week church meeting hosted by World Vision. There was a terrible plight of hungry, poverty-stricken people in Calcutta, India. These people were camped around a pond of water, which they were using for their drinking water, their washing and for their ablutions, because they had nothing else. It was absolutely horrific to see. I'll never forget my wife, Jill, saying, "But Angus, did you see the look in the people's eyes?" Apart from them being emaciated because they were hungry and underfed, and the squalor, which was unbelievable, there was something that was even worse. There was hopelessness in the eyes of those people. They needed Jesus Christ.

As I write this book, we have one more trip to do into Central Africa. We started in Cape Town and we've moved up through most African countries, up the eastern side of Africa, and got as far as Uganda. We've got to do Sudan, Egypt, and then into Israel. That's a mandate that God gave us. When we go into Central Africa and right into the rural areas where there's nothing, the people there are craving Bibles. It's the Word of God they want. They're not craving the food or clothes which we take with us, but Bibles. It's not even Gospels, the Gospel of John, or just the New

Testament they want. They want the whole Bible – the Old Testament, the New Testament, and the Psalms. They have an absolute hunger for the Word of God, because they know that's where their hope lies.

God has put eternity in the hearts of man. It doesn't matter if he's in the middle of the Amazon jungle or the middle of the Congo, he knows in his heart about eternity. He has an insatiable hunger to know his Creator in a personal way. That's why it's so exciting for me as a preacher, as an evangelist, to be living at this time. I've now been preaching the Gospel of Jesus Christ for close on thirty years, and yet never before in my life have I seen such a desire in people to know about the Living God.

This world is filled with people who are living with a poverty mentality when it comes to their future and eternal life. There is a continual hunger that is generated in a man's spirit when the Spirit of God is not present in his life. Everything else becomes obsolete, uninteresting and totally boring, until we find our purpose in this life for living. It's not just about getting up every morning and eating. There's more to life than just eating, drinking and being merry.

Young people are desperately searching at the moment. That, in my humble opinion, is where the greatest poverty in the world is today. There's no reason for getting out of bed in the morning, no reason for training and getting yourself physically and mentally fit, because you have no purpose in life. Of course, you know the old saying: The devil always makes work for idle hands.

On a plane trip back from Australia a couple of years ago, I saw a movie that I first thought was a wildlife documentary, it was so magnificent. It was actually the true story of a young American university graduate. It touched me so deeply. This young man was diligent at school, and university, where he graduated with flying colours. His mother and father were there at the graduation.

He had a beat-up old secondhand motorcar that he'd bought, obviously through working after hours. They went out for a meal. His father and mother were so proud of him. His father wanted to know what he was going to do with his life now. He said that he was still trying to find out what his purpose was. You could see that his Dad was quite impatient because he was, I think, a nuclear scientist or something similar. He was quite embarrassed about his son's old motorcar. He said, "Well, we're going to have to get you a decent car."

That was the last straw for his son. He got into that old motorcar and drove out of town, as far as he could into the Rocky Mountains, one of the most beautiful areas I've ever seen. He just kept driving until the car couldn't go any more. Then he parked it in the bush, took off the number plates and burnt them, so that there was no trace as to who owned the vehicle. He got a rucksack and a rifle and went into the Rockies to go and live by himself, and to try and find out what his purpose in life was.

He found an old broken-down bus that had no wheels, or axles or anything, right in the middle of nowhere and used that for his shack. His parents by this time, of course, had called the police. They tried to find him but couldn't trace him. It was a very sad but very real story.

The story unravels that he used that bus as his base camp and travelled around America. He worked for all types of people. I remember he worked for a harvesting contractor with his big combine harvesters and trucks – a rough but genuine guy – for a while. He ended up getting a lift with some hippies, who took care of him for a time. But they were real people. What had happened, you see, was that he'd come from a home that wasn't real. There were flashbacks of when he was a child, and you'd see how his mother and father used to fight and scream at each other and get violent with each other. These things had burnt a tremendous sense of insecurity into this young man.

I think this is where there is much poverty at the moment, especially in western society. The pressure is so great for Dad to make payments on all these new-fangled gadgets, although half of them are not even necessary, that he has to work those extra hours. He becomes impatient and tired, and as result Mom and the children suffer. He actually thinks that he's doing the right thing. It's a tragedy. I believe that the devil himself is behind it, trying to keep us on that treadmill and work us to the bone until we can't even think straight any more, and then gradually, but surely, break down the family completely.

This movie unfortunately didn't have a happy ending. The young man was very much into herbs and natural food. He'd mistaken some poisonous plants for edible ones, accidentally poisoned himself and died. Because of the tragedy of his death, his mother and father became believers. All he had wanted was a purpose. He wanted a goal. He wanted something to live for. He wanted something constructive.

The poverty that I'm talking about, the real poverty in life, can only be overcome when a man meets that Carpenter from Galilee, who is the Bread of Life. He says: "He who eats of Me will never hunger again. He who drinks of the water which I give will never thirst again."

Chapter 15
Speak your heart

It is only when you've come face to face with meeting the Lord in heaven and have then been given a reprieve that you realize how important it is in life not to waste time. Don't put off for tomorrow what you can do today.

I remember the story in the Bible of the rich man who lived a terrible life (Luke 16:19–31). Remember, Lazarus was the poor man who lay at his gates and begged, and even the dogs came and licked his sores. Lazarus was a poor man but he loved God. He died and went to heaven, where he was comforted by Father Abraham. In time, the rich man also died. He went to hell. The Bible says that he looked up and saw Abraham far away, with Lazarus by his side. Across the chasm that separated them, the rich man cried out to Father Abraham, "Please send Lazarus to tell my brothers to mend their ways so that they don't come to this place!"

Relationships are so important. Don't put off for tomorrow what you can do today, especially in the area of relationships. We cannot afford to have unsettled business lingering and say: "Well, we'll let him sweat a little bit," or, "We'll wait a while and let him suffer a bit." Rather forgive and put relationships right and move on, because life is short.

We've got to learn to speak our heart. Many of us were brought up in the old system: stiff upper lip; boys don't cry; don't show your feelings; don't cry in public; don't make a fool of yourself. But, you know, all that is wrong. The Lord Jesus Christ wept in public, and He's God! He spoke His heart. It cost Him His life. Gone are the days of sweeping things under the carpet. That's the old Victorian way that never worked anyway. Our children need to see who we are. They need to know our heart. They need to know our strengths and our weaknesses. We've got to start speaking our heart, especially to our spouse, our children, and our loved ones. If there is someone who is doing something that is upsetting you, go and speak to them so that they can put it right, and your relationship can continue to grow.

We need to speak our hearts if we want, in any way, to impact people. Isaiah 40:2 says: "Speak to the heart of Jerusalem..." I think that the Lord is saying that it's not head knowledge that will get a person converted, it's heart knowledge. I went to a church service yesterday morning and one of my spiritual sons preached for the first time. He's a very successful businessman, and was also a very successful sportsman in his time, but this was a first for him and I could sense, when we prayed for him before the service, that he was extremely excited and maybe also a little bit nervous. Yet he got up on the platform, and when he started to speak his heart, he touched lives. It was a very special service. When people see Jesus in you, that's when they will respond.

Then, as we see the time is getting shorter before the coming of the Lord, we need to do what we've always dreamed of doing. I always dreamed of becoming an evangelist. I used to go through all the motions. I used to get in the back of the pick-up. I used to preach to the maize plants. They used to bow their heads and accept Jesus Christ as Saviour. The wind would just blow through that maize crop. I used to laugh and cry and dream of it. I've been dreaming of that since I was sixteen years old. Now my dream has come to pass, and I'm preaching to more people than I ever thought I would have the privilege of preaching to. It's because I followed hard after that dream.

You need to dream. There's nothing sadder than to see a man who's come of age and is bitter and very disappointed because he didn't do what he wanted to do; he didn't fulfil his dream. I can honestly say that I have lived life to the full and have no regrets. The Lord has been so gracious to me.

How do you complete a thousand-kilometre journey? By taking the first step! Even now, as I'm writing this book, I'm about to have a meeting with three young men who are going to help me fulfil a part of the dream which God gave to me. That was to take a twenty-ton Mercedes-Benz lorry full of Bibles from Cape Town to Jerusalem. As I said earlier, we've got as far as Uganda. We've hoping that in 2011 we'll finish the trip. But it needs to be planned. It needs to be shared – and I need to encourage the men to fulfil the dream. I have many volunteers but I'm going to be very sensitive about whom I choose, because it is a very serious commitment and it's going to cost a lot in time, money and energy. That's what makes a man tick, doing the will of Him who sent us, and finishing His work. That's what Jesus said in John 4:34 (KJV): "My meat is to do the will of Him that sent me, and to finish His work."

The main reason I talk about relationships is because our journey here on earth is hard enough as it is, without carrying unforgiveness on our shoulders. It's like that proverbial fifty-kilogram bag of cement, which gets heavier as we continue. We need to put it down at the foot of the Cross and move on.

Some of you may say, "Well, the person won't forgive me." That's not your responsibility. You have to forgive them and release them and give them an opportunity to make right. Then move on with your life. Nobody in his right mind wants to have enemies in this world, but the more you stand up for Jesus, the more the enemies will come. You don't even have to try. They will just come, because the devil hates what God is doing and he'll come against anybody who is standing up for the principles of the Gospel of Jesus Christ.

In the little Methodist church in Greytown where I met the Lord as my personal Saviour, the minister, Errol Hind, did a lot of follow-up work with me and became a dear friend. He still is to this day. We had a misunderstanding once. I was running a youth camp for him and the kids got a bit out of hand. One of them was my own son. A mirror was broken in the gents' bathroom and a sewerage pipe outside was broken when one of the boys ran a tyre up against it.

When I went back after the weekend, I told him about all the boys who had given their lives to Christ. I was so excited. He told me that the owner of the youth camp had been in touch with him and said that there had been a bit of damage: "Please try and be more careful."

I took personal offence. I said that I couldn't really care about how much damage took place; kids gave their lives to Christ. Of course, now, as a mature man, I realize the importance of responsibility. I was prepared to pay for all the damages but it caused a bit of a rift between the two of us. I think he thought I was a bit irresponsible, and probably quite rightly so, and I was quite put off because I was so excited about those boys who had given their lives to Christ.

The minister decided to have a day of prayer. I think it was coming up to Easter. The church was open all day and people could come in and out and pray as the Holy Spirit led them. I came in to pray in the middle of the day, in my work clothes. I think I was in my overalls, still trying to build that farm. As I was going up to the altar rail to kneel and pray, out of the corner of my eye I saw the minister sitting in the front row having a time of prayer.

You know, I could not pray to the Lord. Nothing came out of my heart. I looked across and it was as if the Holy Spirit said to me, "Go and settle your differences." As I stood up, the minister stood up and we came together, embraced each other and wept in each other's arms. Then, when I started to pray, the prayers just touched the throne room of heaven.

When there is unforgiveness, it puts a barrier between God and us. Deal with that unforgiveness, so that you can move on and redeem the time. Time is of the essence. There are so many people out there who need to hear the good news of Jesus Christ. If it doesn't come through us, who is it going to come through? I have come to realize in my own life that if the Christian doesn't set the standard by forgiving his brother, or going the extra mile, or by setting a moral standard, who's going to do it?

I think that many of the problems that we have in the world today are because Christians do not stand up and call sin by its name. We cannot serve two masters. Jesus said clearly in Matthew 12:30: "He who is not for Me is against Me, and he who does not gather with Me scatters abroad." We need to set the precedent. We need to ask forgiveness from our brother, we need to turn the other cheek and we need to go the extra mile, so that people in the world can do

Mighty Men Conference 09

Real men praising God

The Buchan Family (except for Paul, Lindi and K Praschma)

Angus about to be airlifted to hospital

Healed – Angus on stage on Sunday morning post heart-attack

Angus in his prayer room

Angus shooting Grassroots episodes for TV screening

Angus and one of his horses

ngus riding Dagga Boy

Angus and Callum – one of his 7 grandchildren

the same. If they see that we condone things like abortion, same-sex marriages, divorce, and so on, they will do so too. It is vital in any country to have a moral standard and the world is busy rejecting that at the moment. It is up to the Christian to set that standard.

The fact that we, as believers, are saved by grace and not by good works is a wonderful gift from God – and nobody is more aware of that fact than I am. However, in James 2:14–17, the Lord asks: "How can you tell a man to go well, and to keep warm, when he has nowhere to lay his head and nothing to eat, and say that you are serving the Lord by faith?" In other words, faith has feet; it is a doing word. Jesus says that you shall know them by the fruit that they produce.

Chapter 16
How the mighty
have fallen

I'm sitting in my quiet time room, early this Sunday morning, meditating on the Word of God the Holy Spirit has spoken into my heart. I'm reading the Word of God, the Bible, which is so sweet to my soul. As I grow older, it seems to mean so much more to me and seems to become so much more applicable and pertinent.

I was reading in 2 Samuel 12, the story of the parable of Nathan, the prophet, and King David's confession. I realized again: When you start out in life, especially when you start your Christian walk, you can become so judgmental, especially if you haven't filled the shoes of the person you are judging. I have often heard a poor man say: "If I had lots of money I wouldn't be as stingy as Bill Gates. He doesn't give enough away," yet I don't think there's a man who gives away more money to charities and needy causes than Bill Gates. The poor man would expect him to give more. The amazing thing is that if that poor man came into the kind of money that Bill Gates has, I'm not so sure he'd give away quite so much!

The point I'm trying to make is that unless you've been there yourself it's better not to say anything. Please, I'm not condoning anything, but I think of some of the celebrities in Hollywood who have been married five, six times. You say that would never happen to you. But, without being nasty, perhaps you're not as good-looking as they are, so perhaps you are not so tempted by a beautiful woman or handsome man. Unless you've been there yourself, it's very easy to judge.

I'm not condoning sin of any description. But I am saying as one has lived longer in this life, you start to realize how easy it is to fall into sin through temptation, through circumstances. It's much easier to have compassion upon people who have fallen into sin than it is when you're young and you've never been tempted, when you've never had the power, the finance, the exposure or the fame that sometimes comes as life goes on. Hence the saying: People who live in glass houses shouldn't throw stones.

It's only by the grace of God that I can tell you that I'm still standing today. When I hear of a mighty man like King David, the greatest king that Israel has ever had – a fine, handsome-looking man, who had an incredible relationship with the Lord, a personal relationship, who spoke to Him, prayed with Him, sang songs for Him, and wrote most of the psalms for Him – when a man of this calibre falls, you feel like saying: "What hope is there for me, Lord?"

I remember so clearly the day when Jimmy Swaggart, the great Gospel singer, fell from grace through immorality. It was about six o'clock in the evening and I was sitting watching the news with my late Dad, before he became a Christian; a tough man who spoke his mind. On the news headlines there was a picture of Jimmy Swaggart, the tears running down his face, saying how he's so sorry, he's let the Lord down, he's let his family down, he's let his fellow believers down.

I didn't know what to do. I was expecting my Dad to say, "You see what I'm saying? A bunch of hypocrites!" But he didn't. He looked at me and said, "Angus, we're all human and every one of us is susceptible to falling." I was so proud of my Dad that day. But, you see, he'd walked a much longer road than I had up to then.

I'm definitely not suggesting that we move the goalposts. Right is right and wrong is wrong. The Bible says very clearly that without holiness no man will see God. However, we live in an impure world and the devil goes about like a roaring lion, seeking whom he may devour. We're all familiar with the three Ps: power, pennies and petticoats. The devil doesn't have to invent anything else, because it's worked so well for him.

What is the moral of the story? When you come of age, you can understand more directly how the devil sets a trap for a successful man or woman of God to fall into – and to be pre-warned is to be pre-armed. That is the point I'm making. King David should have been away at war with his men. He stayed at home. He was idle. The devil always makes work for idle hands. If you have a problem in any area that you battle with, get yourself busy with the things of God. That'll be the greatest deterrent for you. If you're always feeling sick, and you think you might be a bit of a hypochondriac, rather go and visit really sick people and start praying for them. I'm telling you, my friend, all of a sudden you'll realize that you're not that sick.

Keep away from the areas and issues where you know you are weak. If you have a problem in any way with lust, don't go near the bookshops that sell pornographic material. If you have a problem with alcohol, don't go into a drinking house, a pub, or a club that sells alcohol. Never visit anybody on your own, especially someone on their own who has called you to come and pray for them. Always take somebody with you. Wherever I go to preach, wherever it is in the world, I will always take one other person with me. By the way, I'm a grandfather. It's got nothing to do with age; it's to do with spiritual warfare. Do not give the enemy half a chance to try and trip you up.

David was on his own when he walked out onto his verandah in the cool of the day and saw that beautiful woman bathing. If he'd been with some of his generals, it would never have happened. If he'd been doing what he was told to do, it would never have happened. I'm not just talking about just any man, I'm talking about the apple of the Lord's eye, a man after God's own heart. We need to be so aware and so conscious of the spiritual warfare that we're involved in.

Don't for a moment believe that no one will find out. That's the oldest trick in the book. It's like a thief who really believes he'll be the first man who will never be caught. Remember the Great Train Robbery, until recently the biggest robbery in the world? The robbers really believed they would never be caught. Every single one of them was caught and jailed. I believe one of them was released from jail just the other day. He's spent his whole life either on the run or in jail.

If you are contemplating having an affair with a woman who is not your wife, or a man who is not your husband, and you think you'll never be caught out, I can tell you that that is the devil's oldest trick in the book. There's a Scripture which says: "Be sure that your sin will find you out" (Numbers 32:23).

You must remember that Nathan was told by God – no one else – what David had done. Nathan approached God's chosen anointed leader and told him a sad story about a poor family that had one sheep. They loved and nurtured that sheep, kept it in the house and fed it. There was another very rich and selfish farmer, who had a whole herd of sheep. A visitor came and the rich farmer wanted to prepare a feast for the visitor. He took the poor man's one and only sheep, slaughtered it and offered it up to his guest.

When Nathan related this to David, David was furious. He demanded to know who the man was, and said he would be dealt with severely. Nathan, the prophet, the man of God, said: "You are that man." With that, David broke down. Nathan continued: "God loves you, and God will forgive you. But, for the rest of your life, in your house there will be tragedy. Even your own family will turn upon you."

David had taken Bathsheba, the woman that he had had the affair with, the woman that he looked down upon from his balcony in the cool of the evening, for his wife. David made her pregnant with his child. So, very discreetly, he had her husband murdered. A number of other soldiers told lies to cover his deeds. Then Bathsheba became David's wife, but their child died at birth. God said that would happen. Of course, unfortunately, it didn't end there. David's own flesh and blood, his son Absalom, whom he loved dearly, hunted down his own father and tried to kill him. It was only David's faithful soldiers who prevented that from happening. Eventually, Absalom himself was killed.

My friend, there is nothing more serious than to take the Lord lightly. Our God is a holy God. He cannot look upon unrighteousness at all. You and I might be fooling everybody else. But we will never fool the Lord, because He lives inside us. He knows our every thought and every breath that we take.

It's an amazing thing. It's almost like sin propagates sin.

I've seen it in some homes, some businesses, and with some people. The tragedy just seems to go on and on. I've seen it in some prominent families in the world. There's such a constant plague of sin. Accidents, people dying unnatural deaths, adultery, divorce, it just seems to proliferate. That is so sad.

On the other hand, those who walk according to the Word of God, who walk in the ways of God, seem to go from one degree of success to another. Yes, there are hardships and setbacks. Tell me about it! But, at the end of the day, the Lord makes things right for those who love Him.

The thing which saved David was the fact that he knew how to repent. He knew how to say sorry, he knew how to seek forgiveness from God. That's exactly what happened. He repented. You can read it in the Psalms. He was so desperate at one stage that he said: "O to have the wings of a bird and fly away!" He understood about the depths of despair – and his enemies really heaped it on him. Isn't it amazing that it's only in times of real desperation, when things are not going well for you, that you really know who your friends are? That's how it was with King David. The tragedy about sin is that it's very costly. You never hear of David doing any great acts after the events of 2 Samuel 12.

You've heard the old saying: "But for the grace of God, there go I." I don't think there's a man alive anywhere in the world who had a closer walk with God than King David did. Yet, unfortunately, he fell. We praise God that he repented, mended his ways, and lived out his life as a man of God.

We need to exercise tremendous grace towards those in Christian leadership who have fallen into sin of one kind or another, and try with all our might to see them totally and completely restored. We can never, ever, condone sin of any description. If that man is not prepared to change his ways, there is nothing more you can do with him than to pray for him. If he persists in his sin, you have to part company. What does light have in common with darkness? Nothing. I do thank God for one thing: James 5:16 says: "The effective, fervent prayer of a righteous man [or woman] avails much." There's tremendous power in prayer. As we pray for those who have fallen by the way, I know that God will save them from eternal damnation. Some of the biggest rogues in society have been used by God to win countless numbers of people to Him. That is why I am so in love with the Lord Jesus Christ.

I praise God that He chooses the "whoevers" to use in the building of His kingdom. He chose a little shepherd boy to defeat a giant who was mocking His name and His people. I remember with great fondness reading the life story of that great man of God, Dwight L Moody, one of the greatest modern evangelists of all times. He lived in the 1800s. He was a very simple, uneducated, farm boy who became a shoe salesman. They say that he was so gifted with his ability to sell things that he would have become a multimillionaire if he hadn't gone into the ministry of preaching the Gospel of Jesus Christ.

He and fellow American Ira Sankey were touring Britain when a huge revival broke out. He went there for a three-week campaign and stayed for three years. Thousands upon thousands of people followed him from meeting to meeting, filling trains to capacity, carrying people who wanted to hear the Gospel of Jesus Christ.

Apparently one night he was going to preach at a church that was absolutely packed out. He got out of his carriage, wearing his top hat and tails, the dress code of that era, walked through a little gate to the church entrance and was about to go up the steps. There were hordes of people around him. He looked over to the one side and noticed a little street urchin sitting on top of a sundial, crying his heart out. He stopped in his tracks. The people were trying to get him into the church to preach. He said, "Just wait a minute." He walked over to the little boy and asked him what the problem was. The child said he wanted to go in and hear the preacher but the church was full and they wouldn't let him in. D L Moody said to him, "You see these coat-tails behind me? Just take hold of them and don't let go."

The little boy held onto his coat-tails and the mighty man of God walked straight in through the church, right down the aisle, past the hundreds of people waiting with great anticipation and excitement for the Word of God to be preached. He walked up the steps to the pulpit. There was a chair in the pulpit for the preacher. He put the little boy on the chair and started to preach. The man who was relating the story was a great preacher himself. He said, "The church where that took place is actually this church that I'm preaching in now. And that little street urchin was actually me. I'm now the minister of this church." That's why I love Jesus so much. He is absolutely no respecter of persons. He says clearly in Romans 10:13 (NASB): "Whoever will call upon the name of the Lord will be saved" [and used].

The same thing happened with a master plumber by the name of Smith Wigglesworth. He was pretty much illiterate. His wife Polly was the preacher. He used to go to the meetings to help her. He would put all the seats straight and sort out the building for her so she could get on with preaching. In the beginning, when he wasn't a Christian and she was, he was so upset with her that he would threaten to lock her out if she came home late at night from the meetings. One night she was, and he actually did lock her out of her house. She really had to plead with him at the back door to open up and let her in.

When God came into his heart, he was as passionate, if not more so, with his preaching, as he was as an artisan, a master plumber. He bought himself a Bible and a dictionary. His wife taught him how to read and write. He was a man who took the Word of God literally, as it is written. He said that's the way it's meant to be. His favourite saying was, "God said it, I believe it, and that settles it."

In fact, Smith Wigglesworth once came out to South Africa and walked into the office of a great South African son by the name of Reverend David du Plessis, who was later nicknamed "Mr Pentecost". He prophesied that David du Plessis would be going all over the world and preaching. And he did. In fact, David du Plessis even went and had an audience with the Pope himself and spoke about the presence and ministry of the Holy Spirit, the third Person of the Trinity.

Smith Wigglesworth would never have a newspaper pass across the threshold of his front gate. If he saw someone coming in with a newspaper under their arm, he would tell them to leave it out on the hedge. He only read the Bible. He used to break bread and have Holy Communion with the Lord every single day. He had a portable communion set and would often take communion with the Lord on the train when he was going to a healing meeting, or wherever he was going. He was a man who said he never prayed for longer than half an hour – and he never let half an hour go by without praying. He was indeed a mighty warrior of Jesus Christ. Just an ordinary man who had a heart for God; a man who knew how to say sorry, how to repent, and how to move on!

Chapter 17
Patience

Patience, they say, is indeed a virtue. Unfortunately, patience cannot be learned in a university. It has to be learned in the school of life, the school of hard knocks. In my quiet time reading early this morning I was reading about Abraham, the man of faith in the Bible. His greatest virtue, apart obviously from believing first and foremost in God, was patience.

Abraham had incredible patience. The writer said that he was pressurized from all sides, even from his own dearest wife, Sarah. She was extremely impatient and pressed Abraham very hard to do something about the child, the son and heir that God had promised them. Remember, it was Sarah who suggested that he sleep with Hagar in order that her shame would be hidden. In those days, it was regarded as a shameful thing if a woman could not have a baby. Abraham had pressure from his wife and from his friends to do something. Yet the Bible says that "he staggered not at the promises of God through unbelief; but was strong in faith, giving glory to God" (Romans 4:20).

Abraham was definitely not an angel, by any means. We know of two accounts in the Bible where, in order to save his own skin, he offered up Sarah as his sister rather than admit she was his wife. Sarah was an extremely beautiful woman and Abraham knew that if Pharaoh thought that he was Sarah's husband, he would murder him in order to take her. So he passed Sarah off as his sister in order to save his own skin. I don't think there are too many men in this day and age who would do that. Abraham did, and still he was known as the friend of God, because he had extreme patience and was prepared to wait for God's promise over his life. God, as always, was steadfast and sure. And Abraham had a son, whom he named Isaac.

Abraham was the father of every believer in the world today. The Lord promised him that he would have more sons than the grains of sand on the seashore, more sons than the stars in the sky. Take a walk outside tonight before you go to bed and see if you can count how many stars there are in the sky! It was an amazing promise that God made. Remember that Abraham was almost a hundred years old, and there was still no sign of any son and heir coming. However, he did not doubt. He trusted God and he was patient.

I think patience is probably the hardest thing for a young person to learn. I know that when I was young I myself had a problem with impatience; in fact I still battle in the same area because of my personality and make-up. By nature I'm an impulsive person and I like to see results – and I like to see them happen now. Since I've come of age, though, I can honestly say that things are changing. I'm learning that anything worth having is worth waiting for.

When you go down to the beach next time, sit on the sand and watch the seasoned fishermen cast the lines from their huge rods into the ocean and stand there, literally for hours, waiting for the first bite to come. If you've ever gone hunting, you'll see that a hunter is an extremely patient man. He will wait, sometimes for hours, for the animal to come along before he shoots it.

A farmer, too, learns to be patient. As I'm writing this

chapter I'm looking out at my son's herd of breeding cows. They are busy calving down at this time. He's away for a few days and he's asked me to keep an eye on them. It's most important that one is patient and waits for these cows to give birth. The most dangerous thing to do is to jump the gun as it were, and when a cow starts to calve to go and help her deliver that calf. That can cause a lot of unnecessary pain, especially when she has not dilated properly. So you sit and you wait. Usually we wait for half an hour for a seasoned cow. If she hasn't calved by then, we assist her. We might give a young heifer a little bit longer before we help her. But this is where patience comes in, to know when to step in and when to just let it go and let that beautiful calf come naturally. It comes from years and years of experience in agriculture.

It's like planting a crop of corn. One plants the crop into nice moist soil and after two or three days, especially in the case of young farmers, one tends to want to dig up the seed to see whether it's germinated, or what's happening. Of course that's not the thing to do. One needs to be patient. And eventually, after two to three weeks, it will germinate. One morning you'll wake up and see the most glorious sight; a field that was brown, with not a blade of grass, or any life on it at all, will have these faint green lines coming through.

It's the most wonderful sight to see, the sight of new life. Just like that little calf coming through into the outside world from its mother's womb. To see it spluttering and take its first breath of air! The mother gets up and, with her rough tongue, starts to clean off all the afterbirth. Within an hour there is a fluffy little calf jumping around, after it's had a good drink on its mother.

Patience!

Chapter 18
The Weather Man

I've had the privilege of seeing the Lord Jesus Christ work through many signs, wonders and miracles. I've seen blind eyes opened, I've seen deaf ears unstopped; I've seen the lame walk. I've seen God heal cancer, I've seen God give barren women babies, and I've seen many other incredible things happen through the prayer of faith. A statement that I make more and more often as I'm getting older is that God is more real to me than life itself.

If there is one area where God has consistently shown Himself faithful to me through the work that He's called me to, it's through the weather. Remember the Scripture where the Lord stilled the storm when the disciples were so concerned that the sailing vessel was filling with water because the waves were so high – and Jesus was sound asleep in the bottom of the boat? They woke Him up: "Lord, don't You care that we're perishing?" The Lord stood up and stretched out His hand. The wind calmed, the waves became still and the Lord rebuked the disciples: "O ye of little faith!"

Just a week ago I returned from Upington, a Southern Kalahari Desert town in the Northern Cape. It was one of the driest areas that I've seen – and I've been to the outback in Australia, and that's pretty remote and dry. But this area! We flew in a light aircraft from the farm all the way around the kingdom of Lesotho to Bloemfontein, where we stopped and refuelled and then carried on flying west, past

Kimberley with its huge diamond fields, towards Namibia on the west coast of Africa. The landscape gradually grew flatter and flatter and more and more arid and desert-like. Eventually it was just plain, unbroken desert. There was nobody there.

I was going to preach at a campaign that had been organized at a rugby stadium, and I was saying to myself: "Lord, where are these people going to come from?" It looked like we were literally in the wilderness.

After approximately another hour of flight, I saw a small little strip, almost like a ribbon, of water in the distance. It was the mighty Orange River. Whereas most of the rivers in Southern Africa – for example, the mighty Zambezi, Limpopo and Tugela Rivers – flow from the west to the east, this river flows from the east to the west. After flying along this river for some time, maybe half an hour, I started seeing beautiful irrigation schemes, the centre-pivots, those big green circles in a dry desert land. Right in the distance we saw the outline of a town. The pilot, Dirk, said to me, "That is Upington."

I really thought: "Lord, where are these people going to come from?" because we were expecting between seven to ten thousand people. When we arrived we were taken for a brief rest and then on to the stadium to start the meeting. I was so pleasantly surprised to see the stadium packed and people waiting anxiously to hear the Word of God. I'd been warned that these people are very conservative, and not to expect too much in terms of actual physical response. But I was completely surprised. There was such a hunger. Obviously the intercessors had done their homework well. From the time that we arrived and the praise and worship started, there was such a sense of expectancy. People were expecting to see the power of God manifested in that place.

I remember preaching from the text, Romans 10:13, which says: "WHOEVER calls on the name of the Lord shall be saved." The message was on the "whoevers". God takes donkeys and makes them into racehorses. I distinctly remember saying that. "Whoever calls..." But we need to call upon His name. We need to cry out to God and to seek forgiveness.

While I was preaching, the Holy Spirit was continually challenging me in my heart to call the people forward to the altar. We'd been given permission to come onto the rugby field. I was very reluctant to do so because: What if...? What if...? However, by the end of the meeting, I was so confident in the Lord. I felt the presence of God, and I called out to the people to come forward to the platform and to repent of their sins and call upon the Lord, and He would save them.

I got one of the biggest surprises of my life. I've been preaching the Gospel for many years now but I've never seen this before – which tells me that the Lord is coming very soon. There is such a hunger for the things of God. After I'd made the altar call it took maybe twenty minutes, maybe half an hour, for the people to come. The whole stadium emptied: all the grandstands. The people just left their personal possessions and started walking towards the platform. It was a sight I'll never forget as long as I live.

The presence of God was almost tangible. We repented and asked God to forgive us our sins. We asked Him to be the Lord of our lives. I said, "Those of you who have today prayed this prayer for the first time, please raise your hands, so that I can see who you are." I want to tell you that over ninety per cent of that crowd indicated that they were accepting Jesus Christ as their Lord and Saviour for the first time. It was a momentous occasion, and one that I'll never forget as long as I live. There was much weeping, much rejoicing and much repentance. To see families standing together, Moms and Dads, boys and girls, was a wonderful sight to behold.

Apparently I'd said in my preaching, "Because God has seen your heart and because you've got a repentant heart, He will send rain." Unbeknown to me, it was right out of season. The rain, when it does come, if it comes, is normally in October/November. This was the middle of September. There was no sign of rain, no clouds, nothing. Remember, it's close to the Kalahari Desert; the sand dunes are approximately twenty kilometres north of Upington.

We went home with much rejoicing. The next day we got in our little light aircraft and started making our way home. It was one of the bumpiest, roughest trips I've ever had in my entire preaching ministry. Even the pilots were nauseous and were really taking strain. Not to mention my two armour-bearers. Both Pierre and Kevin were in a cold sweat, and so was I. It was because there was so much turbulence in the air. But it was worth it. We touched down on terra firma at the airstrip next to Shalom, had a word of prayer and then departed.

The most amazing thing was that the next morning I got an SMS saying: "It is raining in Upington." You need to understand that this doesn't happen. It's not a desert by coincidence. It's a desert because it never rains there. Those people go for years without rain. Within twenty-four hours of people giving their lives to Christ and repenting, the rain came. I think I was more excited than anybody else. I was jumping up and down again and saying, "Lord, You are so good, so good!"

The very next day I got an SMS to say that the churches were full to overflowing in Upington. They had to bring in more chairs. The people were talking about Jesus in the streets and in the supermarkets. Indeed, genuine revival. I believe that God just sealed it by sending that shower of rain totally out of season. He is the Rainmaker. About that, I have no doubt.

The exact same thing happened when I arrived back from the UK a few months ago. I got an urgent phone call from a young man in the Eastern Cape, Malcolm McKenzie, who said, "Please, Angus, the dairy farmers are absolutely at their wit's end. There is nothing, nothing left to eat. The grass is finished, the water's finished. We need rain. Please come."

It was such an impassioned plea that I could not refuse. I felt the Lord told me to go. I got in the plane with one armour-bearer and off we flew. As we were coming in to Port Elizabeth to land, I saw what seemed to be like mist right across the airstrip. I thought: "Hallelujah, Lord, You've brought the rain on before we've even arrived!" But it was smoke. In the middle of the supposed rainy season, there was a bushfire in the *fynbos* (the natural bush) in that area. The Eastern Cape was on fire. It was so dry it was burning.

We were taken off to the meeting place, which was an indoor sports arena in Uitenhage. Needless to say, it was packed to capacity. There's nothing like hardship, tribulation, pain and suffering to draw people to God. We didn't even speak about rain. We spoke about repentance. We preached about salvation. We prayed for the sick. We prayed for bad habits to be broken. We prayed for people to have an intimate relationship with God. Right at the end, we had an open prayer time. People started to pray that God would bring rain to the Eastern Cape and to that area. Then we closed off the meeting.

As I walked outside, the sun was still shining. There was no cloud in the sky but I knew in my heart that the Weather Man had already started to work. Within twenty minutes, we had our first SMS to say that a town fifty, sixty kilometres away had already had forty millimetres of rain. So it went on. We got onto the plane and flew home. I watched the weather report for a good week after that. Every single day, it rained in that area. It rained and rained and rained. And God got all the glory!

What happened in a place named Willowmore is an experience that I'll probably take to heaven with me. A little while ago I was invited to go to this small town in what they call the Klein Karoo (the Little Karoo). Again, just beautiful country folk; farmers, who were also experiencing a very, very severe drought. They'd called us there for a campaign, which was held in the Voortrekker Saal (the Farmers' Hall). From the first meeting, it was packed to capacity. Again, we saw repentance. We saw people coming back to God. We saw people who never knew about divine healing getting healed. It was a wonderful, wonderful experience.

We prayed for rain. They'd had no rain for – I don't know if it was three months, or six months. The place was in a terrible state of drought. Lo and behold, on the Saturday night it started to drizzle. Nice, gentle rain. You must remember that in these marginal areas the soil is so loose, and the sand is so sensitive, that if there's a cloudburst it can do a tremendous amount of damage. God brought gentle rain. It rained that whole night. The next morning when we woke up it was still raining. We went to the service. There were pools of water everywhere. It rained that whole day. It rained the next day.

They took my daughter and me to the airport and put us on the plane to come home. It was still raining. They got over eighty millimetres (close on four inches) of rain. It changed the veld (the bush) into an absolute Garden of Eden. Michael Kroon, the farmer at whose home I stayed, said that the veld looked better than his wife's garden, and she had a beautiful garden. Those wildflowers just came alive. Once again, God was glorified.

This didn't just happen in South Africa. A few years ago, in the outback of Australia, in a place called Roma, a minister read our story *Faith like Potatoes* and asked us to come across and to pray, because the people were in a desperate state. Which we subsequently did. I'll never forget flying across that huge continent of Australia, from Perth to Sydney on the east coast, then catching a connecting flight up to Brisbane. From Brisbane we flew inland in a turboprop aeroplane and touched down at Roma. I think it was about an hour or two inland.

While I was flying across, I looked out of the window of the aeroplane. I saw vast areas of natural eucalyptus trees lying flat on the ground and wondered what had happened, whether there had been a hurricane or something. When we finally landed, I started speaking to some of the cattle farmers, who told us that every day they would take out their huge D8 bulldozers and push down lines and lines of trees so that their cattle could eat the leaves just to stay alive. That's how bad it was.

We got ready for the meeting in the little town hall. I'll

never forget the excitement, seeing farmers coming in from many kilometres away with their wives and children, laying out the blankets and the children getting bedded down in the hall. It was a wonderful sight to see. Some of them had come hundreds of kilometres. They'd come expectant. These men and women were decent country folk but totally "unchurched", as it were, in terms of the charismatic renewal and the demonstrative way of worshipping God. They were very, very conservative, very humble and beautiful people.

I realized that I only had that weekend, so we couldn't waste any time. Right from the first meeting, we preached repentance and the love of God, the need to have faith to please God. We made the altar call and literally everyone in the hall came to the front and accepted Christ as Saviour. We prayed for the sick, for the forgiveness of sins, for healing.

The next day we spoke in another little town in the outback and the rain started. The more the thunder clapped and the rain fell, the more excited I got. I think I was more excited than the Australians! Again, my Jesus, the Weather Man, was coming through loud and clear, force five. It rained and rained and rained. When we left that place, it was still raining. They drove us all the way back to the town of Toowoomba and then eventually to Brisbane.

In Toowoomba we met in the agricultural hall – a huge hall with a tin roof. There must have been at least one or two thousand people there. The noise was so loud with the rain falling on the roof that I could hardly hear myself speaking. Again, the people were absolutely elated. I don't think they even needed to hear the message. Just the sound of the rain on the roof was enough. Again, Jesus Christ was glorified to the uttermost. We got reports from Australia

– and again this is all to do with the Lord and His goodness towards us – from the outback right through to the coast, that they had the most amazing wheat crops that year, and good steady rain. It matched the very trip that we'd taken, like a line from where we'd been preaching!

God always answers prayer. There's absolutely no doubt whatsoever. He is a good God. He's for us. He's not against us. I cannot exhort you enough, my dear friend reading this book, to put your trust in the Lord Jesus Christ. I have so many different illustrations to share with you on how the Lord has come through for us, especially in the area of the weather. And why not! Moses just stretched out his arm as the Lord told him to, and the mighty Red Sea parted. The whole nation of two-and-a-half million Jews went through on dry land. Then He closed up the sea on top of the enemy and they were drowned.

Moses called upon the Lord to give His people food – and manna came down from heaven. By the way, the word "manna" means "what?" because they didn't know what it was; they'd never seen it before. I believe it was a beautiful, flaky type of food that settled on the grass in the morning almost like a frost, and apparently it was delicious to eat. It had a wafer texture with the flavour of honey. Most delicious!

God is so interested in you and me. All He wants us to do is to call upon His name, like the people in Upington did. It's not just about calling upon His name, though; it's calling upon His name by faith. That is the most important part of all. We need to pray the prayer of faith and the Lord Jesus Christ will do the rest.

We had a Mighty Men Conference here in 2008, which took place on a Friday and a Saturday, with a final service on the Sunday morning. We hired the biggest tent in the whole world and it only seated half of the men. The other half had to sit outside. There were over sixty thousand men here. Just like Elijah had told King Ahab: "Gird up your loins, because the rain is coming" (that was after three-and-a-half years of drought), I felt led by the Holy Spirit to tell the men: "Gentlemen, tomorrow morning, after the service, don't hang around. The rain is coming."

At four o'clock on the Sunday morning I was in my prayer room, getting ready for the last message. I heard the big Crown buses start up their engines and begin to move out. You know, it's amazing how one can doubt (and I have asked God to forgive me). I thought: Oh dear. The people are leaving before the last meeting. But they weren't. They'd heard what I'd said from the platform the night before. They were all parking their buses nose-to-bumper on the district road outside the farm so that, when the rain came, they'd be ready to move out, to go out into all the different parts of South Africa and not be bogged down in the rain.

Bear in mind that we'd had the most beautiful weekend, a full moon on the Friday night. The men didn't even need torches. There were no mosquitoes, just a nice, gentle breeze. On the Sunday morning, just as I was closing off and had wished all the men well, a gentle rain began to fall. It began as a gentle drizzle and then just grew stronger and stronger. By mid-afternoon, when most of the heavy traffic had left, thunderstorms, accompanied by thunder and lightning, started to build up over the farm.

As you can imagine, after having sixty thousand men camping all over the farm for a full weekend, and some for even longer, the farm was rather dirty. It rained nonstop for three days and three nights and washed that farm absolutely clean.

You can sit there and say that was another coincidence but you can't keep saying that, my dear friend. Why didn't it rain over the weekend of the campaign? Why didn't it rain two weeks after the campaign? Why didn't it rain two weeks before the campaign? It rained then, because God was giving us a sign that He was well pleased with His people. That's why I love Him so much.

I've never had the privilege of seeing Him. I've never had the privilege of hearing His voice speak. In fact, Moses himself only got a glimpse of the back of the Lord after the Lord had hidden him in the cleft of the rock, because of the Glory of the Lord. Moses had to wear a veil over his face for three weeks after that, because his face was shining so brightly that the people could not look upon it.

What I'm talking about is not something that's foreign to the Word of God. Jesus said very clearly: "And these signs will follow those who preach the Gospel: miracles, signs and wonders. They will lay their hands upon the sick and they will recover. They will cast out demons." That's exactly what's happening. These miracles always follow the preaching of God's undiluted Word. But one thing I've learned is that God cannot stand compromise. If you want God to use you, and you want to see the miraculous take place after preaching the Gospel, be careful that you don't fall short of preaching the whole Gospel. There is no other God. There never was and never will be, save the Son of God, Jesus Christ, our Lord and Saviour.

Now we go to the other extreme. Just last year we planned, with a huge organizing committee, to go to the southern tip of the continent of Africa, to Cape Town, and to have a two-day event at the cricket stadium, because we were unable to book the rugby stadium at that time. We were blessed again. We had a full-capacity crowd of thirty thousand on both the Friday and the Saturday nights. It was something I'll never forget.

But the build-up to that campaign was quite extraordinary, to put it mildly. It had rained solidly for two weeks before we even got there. We were to start preaching on the Friday night. We arrived on the Friday morning and on that day the rain stopped and the sun came out. When the plane touched down at the airport we saw sheets of water lying everywhere as far as the eye could see. Yet the sun was out.

The Friday night was a most magnificent night. Saturday night there was a strong wind blowing. In fact it blew so hard that it blew the pulpit right over. Normally, I lose my notes. I think God has been trying to tell me for a number of years that I mustn't use notes because usually when I open my Bible at any campaign, the notes get blown away! This time the notes and the pulpit got blown over. Yet we had an amazing meeting. We saw many, many souls come to Christ.

We prayed again that God would just hold the weather. You know, there was no rain until I got onto that big silver bird the very next day to fly back to our beloved green hills of KwaZulu-Natal. As that plane took off, the rain started. When I got home I received an SMS from Sias, one of my spiritual sons in the Cape, to say that it was pouring with rain again. It rained for another two weeks. In the middle of that period of some two months of incessant rain, the Lord gave us two clear nights for His Gospel to be preached. The most incredible miracle, again! God is so good.

I must end off this chapter by being quite honest. I made a commitment to Christ that I would preach His Gospel in fair weather and in foul. The Lord says it; I believe it and that settles it. I refuse to be called a fair-weather Christian.

I went to Johannesburg right in the middle of the rainy season, but we trusted the Lord concerning the weather. There was a huge crowd of over fifty thousand people at the Coca Cola (Absa) Stadium, the largest stadium there. Guess what? After the praise and worship, we saw the clouds building. When it was time for me to preach, it started to rain. I thought: "There's no way that I'm going to stand underneath an umbrella." They tried to put up an umbrella on the platform for me and I saw people all over the rugby field sitting out in the rain, not prepared to move, some in wheelchairs. There were sick people; old people; young people. I declined the umbrella and said, "How can I keep myself dry when these blessed souls are getting soaking wet?" Praise God, at least the rain was warm. It was a hot afternoon.

Then I did something I should never have done. I heard a crack of thunder and I said, "Bring it on, Jesus!" Oh, I love the Lord so much. He has said: "Call to Me, and I will answer you, and I will show you great and mighty things, which you do not know" (Jeremiah 33:3). The Lord obviously did exactly what I'd asked Him to and He opened a valve. I tell you what, the heavens opened up. It rained sheets of white, pure rain. It pelted down.

I carried on preaching. There must have been about an 25 millimetres (an inch) of water on the platform. All of us were totally saturated. Eventually, the sound system blew. We were live on television, worldwide. The whole technical part of the event just blew out and the rain came down. We made the altar call and many, many souls gave their lives to Christ that afternoon. We gave thanks to God that day when we went home.

As a farmer, you will never frighten me with rain. Rain, to me, signifies life. Where there is rain, there is life. A farmer can work through a flood but not through a drought. A drought is the most disheartening situation to be in, because it lingers on and on and on. I've watched crops just slowly but surely curl up and die. With rain, there's life. I thank Him for the numerous times He has brought rain onto our farm, Shalom, when the crops have been at their worst and we've said, "Lord, if it doesn't happen we're literally going to go bankrupt." And He's done it every single time.

So many times we've gone to the little town hall in Greytown to pray for rain. Some of the older people – I love them – used to go with their gumboots, their raincoats and their umbrellas. Nine times out of ten, we'd walk out of that little town hall and hear the rumble of thunder. Often it was actually raining before we even left the hall. The Lord just so much wants you and me to call upon Him. And He will, indeed, save us to the uttermost.

Chapter 19

The watchman

Ezekiel 3:17 says: "Son of man, I have made you a watchman for the house of Israel; therefore hear a word from My mouth and give them warning from Me."

As Christians, you and I have an obligation to tell people that it is time to get our houses in order, because the Lord is coming very soon. Maybe that's the one element – the time factor – that is standing out for me more now than ever before. God is not interested in what happened yesterday. He's not even concerned about tomorrow. He's concerned about how you are today. As watchmen unto the house of Israel, we need to give the people warning. We need to tell them that the enemy is going around like a roaring lion, seeking whom he may devour.

Many years ago the Lord gave me a picture. I remember us making a huge banner depicting it, painting it and hanging it up in a big church in Pietermaritzburg. The picture was of an old medieval castle with all its turrets stretching out up to the sky, flags flying out. On the top was a sentry – a guard, a watchman – with a huge ram's horn, a shofar. This watchman had gone to sleep. His job was to blow the horn when he saw the enemy coming.

Inside that huge castle, people were sleeping. There were soldiers and there were men, women and children, all sound asleep. In the picture there were hordes of the enemy, multitudes of the demons of hell, coming to the ramparts of the castle. They were putting up huge ladders, climbing up and were just about coming over the top to surprise the people. The watchman was fast asleep. That's when I woke up. It had been a nightmare.

The Lord has called us to blow the trumpet in Zion and to sound the alarm. We really need to speak up in these last days. I conducted a funeral a week ago of a dear, grand old lady, who died a few months before her birthday. She would have been a hundred and two. I made the altar call at that funeral because the old lady loved Jesus very much. Her family responded to the Gospel of Christ. They all stood up and prayed the sinner's prayer aloud. There was nothing secretive about it.

You might say: "And then what happened after that?"

The answer is that I really do not know, because I'm an evangelist, I'm not a pastor. They all went their different ways. They came from all over the world. But they've at least had the opportunity to prepare themselves for the coming of the Lord, to prepare themselves and to arm themselves against the wiles of the devil. You know what they say: To be forewarned is to be forearmed. People need to know that we are living in perilous times.

After the funeral, I got a letter from a senior citizen thanking us for the service. I was quite taken aback because this is a very conservative, very lovely lady, probably in her late seventies. By the sound of her letter she loves the Lord but she's not the type of lady I would have thought would have enjoyed that kind of message. She thanked me for preaching the truth. She also wanted to introduce me to her priest, and said, "Please, I've got such a heart for the young people. They are so lost, so caught up with so many temptations on television, the internet, cellphones, and so on. There are no moral standards any more. Please, please, can you hold a campaign just for young people?"

Again, I thought: "Father, we need to be better watchmen for the house of Israel."

People are absolutely destitute in so many ways. Even as I'm writing this book, I've just had a phone call from a young man living in Bloemfontein, some six, seven hours drive away, who is desperate. His marriage is on the rocks. He needs help. He wants to come. My PA advised him that there are no more appointments, because I'm fully booked at the moment. But my heart went out to this young man and I said, "Come". Next Friday, he and his wife will meet with me. They are about to get divorced but I'm believing God for a miracle in their lives.

As Edmund Burke said, all that is necessary for evil to triumph is that good men do nothing. That is so true. Faith has feet. It's a doing word. We need to be more outspoken. Even as the Gospel will set you and me free, that very same Gospel will condemn us on the Day of Judgment, when God asks us one question: "What did you do with what I gave you?"

All we have to do is tell people that Jesus Christ can save them to the uttermost; that Jesus Christ is a Friend indeed. We've got to stand up and be counted. We need to take authority in our homes, on our farms, in our businesses, on the sports fields, in the schools, in the universities. Remember one thing, my dear friend: It's not important that people like you. What is most important is that people respect you. You know something? When you stand up for righteousness and holiness, people will respect you.

While out jogging with my wife the other morning, she said something that really jolted and challenged me in my innermost man. She said, "You know, we also have to be watchmen over our thought life."

Isn't that so true? We have a responsibility to watch over what we are thinking. As you read this, have you thought about what could happen if God said: "I want to put your thought life on a big screen, so that everybody in your town can see what you're thinking"? It might be a most embarrassing and frightening experience.

We need to be careful what we are watching and what we are listening to. That flicking through the TV channels is dangerous. The computer and the cellphone can also be extremely dangerous instruments if not used in the correct manner. Of course, on the other hand, TV can be used very powerfully for the Gospel of Jesus Christ. Most of our ministry at Shalom is through television.

Just as a good athlete will train properly and eat correctly, we too need to lead disciplined lives. We need to watch what we are reading and what we are getting involved with, because these things can have very detrimental effects on our witness for Christ. Remember, out of the heart the mouth speaks. If you are continually reading rubbish and taking in immoral movies, reading immoral books and looking at immoral programmes, that will get to you and begin to produce a very bad crop, which could eventually lead you into direct sin.

I believe one of the greatest deterrents against getting caught up in immorality and an impure thought life is to have good quiet times with the Lord Jesus Christ every single morning; clearing the desk as it were and starting afresh. Without my quiet time, I cannot live. The more God uses me, the longer my quiet times are becoming. When I read the Word of God and I pray and I read Christian literature, it is healthy. It is like eating good, wholesome food. It gets rid of all the junk in my life.

Maybe, when you've finished reading this chapter, you need to pray that God will simply erase any evil thoughts or pictures that you have in your mind of things that you'd be embarrassed to share with other people. Speak to Jesus and encourage yourself with the Word of God. He will never leave you, nor forsake you.

Chapter 20
Nothing will be impossible for you

If there is one thing that I've learned in my Christian walk with the Lord Jesus Christ over the last thirty years, it's that there's nothing impossible for God. In Genesis 18:14, the Lord asks the question of Abraham and Sarah: "Is there anything too hard for [Me]?" The answer is quite simply, no. There is nothing that is too hard for God. The problem lies with us. The only thing that restricts God is unbelief.

Apart from the love of God, which obviously goes without saying, the most significant thing I have learned as a believer, after walking with the Lord Jesus Christ for thirty years, is that God always honours faith. Just look at the great patriarchs who went before us. Look at Abraham, the father of faith; at Moses, a great man of faith; at Noah, an obedient man of faith. Think of the great prophets, Elijah and Elisha, and of King David, the greatest king next to Jesus Himself, who has ever lived in Israel. Think of Daniel, a holy man; of Samson, and of Solomon, the wisest man who ever lived. These were men of faith. They literally took God at His Word and obeyed Him. What was the outcome? Unparalleled, miraculous success!

The only regret that I have in this life is that it has taken me so long to realize that we have a living God, who is more than prepared to answer our prayer requests, and who is more than able and prepared to be our Friend who sticks closer than a brother. The more we step out of the boat and walk on the water, the closer He is to us.

There's no short cut to learning faith. I wish there was. If there was, it would be my greatest pleasure to tell young people in particular the secret, the recipe, for growing in faith. But unfortunately there is no secret recipe. It has to be learned through the trials of life, through making mistakes, through hardships.

As I said in a previous chapter, I have so many vivid memories of God moving the elements to show us His glory. In a few days time I've been asked to go down to a coastal town in the Southern Cape that is experiencing an unprecedented drought. The municipality has said it is the worst drought in a hundred and fifty years. For the last three years, they've had almost nothing in terms of rain. Even the drinking water in the town has now been restricted. I have been asked to go down and join them and pray and ask the Lord to send rain on the town. The people are very serious about it. They are literally closing that huge town down completely. They are closing all the shops, all the schools and the municipal offices. All the farmers are coming to town and they are going to meet at the local rugby stadium. Some men are coming from the Great Karoo, which has also experienced this horrific drought. They will be standing proxy for their respective regions. We are expecting thousands and thousands of people. Once again, we are walking on water – because unless the Lord brings the rain, it's not going to come.

If there's one thing I have learned about the Lord, it's that He's a jealous God. I have said to the organizers, "I will not share the platform with any other men representing any other faiths, save that of our Lord Jesus Christ." I also stipulated that it was preferable to have the event in the middle of the day, so that there is a price to pay. Everyone must close up shop and be prepared to make a conscious stand for the Lord. Then, if it's possible, I'd like to fly home the same night. I seem to be spending so much time away from my wife Jill at this time.

I believe that God will answer our prayers and I believe that it will rain, and it will rain incessantly, so that no one will be under any illusion as to who brought the rain. I also believe that it won't rain while I'm there. I believe it will rain once we leave, because no man must touch God's glory.

It is so important that we don't ever try to manipulate or use God. Because if we remember the Scriptures, when the Pharisees (the churchmen) said to the Lord: "Just show us one more sign and we'll believe that You were sent by God", He said: "You'll see no more signs from Me!" You cannot in any way manipulate or try to use God. He will not be used. But He loves us so much that He will give us as many signs as we need to prove to us that He is our Lord and Saviour.

We read in Judges 6:36–40 of Gideon, another great warrior of the Lord, who cast a fleece before the Lord and said: "Lord, please give me a sign. Tomorrow morning, when I wake up, if the fleece is wet and the ground around it is dry, I'll believe that You sent me." The next morning he squeezed out the fleece and got a container full of water out of it. Still, he asked the Lord: "Lord, please just show me once more that You've called me." He said, "Tomorrow I want the fleece to be dry and dew to be on the ground." Sure enough, the next morning it was as dry and fluffy as any fleece coming out of a tumble drier could be, yet the ground around the fleece was soaking wet.

Oh my friend, God will use as many signs as we need to

convince us and show us that He loves us. More than that, He wants us to succeed. He wants us to do what is right. But we need to be obedient and we need to listen to the prompting of His Holy Spirit.

I've heard people say that you spell FAITH, "R-I-S-K". I don't believe that at all. In fact, I think it's the opposite. I think the surest thing that we have in this life is faith in God. That's what Jesus said in Mark 11:22: "Have faith in God." That's probably the most important lesson of all that the Lord has taught me when it comes to growing up and coming of age. At the end of the day He is the only One who is steadfast, who is true, who is trustworthy and who is faithful. What He says, He will do, unconditionally. What He requires of us is quite simply to believe.

Chapter 21
Taking your responsibility seriously

I believe that every Christian has different seasons in his life. The first season is when you fall in love with the Master for the first time, when you bow the knee, bow your head, raise your hand, and you come to the altar and say: "Jesus, I repent of all my sin and from today onwards I want You to be my Lord and Saviour. I will follow no other gods but You."

After that comes the honeymoon, the most wonderful time in any Christian's life. It's as if you're looking through rose-tinted glasses at everything you see. God seems to send the right people across your path, people to encourage and to uplift you, and your life seems to be going better. The biggest thing, of course, is that tremendous release and freedom from carrying the burden of unconfessed sin in your life. You wake up one morning and that fifty-kilogram bag of cement is no longer strapped to your back. You want to run like a deer. You are fleet of foot, because there are no more shackles binding you. The devil has left you, because Jesus is dominating and filling your life with joy. You feel that you can scale a mountain; that you can run like the wind. There's no more shyness in your life. You are not self-conscious. You couldn't care less what people think of you because Jesus has reassured you that your name is written in the Lamb's Book of Life. It is the most exhilarating time in a young believer's life. All the cares of this world are no longer of any consequence. You have refocused. Your eyes are now focused on heaven and you realize that you are only a sojourner in this life. You are just passing through. That sometimes lasts for six months, maybe even longer. Maybe it should last always.

Then comes the conviction! Not condemnation. Condemnation comes from the devil. The Lord says to us in Romans 8:1: "There is therefore now no condemnation to those who are in Christ Jesus." But the Lord starts to convict you because He's a holy God and He cannot look upon sin of any description. Just think about what happened with His only Son, His dearly beloved Son. When He was hanging on the Cross, dying, He cried out: *"Eloi, Eloi, lama sabachthani?"* which means: "My God, My God, why have You forsaken Me?" At that moment in time our heavenly Father had to turn away from His own Son, because His Son was carrying the sin of the world on His shoulders; your sin and my sin.

If God cannot look upon His own Son because of sin, then He cannot look upon anybody who is full of sin. The time of conviction then comes into a Christian's life. The Holy Spirit slowly but surely starts to pinpoint areas in your life that are displeasing to God. He is sometimes referred to as the Hound of Heaven. (My wife doesn't like that terminology whatsoever!) However, He persists. He will not let up until you deal with certain areas in your life. It might be an area of alcohol that you've never before been convicted of and now you realize that you actually don't need to drink strong liquor to calm your nerves or to pacify you, because you've got Jesus.

After I'd served the Lord for about three months, one

day I woke up and said, "Jill, we don't need this any more." I was a very sociable person. I was a good host; Jill was a good hostess. When someone came to my house there was any drink that he might want, whisky, beer, wine, Drambuie, you name it – and it was worth quite a substantial amount of money. I got all the alcohol out of our cupboard, poured the whole lot down the toilet and flushed it away. From that day to this, I've never partaken of any alcohol, simply because I didn't need it. Of course, after that, Jill and I spent a lot of time helping alcoholics. Once you spend time with them, you have a problem condoning alcohol.

The Lord began to convict me about my attitude towards people with different standards of life, different walks of life, different colours, classes and creeds. The Holy Spirit really took me to task and made me realize that I indeed am the greatest sinner of all, the least in the kingdom of God. The apostle Paul said that about himself too (Ephesians 3:8). God gave me a new love for people, especially the poor, the needy, the widows and the orphans. We started our children's home.

The next season followed. When you have really come of age you have to begin to take responsibility. You cannot turn a blind eye to blatant sin and still call yourself a Christian. You have to put your hand up. You have to say: "That is not correct." In John 14:6, Jesus says very clearly: "I am the way, the truth, and the life. No one comes to the Father except through Me."

If we take just that one verse literally and we believe it and we live it and we preach it, we will be severely chastised by this world. What that Scripture says is simply that there is no other God save the God of Israel. His name is Jehovah. He is known as the great I AM. He has one Son and His name is Jesus Christ. He died for your sins and my sins. We have the Comforter, the Helper, our Lord Holy Spirit. That is it. When you preach that in certain countries in the world today you could very well end up in jail, because they will straight away accuse you of insulting the minor faiths, of causing religious strife. I don't like the word 'religious', but I'm using it carefully in this context.

We begin to see the principles of God in a new light because we've come of age. The Lord says that He hates divorce. That is quite straightforward and quite simple. We need to work through difficulties in our marriages. For a born-again Christian, divorce is not an option. If you divorce, then you must know that there are penalties that are imposed by God.

The Lord says: "Thou shalt not kill." If we as believers condone abortion, we are condoning legalized murder. Remember, in order for evil to abound, all that good people have to do is nothing. When you become a Christian you may not remain neutral any more. You are either for God, or against Him. This is where the responsibility comes in.

The Lord is very clear on homosexuality. In Leviticus 18:22, the Lord says that a male may not lie with a male as with a woman. And if he does, it is an abomination. The same thing applies to the female, as you will see if you read Romans 1:26.

We incur the wrath of God when we purposely and wilfully go against His standards. This applies to immorality of any description, as well as division caused by strife. It's not of God. We need to work out our problems between us. The hardest place to be a Christian is in your own home. We need to work at our marriages. We need to work at our relationships with our loved ones. We cannot have aught

233

against our brother. We use the excuse: "Well, it wasn't my fault" or, "I've done what I can." But we need to persevere. We need to keep on, especially if we want to receive the blessings of God upon our lives and indeed in everything that we do.

We've got to call sin by its name. That's probably one of the hardest things to do, especially in your own family. You don't ever hate the sinner, you hate the sin. You know the old saying: People who live in glass houses shouldn't throw stones. However, as soon as you condone sin, you're actually in effect turning your back on God. When you come of age you need to make the choice that, irrespective of what people think, you will stand your ground. Once you begin to erode the statutes and the commandments of God, you have nothing left. It's either all or nothing with the Lord Jesus Christ.

He is indeed a radical God. But He's such a merciful and loving God. He died for sinners like you and me; that we know. When we've been redeemed we've been forgiven, just like the woman caught in adultery, who hid behind Jesus. Jesus stood in front of her. All her accusers were there, with their stones and rocks. They were going to stone her to death, as was the custom according to the Law of Moses.

Jesus started to write in the sand. I would love to know what He wrote in the sand. He said: "He that is without sin among you, let him first cast a stone at her." Slowly but surely, every one of them dropped their stones and walked away, until just she and Jesus were left standing there. Jesus told the woman that her sins were forgiven but that she was to go and sin no more.

Grace means undeserved loving-kindness, unmerited favour. God has given us tremendous grace. But that grace must never be misinterpreted as an excuse to carry on living like before. Once our sins are forgiven, we need to move on. Yes, we continue to fall down. Of course we do; I do and you do too, but we cannot condone blatant sin.

In a few days time I will be going down to the coastal town in the Southern Cape that is experiencing its worst drought in a hundred and fifty years. Affliction can sometimes almost be a blessing, because it brings people to their senses. They begin to realize that we really have to call on God Almighty to intervene, because we can do nothing ourselves. We can have all our irrigation systems, all our centre-pivots, and all our high-tech irrigation equipment. But – if there is no water in the ground, the water-table is dropping, and the dams are empty – they actually don't help at all.

I have had quite a few e-mails in the last couple of days asking me to address certain areas of sin in that town when I go there. I'm really seeking the Lord as to what I'm going to say. I'm a sinner saved by much grace. God has done so much in my life. I love people. I just want to encourage people and see them grow in the Lord. I love exhorting people to raise the bar and to enlarge their vision. I remind them of the God of forgiveness and love, the God of great potential for each one of us. That is my meat. That is what I love doing.

However, this time I feel that I have a tremendous responsibility to the people who have invited me down to this area. Obviously though, my first responsibility is to God. I'll have to preach the truth in God's love. I feel that I'm going to have to go there and remind the people that God hates sin, and that we cannot expect Him to bless an area with rain if people blatantly disregard the Word of

God. I'm going to have to mention things like division in the leadership, the homosexual question, and other very sensitive areas like the marriage situation and the racial issue.

I'm really going to trust that God will honour that area with abundant rain as I humbly, but straightforwardly, relay the Word of God to them. I know that He will, because He continually does that. It's happened so many times in my Christian walk. God is more than able and willing to bring rain to that dry and thirsty land, but He does require the people to repent publicly so that He can bring that blessing.

2 Chronicles 7:14 is a verse in the Bible that's very, very close to my heart. It says: "If My people..." Who are God's people? They are the believers. They are not the churchgoers, they are not the casual enquirers, they are not the pew-fillers, they are not the bench-warmers; they are the believers. By the way, in the early Church the followers of Jesus Christ were called believers, not Christians. That terminology came much, much later. "If My people [the believers], who are called by My name, will humble themselves..."

Pride is probably the biggest sin in the Bible. It was pride that caused Lucifer, the choirmaster of heaven, to be thrown out of heaven together with a third of the angels of heaven, because he actually got to the stage where he thought he was bigger and better than God. That is an extremely serious offence to God. The Bible says that God resists the proud and gives grace to the humble. You'll find that wherever Jesus went, He spent time with the widows and orphans; He spent time with the down-and-outs, the nobodies, the prostitutes, the alcoholics. He didn't spend too much time with the hierarchy in the church or indeed, in society. He was for the people. He was a people's Man.

The verse continues: "...will humble themselves and pray..." We have to pray the prayer of faith. It's no good just praying mechanically, going through the prayer book, or praying a prayer that you've prayed many times before and you don't even believe is going to happen. God never answers that type of prayer. He only answers the prayer of faith. James 5:16 says: "The effective, fervent prayer of a righteous man availeth much."

Returning to our Scripture in 2 Chronicles 7:14, we read: "...and seek My face, and turn from their wicked ways..." That means to put the things of this world to one side; to really seek the face of God and to turn away from any known wickedness and sin; things like hatred, unforgiveness, theft, murder, homosexuality, abortion and racialism. The Lord says that if we turn away from these things, then He will hear from heaven, He will forgive our sins and He will heal the land.

As a farmer, I understand what that means. To heal the land literally means to bring rain because, without rain, nothing happens. The ground becomes sterile and literally dies. A farmer can work in a flood situation; he can divert the water. But in a drought situation there is absolutely nothing that anybody can do.

I'm really praying that the Lord will give me the courage to stand up for righteousness and to call sin by its name when I go down to that large coastal town in the Southern Cape in a few days time. Not to condemn people, but to convict people, so that they change; so that God can heal the land. It's going to take a lot of courage, a lot of discipline and most of all, a lot of love, because it's only in love that one can bring a message as strong as that. My prayer is that the Lord will keep me humble; that I will not become arrogant and self-righteous. I pray that I will also be a good ambassador for Christ, so that no one will leave that rugby stadium in any doubt of what it means to belong to Jesus, and the responsibility that we have as Christians; towards God first, and then our spouses, our children, our fellow man, our ministry and our profession.

If there's one thing I have learned in these past thirty years, it's that God loves us with such an amazing love, an everlasting love. He says: "Greater love has no man than this, than a man lay down his life for his friends" (John 15:13, KJV). That's exactly what Jesus Christ did for you and me. He died for us, by the way, while we were still sinners. He doesn't have to prove to you or me how much He loves us. It's like me giving a man a chequebook full of signed, blank, uncrossed cheques. I don't have to tell that man that I trust him. I've just given him access to my complete bank account. He doesn't have to hear whether I appreciate him, love him or trust him, because, by that very act, I've done everything.

By that act of dying for our sins, Jesus has done everything for us. He wants us to succeed in everything we do. He wants us to succeed in our lives, our marriages, our businesses, our farming enterprises, and our sport. He wants us to live life abundantly. He says to us very clearly that the devil comes only to steal and kill and destroy, but that He wants us to have life, and to have it more abundantly (John 10:10). We cannot have that more abundant life if we do not live and walk in righteousness.

How is a person supposed to know how to walk in righteousness unless he's been told? Many years ago, a man wrote me a letter and told me about a dream he'd had. He dreamed that he went to hell. He said that as he walked in hell it was like walking in liquid mud. There were bubbles coming to the surface all over. There was steam rising and there were dead people lying in the mud. There were people struggling to breathe, going down for the last time. Some people were floating on the top and others were frantically trying to keep above the mud. He saw a man wading chest-deep through the mud, picking up people's heads, looking at their faces and then putting them back down in the mud.

He asked the man in his dream: "What are you doing?"

He said: "I'm looking for the preacher who put me in this place."

When we come of age we have a responsibility, first of all to God, then to our fellow man. We can't convert anybody. Only the Holy Spirit can do that. What we can do though, is present the Gospel clearly and simply. Not in a condemning way, but not in a compromising way either. People need to know what it means to live a holy life. The Bible is very clear about that. Without holiness, no man will see God. They need an opportunity to repent, just like I had the opportunity.

One of the Scriptures with which the Lord Jesus Christ called me to preach is found in Ezekiel 3:17–19. It starts off: "Son of man, I have made you a watchman for the house of Israel; therefore ... give them warning from Me." The house of Israel is the believer. The Lord has called me to give my fellow Christians a warning. If I do not do that, I will end up with their blood on my hands when they go to hell and I, in turn, will have to give an account to God for that. But if I have warned them, and they have not responded or listened, they'll go to hell but I will have redeemed my own soul. So, as believers, we have a responsibility to warn people of what it means to live a sinful life and to end up in hell; or to live a redeemed life and end up in heaven.

Jesus said that if we confess with our mouths the Lord Jesus Christ, and believe in our hearts that He's been raised from the dead, we shall be saved (Romans 10:9). That's all I'm going to tell them in this little town in the Southern Cape. After that, there will be no need to say anything more. I'm believing that our Almighty God, the Rainmaker, will honour His Word and it will rain.

One of my role models is Martin Luther. He helped us to understand the meaning of grace. Before Martin Luther, everybody was trying to work their way to heaven by good works; trying to behave themselves, trying to put the flesh down. He was a Roman Catholic monk, and very sincere. He was also a doctor of theology, a very intelligent young man. And, try as he would, he could never, ever seem to overcome the flesh. He would beat himself, he would starve himself, he would wear horsehair shirts to try and get the flesh to submit – and he failed miserably. Then he stumbled on that beautiful Scripture in Romans 1:17: "For therein is the righteousness of God revealed from faith to faith: as it is written, The just shall live by faith" (KJV).

It changed his whole outlook and his whole life. From then on, Luther walked by faith and not by people's opinions. He had no more fear of man. In fact he said: "I was born to fight factions and devils. It was my work to cut down thorn trees, fill quagmires and make rough roads smooth. But, if I must have one failure in life, then let it be that I've preached the Gospel too severely rather than to have been a hypocrite and denied the truth."

He was a man who had a tremendous heart for the poor

and the needy. He stood against the establishment of the time and proclaimed the Gospel of Jesus Christ: that the righteous and the just shall live by faith.

That is exactly what I, by the grace of God, intend to do, because I realize now that I've come of age that time is actually no longer on my side. That applies to all of us. Isn't it amazing? We can preach it, we can read it, we can write it, but until we've actually been to the Pearly Gates (heaven's gates), we don't really understand about the brevity of life. I don't have time to repeat it. I have to get it right the first time. There'll be thousands of people who will be standing there in the balance on that day. The amazing thing is that it's not the rain or the water that is my concern; it's people's souls. Because people will repent – they always do when the Word of God is preached. They will be saved, and then the rain will literally come and wash away the sin of that place.

Chapter 22
Flying from the nest

God has really been so gracious, so gentle, with Jill and me, maybe because we are very family-orientated and have extremely soft hearts when it comes to our children. Of the five children that the Lord has given us, every single one of them has grown up within almost a forty- or fifty-kilometre radius. My older son is farming a stone's throw away from where I stay; my other son is also a very short distance away. My youngest daughter and her husband live not even half a kilometre away, all on the same farm. My middle daughter is married to a timber farmer and they live about fifty kilometres away. My oldest daughter and their family are basically living in the next town. We have been extremely blessed, but there comes a time in everybody's life when change comes.

As I've said before, many a time change is here to stay. This morning, while I was sitting quietly in my prayer room, my son-in-law phoned me and asked if he, my youngest daughter and their two little sons could come down and see *khulu* and *ugogo* (Zulu for grandfather and grandmother). They arrived, sat down and indicated that they feel that God is calling them to move on. At the present time my son-in-law and daughter are working with my younger son on the home farm but they feel very strongly that the Holy Spirit is guiding them to move on, possibly to another country.

Again, it brought me to the realization that, outside of Jesus Christ, there's nothing permanent in this life.

Of course there were many tears, because we love them so much, and they love us. I looked at my two little grandsons; the one is nearly two years old, the other a babe in arms, and thought to myself: How often will I see them now if they relocate to another country? I had to check myself and thought: I'm being extremely selfish.

It's actually not about me. It's all about them. It's all about laying it all down again at the foot of the Cross. Isn't it amazing, my friend, how, when you think you have just come of age and you think you've dealt with issues in your life, you get a challenge like this? It basically takes you right back to square one again. You feel like a new Christian. You become emotional. All kinds of emotions and thoughts invade your mind. You actually even almost become a bit angry – and of course there's absolutely no reason for that. It is purely a selfish attitude, because our children have got to move on. They've got to make their way. My son-in-law has always had a heart to own his own farm. This is the move he wants to make.

My wife and I thought it was all settled and that we were all going to live happily ever after together on the same farm. But that's not to be. I had to repent and say, "Lord, please forgive me for being so selfish." I had to encourage my daughter and her husband to press on, because I saw myself, of course. That's exactly what my wife and I did when we were the same age they are now. And, in fact, we had three children, with one on the way, when we arrived at a piece of overgrown bush and made it our new home. Of course the children will do what you do, not what you tell them, so I suppose that it's my fault that this is happening.

But that doesn't make it any easier.

We had a good cry, me crying mostly inside. My wife is such a home bird, and sees our grandchildren, daughters and sons at least once or twice a day. In fact we both said, after they'd left, that we're extremely selfish when we think of how many of our counterparts have children living all over the world. Sometimes they might only see them once or twice in a couple of years, and we see our children literally every day. That's going to change, especially with this little family, as they move on. I think of that Scripture again: "It is more blessed to give than to receive." It's actually in releasing that we receive blessing. I sat there and said to my son-in-law, "I'm just so thankful to God that you're Christians, because we can talk these things through, we can pray for each other, we can still be united in the Spirit, even though we're parted by distance."

Many of you reading this book will know exactly what I'm going through at this time, because you may either be the children who have had to leave, or the parents who have had to stay behind. A very, very close couple, best friends, who live in Zimbabwe, had to say goodbye to their children recently. One couple now lives in London, the other in Australia.

The stress and the pain of saying goodbye are extreme, more painful than any physical ailment could ever be. Yet they say that absence makes the heart grow fonder. I'm sure it does. But of course, because we're flesh and blood, we'd rather have our loved ones closer to us. I think of the Lord Jesus Christ when He had to leave heaven and His Father and come to earth in the form of a defenceless babe. The tremendous price He paid! Then I think of the greater price – maybe because I'm in that position now – the price

244

that Father had to pay to release His Son, knowing full well what He was going to be subjected to on this earth. That is enormous love.

God is teaching me one very important lesson, and that is to seize the day. *Carpe diem!* Do not worry about what tomorrow brings, don't be concerned about yesterday, because it's gone, but enjoy the moment. That's exactly what I intend to do. I intend to enjoy my family, all of them, every day that God gives us. God will take care of the rest. Now I can understand how the early believers always looked forward to home-time; the time when they would be at home in heaven with Jesus, forever. No more suffering, no more pain, no more sharing of tears, no more goodbyes.

I don't enjoy airports or train stations or seaports because, preaching the way I am at the moment, I seem to be forever sitting at one of them, either waiting to come home, or waiting for a plane to take me away. I often sit there and see families weeping. I see Mom trying to be so brave and wiping the tears away. I see the young children looking up, trying to cover those tears. I see the old patriarch, Dad, his face ashen-white, trying to be brave, trying to put on a smile. I see them drawing out that last cup of coffee as long as they can when the final announcement has been made for them to board. I see them stretching across the table, touching each other's hands, holding hands, kissing their grandchildren, holding their daughter, their son. No words to speak; then slowly walking towards the boarding gate, standing there; waving to each other as they walk away into the distance.

Oh my dear friend, there is no time left in this world to fight and argue. Let us redeem the time together. Let us love one another while we still can, bury our differences and put Jesus Christ firmly in the centre of our families and homes.

Chapter 23
Unconventional people

Last weekend I returned from Durban, where I saw the Lord do an amazing work. I was invited to address the final session of a huge group of churches that were having their annual convention. They gave me free rein as to what topic I would use. The text that I used is from Mark 11:24, where the Lord says: "Therefore I say to you, whatever things you ask when you pray, *believe* that you will receive them and you will have them."

When I arrived I was treated so beautifully by my brothers and sisters in Christ. I started to share my heart and told them how, many years ago, as a young Christian I went to a conference where the main speaker was a fine man from America, who used an illustration which didn't gel with me. I was a brand-new Christian. He said, "You will never, ever make a racehorse out of a donkey." I sat there, bewildered.

I went home that night and didn't sleep so well. I thought: "But, Lord, I am a donkey, and You've made me into one of Your racehorses!" I really believe that that man of God got it the wrong way around. God delights in using nobodies and making them into somebodies. After all, wasn't it a humble donkey that brought Jesus into Jerusalem as the Saviour of the world? Didn't God use David, the youngest of eight brothers, to be the greatest king that Israel had ever had up until the time of Jesus Himself? Didn't Jesus use untrained, uneducated disciples, ordinary artisans, fishermen, tax collectors, even a zealot (a terrorist), to bring salvation to a lost world?

The Lord is truly no respecter of persons. That's exactly what I experienced over this weekend; just ordinary men and women, many of them being used mightily by God in this particular church grouping, but just ordinary people. Some of them are professional men, others are working men. God is using them to touch the world. We had an amazing meeting that evening. There was much repenting and, I believe, much scrapping of programmes in the spiritual realm, and just trusting God unconditionally.

I've just finished reading a delightful and very encouraging small little book *The Barbarian Way* by Erwin McManus, in which the author uses the example of Jephthah the Gileadite (Judges 11). He was a mighty warrior, but the son of a harlot. Gilead's wife bore him sons, and of course when the sons grew up, they chased Jephthah out. They said, "You'll never, ever, inherit anything from our father." Jephthah was then sent out to the land of Tob. A worthless band of men followed him and went out raiding with him. However, when Israel was in trouble, they sent for Jephthah to come and help them deliver Israel.

The writer was actually saying: "What's new in society today?" The so-called "barbarians", the misfits of society, the loudmouths, the gangsters (I'll never forget one old evangelist telling me, tongue in cheek, that every evangelist is a gangster before he gets saved) is just the way God has done it. The so-called organized church gets a bit embarrassed when these barbarians come to church. The amazing thing is that they're normally the ones who bring revival; they bring in the unbelievers and are the men who get things done. Yet we tend to disregard them – and sometimes they embarrass us by their appearance, or by their personalities or mannerisms. Can you imagine the disciples when they went out to preach the Gospel? Whenever Peter came into a room, or into a situation, everybody knew that he had arrived. Men of distinct characteristics, but largely unchurched...

It's so sad that we sometimes judge people by their appearance. I think that if John the Baptist, or Elijah the Tishbite, the prophet of Israel, came to a church service it would be hugely embarrassing, first of all, to identify with their attire. John the Baptist was a man, obviously with a long, trailing beard, who lived in the desert, on wild honey and locusts. He was a tough man who had the same spirit as his predecessor Elijah, who was called "the hairy man with the leather belt". The king of Israel, King Ahab, was very afraid of Elijah, as was King Herod afraid of John the Baptist.

But we praise God that the Lord is no respecter of persons and that He uses different men for different jobs. When it comes to pioneering jobs and confronting the enemy head-on, He has to use His elite corps of men who fear nothing but sin and desire no one but God. John Wesley said, "Give me a hundred men who fear nothing but sin and desire no one but God. I care not one straw whether they be laymen or clergymen. With those hundred men I will rattle the gates of hell and bring heaven down to earth."

God has taught me over the years not to judge a book by its cover. By the way, those men that I've spoken about might not even have been able to read or write. I don't think they could. But they had the privilege of walking with, and getting to know, the Author of the Book. In fact, in 1 John 5:7, it says: "For there are three that bear witness in heaven, the Father, the Word and the Holy Spirit; and these three are one." So Jesus is the Word in print. They didn't have to read the Book, they lived with the Book.

In closing, I include the beautiful testimony of a very unconventional young man who has recently come of age:

Oom Angus

I shouldn't really call you "oom" since we are the same age [spiritually]. I attended your MMC 2009 the other day, and a few days after that I bought two of your books, "Fathers and Sons" and "Revival". I am reading both at the same time now. I had a bit of time on my hands to think and I thought I would write you this letter, because trying to explain to an ordinary person what has happened in my life is very difficult; my life is different from most normal lives. I am sure you have met all kinds in the world, and I bet everyone's life is different, but I would like you to know anyway.

I am a Boereseun [country boy] from the Western Cape. I don't farm, not yet, but I am as true a South African as you can get. I would like to tell you a little bit about my life, in order for you to understand why it is so important for me that you know how YOUR life changed MY life.

I matriculated in 1991, and on the 8th of January 1992, I joined up for national service at Voortrekker Hoogte. I grew up in an ordinary house, with very loving parents; the best in the world, me and my dad are very close. Anyway, I got posted to Heidelberg Army Gymnasium, where I joined the Signals Core.

I did 6 months and decided that I wanted to get the

best out of my military career, so I signed up to go for the pre-selections for Special Forces. We were 4 guys out of our whole regiment that went for this.

We arrived at Speskop in Pretoria, where there were about 2,000 men lined up for pre-selection; this was a one-day event, just fitness and medical. 351 of us made it, and we were given two weeks to return to base for the proper selection phase, which was going to be a week. We had to report at 1 Reconnaissance Commando in Durban, from there we were taken to places called Duku-Duku and Hellsgate, near Matubatuba in Natal, to do the selection.

I had read an article about the "Recces" and their selection and how tough it was, this article was published in the June 1988 edition of the Scope magazine. I got hold of the article; the rest of the magazine was absorbed by my fellow countrymen.

This article made it very clear to me that this is no game, and made me realize that there is no turning back, because I am a very proud person, failure was not an option. We had some tough times as a family, financial-wise, and I just could not go back to my old base and face the rest, as a failure. My biggest inspiration to succeed was my dad, he had never failed me, he had pulled us through some pretty tough times, and he never ever even thought about giving up, and I was more determined to make my dad proud than ever before.

I grew up in a Christian family, doing all the right things like we were supposed to do, we were good people, I was a "good person", mom and dad were "believers" but I was a good person, and I only realized a week ago, that

251

"good people don't go to heaven, believers do", and that I was not a "believer" but just another "good person".

Arriving in Durban, we had two days to prepare mentally for our selection phase, which would follow a week later with one full year of specialized training. I knew that I had to spend some time with the Lord alone to get my head strong for this selection, because the aim of this training is to break everyone down to such a point that only the strongest survive. This wasn't about physical strength any more, we were all super fit; this was about mental strength and endurance. I knew I would have to get out of my head for the next week, and the only way I could do this was to ask God to help me. I spent hours praying all by myself, and I felt strong and ready, still scared though, but prepared.

We did the selection and twelve out of the 351 of us made it, we had one week to go home and rest and then returned to base for departure to different training areas for the next year, to specialize in all sorts of warfare.

I was really proud of myself, and so was my dad, my mom never knew what I was doing, me and my dad kept it a secret, we told her a year later. I felt like I was the best, I felt strong, and I was grateful that God helped me, and I knew that the following 12 months were going to be very hard and very long. I did my training, along with God; all our training was about the grace of God, we started every day with reading from the Bible and prayers, like the old days you mentioned on the MMC.

All of us, the handful that we were, acknowledged God for carrying us through this very tough time. Then we reached the end of our training and we qualified, one year later, as Special Forces Operators. We were untouchable, on top of the world, the best of the best, and then began my life as a Special Forces soldier.

I got posted to Langebaan on the West Coast, 4 Reconnaissance Commando; most of us from that training group went there. Soon I had forgotten where I got my strength from to come this far, and how I got there. All of us did. We became operators in the commando with the old boys and we started seeing the world; we did everything people can only dream about, things money can not buy; we got so much exposure to life, we were literally living life in the fast lane. The more experience we got, the stronger we got, the more we forgot about God. Trying to explain to someone what it feels like to be "untouchable" is not easy. We thought we were untouchable, in all human eyes we were just that.

We were a gift to the world, so to speak, that is what we thought. We had a Special Forces Creed, which reads "Live by chance, Love by choice and Kill by profession" for those who dare, life has a flavour the protected will never know... and it was like that indeed. We had the most beautiful women coming from Cape Town every weekend, just to see if they could "catch" one of us; everyone wanted to be our friend, we were the guys to hang out with; we were the iron boys, at least for the small periods of time we were there anyway; the rest of the time somewhere in the middle of nowhere.

I spent 8 years in this unit, and qualified as one of the best in the world. The politics changed and in 1998 I terminated my services with the South African Defence Force. I went straight into Angola, where many of my friends had been already. We became soldiers of fortune, fighting for money. I lost many friends in Angola, but I *was tough and we were built to go on with life. I have attended more funerals in my life than weddings and baptisms all together, but I always kept strong.*

I spent three years in Angola, one year in Uganda, four years in Iraq. I had some tough times in my life, sometimes I really thought, "this is it." I saw many people die. I always spoke to God before every mission I went on, I spoke to God, and I had a real good relationship with Him. He takes care of me; I take care of my men. In Iraq I was the team leader for an international company's corporate team, the biggest company in the world. I had their directors as my VIPs, I had to protect them every day, and take them from point A to B without a scratch. These are billion-dollar people, irreplaceable; they could absolutely not get hurt. This was very stressful, but every time I hit the road, I spoke to God, and he never failed me once, some times were very close, but I am still here. I had the privilege of deploying with the US Army's 601 Brigade from the 1st Airborne Division. This was the same 601 Unit that first set foot in Vietnam in the time of the war. I was the only civilian ever to have the opportunity to go out on patrol with these guys in Ramadi, the hottest war zone in the whole of Iraq, because they asked me to, they respected me for who I am.

Now comes the tricky part, I have had such an adventurous life, and I have experienced so many things normal people don't experience in everyday life. I have become so wise about my own survival and life has taught me so many lessons, and showed me so many ways NOT to go about. I have survived three different war zones in the past 10 years, where I have lost good friends, but I am still here. Men of war become hard; it is not for any man to push a soldier like me down on my knees. I have had too much exposure in life, which made me very strong in my mind, my skin as thick as a rhino's, because a "Special Forces" soldier's life ain't for sissies, and unless you have endured what I did, you will never break through to me.

You see, oom Angus, that was what I thought. I tried to be as normal as possible; I left all the warfare, trying to make a normal living. I have a construction business in Africa now, still new, struggling here and there, but surviving. I am in Angola as I write this letter; I came to help a friend who is doing a survey for an international company. I thought I would accept the invitation, as it was 10 years since I left Angola. I came to see how it changed.

Just before I got my invitation to Angola, I had booked two tickets for the MMC, one for me and one for my brother, two years older than me, also a military man. I got the invite from my friend and an email came through that I had to be in Luanda ASAP.

I gave my ticket to my dad and asked him to make sure that my brother got to this MMC, because I thought he needed it. My dad is pretty OK with God, but I thought, "let them go instead of my ticket going to waste." I got to Johannesburg, and realized that I had another few days before my visa would be ready, so I wanted to head back home to my wife. I have a wife – in all my ventures and rages; chasing one war after the other, I met a girl 13 years ago, whom I have lost a couple of times along the way, or shall I say, along MY way, but we are married today, almost 5 years now.

I got more news on my visa for Luanda and realized that I had 4 days until departure. I still wanted to go back to my wife. I was very keen on the MMC when I booked it; and then when the Angola invitation came, I lost interest. Now with time on my hands, I wanted to head back home, but instead I decided to purchase another ticket for MMC; and I informed my wife I was going to this conference, with my dad and my brother. I wasn't really into this any more, my head was already on another job, but I did this for my dad.

I can honestly tell you right now that this was the best choice in my life. I never ever expected it to be like it was. I heard guys talking about the MMC, "It's an appointed time with the Holy Spirit!" "God makes a personal appointment with everyone there!"

I heard all of this, and I thought to myself, "I have been close to God, I have experienced miracles in life, I have escaped death by the mercy of God" – things these guys have never experienced. I know what it feels like to have the hair on your neck stand up; and only God can save you, and He did; I thought I was OK with God.

But I WASN'T, because that day you collapsed on stage, and we went back to pray for you while you were waiting for the chopper, I felt the Holy Spirit work amongst all those men. From the time I started praying that afternoon, I felt very strange; I withdrew from my dad and my brother for a while. The next day I went to the stage by myself, and when you came onto that stage, and you put your arms in the air, looking at God; I felt for the first time in my life what it really feels like to be filled with the love of Jesus. I cried that day. The feeling I experienced when you showed your gratefulness to

God on that stage, is the feeling of being loved by God, and that is what it feels to love God back, as much as He loves you. I decided that this is what I want to feel every day, this is better than any adrenaline rush I have ever experienced in my entire life. None of my previous experiences, narrow escapes, anything, was even close to this – this is the ultimate. I'd had the privilege in life to experience what very few people ever experience, I thought I was special, but the love of God is far beyond that. The best about this love is – anyone can have it. What life made me experience; and the flavour I got was only for the chosen few, the ones who made it. In my world it was like this, but in God's world everyone is special.

I decided on the Sunday when we left the MMC that I wanted to take this further, so I went the Monday and bought your books, "Father and Son" and "Revival". I also bought the DVD "Fireproof" which I watched last night.

I was sad that I couldn't go back to my wife and share my experience with her because my flight was for the Tuesday after the MMC. She has to wait 2 months now before I can share this with her, but on the plane to Luanda, where I am now, I realized that I have shared so many emotions with my wife in the past 10 years and she took it all as it came. But this one is different, this is not an emotion, this is a new life, a new beginning. I figured that God knows me well enough not to have me go home now, but to spend time and grow and get stronger, so that by the time I do get home, I will have the right words, to explain to my wife that I have given my life, her life and my whole house to Jesus; He is in control of this now, and there are so many things in my life that will have to change from now onwards.

My wife used to be very religious, but I have realized that I have changed her, she has become like me – hard, aggressive, a fighter; I turned her into a soldier like me. She was a very soft, humble and religious girl when I met her. I turned her to become like me, which I thought was the right thing, but in fact, that is what the devil wants you to believe. He makes you believe that you are doing the right thing, and now that I have given my life to Jesus, I realize how stupid I was. I am now seeing clearly what the devil does and the way he gets things done his way. My wife is being difficult due to the changes I want in our lives, changes that Jesus wants; He told me to make them. The devil makes her say things that normally would blow my lid straight away, but I realized this isn't her talking and I just let it be. I am praying for her, that she can ask Jesus to clean up the mess in her heart that I left. I have asked for forgiveness, God forgave me and my life goes on, but I pray that she will also find forgiveness, and that she will forgive me and that Jesus will move back into her heart and live there; where He used to live, before I drove Him away. She always prayed for me, but ironically, it's me having to pray for her now, but it is my fault that she ended up where she is now. I left her alone when I should have been there for her; I showed her a side of life which she was never meant to see.

I have always been a good person, oom Angus, I have always helped where I can, I have given money where it was needed, I always thought about other people, if you had bumped into me in the street, you would have thought that I was a super-nice guy, and I was, but not at home. All the things in my life I regret are things that happened at my home. Outside of my home I was a good guy, not a believer, just a good guy, good to other people, only people, not God.

And now I hope you understand, oom Angus, why I say it is difficult to explain to an ordinary person, how my life has changed, from being a soldier of fortune, a dog of war, to be on my way to becoming a soldier for Jesus – a Special Forces soldier. If I had put as much effort into being a soldier for God, as what I have into being a soldier of fortune, I would have been His general by now – but I will be. I need to get things right, I know what to do, and because of you, oom Angus – you, because God chose you, I am a new man today. The work that you do through Jesus is second to none.

People always tell me I should write a book about my experiences in life, but you know what, I only started living last week, so there is nothing to tell. I feel like I am in a race, and I fell asleep at the starting point, and when I woke up, everybody was gone. I am the very last one to pull off. Now I feel like I have to run so fast, work so hard, just to catch up with the group. I have to catch up, I have to get ahead. I feel like I have so much to say to God all at once I don't know where to begin. But I love it, because I feel the Spirit in me grow every day.

Please pray for my wife, she was the "believer" and I was the "good person", but now I am the believer and she is the good person, and all of this is only my doing, no one else; my own work – nothing to be proud of, just ashamed, so very ashamed. I need to fix it, and I hope that Jesus touches her like He has touched me. I am going to bring my wife to your farm one day. The Sunday I left there after the MMC, I was very sad to leave, and the further I drove away, the more sad I became, and the Monday I felt lost. I wanted to go back to your farm, because I wanted to experience the touch of Jesus again, but then I realized, He is here with me. On my way to the airport that Tuesday morning, I knew He was going to fly with me to Angola, to help me prepare for my new life with my wife.

My heart is melting just to think that my wife has to be alone for the next 2 months. She is used to it, but like you said at the MMC, if you become a Christian, the devil makes it very difficult for you, he keeps on attacking you. I am a soldier, I can handle his attacks, but now he attacks my wife, to try and break me. He will keep on failing in doing so, but I really hope that by the time I get back home, Jesus would have moved into His place, where He was living 13 years ago, in her heart, before I came and drove Him away.

I pray for this, and you know Jesus so much better than I do, I am a new troop, just signed up for service; you are a general. Please ask Him to send the Holy Spirit to my house, there is someone inside who desperately needs to get in touch. I don't think she can do this by herself.

God bless you oom Angus.

All the Best
John D (Not his real name).

Chapter 24
Being rather than doing

My younger son Fergie has a very special gift with horses. Right from before he could walk, I had him on a horse. He has an amazing ability to identify with an animal. Often a young person will try to see how fast a horse can run, how high he can rear, how many times he can buck, often making a horse very, very spirited and nervous. That's called "a hot seat". A person has that kind of character. As soon as he gets on the horse, it gets edgy and starts jumping around. Fergie has the opposite effect on a horse. He has a cool saddle. He's a big, strong boy but when he gets on a horse it calms down completely. You don't see him pulling at the reins or in any way trying to manhandle the horse. He just sits into the horse and the horse does the work.

That's what God has been laying on my heart recently. There are too many of us Christians striving to be like Jesus, striving to earn God's favour, striving to make a mark, instead of just being. Being totally relaxed in His presence and allowing the Lord to use us in whatever way He sees fit. I think many of us wear ourselves out, a bit like Martha and Mary. Martha was the one who was always trying to do, for Jesus. She was running around the house. She was doing the cooking. She was making sure everything was clean. She was making sure the guests always had something to eat, especially when the Lord came. She was in and out of the kitchen.

But Mary sat at His feet. She was the wise woman,

because she knew that her time on this earth with her Saviour was limited. She just sat at His feet and drank in all the Words of wisdom, and the life, and looked upon His countenance. Her sister, however, was trying to be a Christian. In the process, she was spending less time with God. Eventually, Jesus Himself had to rebuke Martha, knowing full well what she was trying to do. She was working hard and spending herself for Him. He had to say that Mary had chosen the better way. I'm realizing, and it's taken me too long, that there's really nothing we can do for God. He's done it all already.

As I'm writing this chapter, two messages have just arrived from the Southern Cape on my cellphone to say that good rain is falling in that area. I am ecstatic. What a mighty God we serve! We went down there not even a week ago and saw the Outeniqua rugby stadium packed to capacity with businessmen, schoolchildren, farmers and their workers, old-age pensioners, policemen, councillors, and the city mayor himself. The premier of the Western Province, the Honourable Helen Zille, and her Members of Parliament were there too. They had all come to beseech Almighty God, the Weather Man, to bring rain to a thirsty and dry land. Then we came home. It did not rain that day. It is now Sunday afternoon and the reports are starting to come in that the rain is falling.

What a faithful God we serve! All He asks is for us to pray and to believe. That's all. He will do the rest. As I'm growing older in the Lord, I'm realizing more and more that it's more about prayer; it's more about sitting at His feet and doing what He's asked us to do. It is more about believing on Him. How can you believe on Him whom you do not know? How can you know Him whom you have not met? How can you meet a person without spending time with Him? Many young people come to me and say that they want more faith. There is no magic formula to gaining faith. It comes simply by sitting at the feet of the Faithful One and drinking in His Holy Word on a daily basis.

How can you get to know someone? How can you ask someone for something if you don't know them? Mary chose the better way. She chose rather to spend time with God while He was there. Martha was so busy trying to earn the love of Jesus that she wasn't even there. She was in the kitchen most of the time.

Paul, the greatest apostle that has ever lived, next to Jesus Christ Himself, said in Philippians 3:10: "...that I might know Him and the power of His resurrection, and the fellowship of His sufferings, being conformed to His death." This was a man who saw Jesus in a vision when he was struck off his horse. He was on his way to Damascus to murder Christians because he thought, being a good Pharisee, that was what he had to do. He really believed Jesus was an impostor. The Master knocked him off his horse and spoke to him.

I have just been watching the accounts of five Muslims who have had a living experience with Jesus Christ of Nazareth. One was a Turk; another, an Arabian; another, from Thailand; and a couple of others, each one of them a Muslim. One was actually at Mecca when he had a vision of Jesus Christ.

I want to tell you, my dear friend reading this book, the Lord Jesus is more real to me than anything else I've ever encountered in my life. He has never once failed me. He has never once let me down, and the more I'm growing to love Him and to know Him, and to see His miracle-working power operating in my life, the more I realize that as a younger Christian I should have done less work, and spent more time with Him. More time being, rather than doing.

One might think that as you grow older in the Lord, and the Lord starts to use you more in signs and wonders and miracles, you don't need to spend quite so much time with God, or you don't need so much faith. That's absolutely wrong. In fact, it's totally the opposite; the more time that you spend with God, and the more He uses you, the more faith you need.

As I write, I'm walking around the area where some five months ago we met with approximately two hundred thousand men. God has told us that the 2010 Mighty Men Conference will be the last one here at Shalom. We're expecting four hundred thousand men. My faith level needs to double. It can only happen if I spend more time sitting at His feet. Not less. God will only bless you with as much faith as you need. Nothing spare, nothing extra, nothing less. When He healed the sick and He set the captives free, Jesus often said: "Be it according to your faith." He said to the woman with the issue of blood: "Your faith has made you well."

When God begins to honour His Word through your faith, you don't have to say anything about it, because the evidence speaks for itself. The people who went to the prayer meeting in George, in the Southern Cape, last Tuesday (five days ago), don't have to say a word about the fact that Jesus Christ is authentic, the fact that Jesus Christ is real, because the miracle is speaking for itself as I write this book. The miracle is saying quite clearly, as the rain is falling out of the sky, as that area is getting drenched in rain, that Jesus is alive and that He answers the faithful prayers of His loved ones.

The more God uses you, the less you have to say. When Lazarus came out of the tomb, his sisters Martha and Mary didn't have to go around telling everybody that Jesus was the miracle worker. They knew that Jesus was the miracle-worker. Let us choose the way of Mary and not the way of Martha. Let us choose to be those who would say less and believe more. Let us choose to be those who would stop rushing around and start sitting at His feet and resting in the faithfulness of the Faithful One.

I don't think you could find a more faith-filled man than James Hudson Taylor, who took the Gospel of Jesus Christ to mainland China. I'm so pleased that he did, because the biggest industrial revolution that is happening in the world today is happening in that region. The biggest population group in the world today is in China – something like just over 1.3 billion Chinese populate the mainland.

James Hudson Taylor, by raw faith, trusted God for one thousand missionary families to go to China. He had no money, no source of income, only faith. They went, and they did an amazing job. Then the Boxer Rebellion broke out. The Chinese people started to massacre the white people. They regarded the white people as foreign devils and started killing them off. Of course most of the people they massacred were missionaries.

At that time, James Hudson Taylor was quite senior in years, very sickly, and recuperating in Switzerland. He would only get a letter every six months, which would talk about this family that had gone missing, that family unaccounted for, that family killed, in the various provinces in China. He got so desperate that he could not concentrate and read his Bible, and he could not even pray.

He wrote a letter to his dear friend George Müller, another man of great faith. Hudson Taylor said that he didn't know what to do, because everything seemed to be going wrong. George Müller wrote back to his dear friend and said, "Just rest in the faithfulness of the Faithful One." That's all.

That's what Hudson Taylor did. After that dark cloud passed over, the sun started shining again – like it always does – and today, through the house church movement, mainland China is having the biggest revival that the world has ever known. There are more Chinese people being born again every day than babies being born in China.

More people are impacted by a believer's life than by the hurrying and scurrying around trying to do things for God and being an ambassador for Christ. In a time when things like stress, depression, anxiety and fear are rampant, the world is looking for those who would just be Jesus to them.

Chapter 25
Bitter-sweet

As I continue to write this book, the Lord is revealing many things to me, as He always does, not necessarily through reading, but through living the experiences that I'm walking through at this time.

I've just returned from Vredendal in the northwestern Cape. It is in the middle of Namaqualand, which is famous for its winter show of flowers as they have winter rains there. It is a desert area and the life-spring of that community depends on the irrigation canals that come from many, many miles away, from great dams built into the rivers, like the Clanwilliam Dam. These are farming people, country folk, whom I love so very much. They are such down-to-earth, genuine folk, who understand about prosperity and poverty. They live life to the full and experience the reality of this world in which we live. I've said before that farming is not for sissies. One day you're a millionaire, the next day you're a pauper. It depends purely on the elements and, of course, these days also on the economics and the politics of any country.

I went down to the land of the Namaqualand daisies. I landed at Cape Town airport with two armour-bearers with me. We were treated like royalty. We were whisked off by a private charter company that put us into a turboprop aeroplane. There was tremendous excitement about what was going to take place. Johnny Louw, one of my spiritual sons, was there to meet us. He's from that area. He said that there was a build-up there that he hadn't experienced before.

Within an hour, we were landing at Vredendal. It was two o'clock in the afternoon. That place gets so hot. Sometimes it goes up to 45 to 50 degrees in the middle of summer, so they had decided to have the event in the evening, starting at five o'clock and going through to about eight. The most miraculous thing of all was that there were two Currie Cup semi-final rugby matches to be played that same afternoon. Talk about competition! Remember, this is an area where rugby is almost like a religion.

I was so happy and so encouraged by the hard work that the organizers had done. When we arrived there they took us to the stadium just to show us how they'd set up everything. People were already seated, waiting for the meeting. It was amazing. Then they took me to a bed-and-breakfast, where I was able to relax and really spend time with God before getting changed for the meeting.

The meeting was amazing. They had a local praise and worship band that did exceptionally well, singing the type of songs that the local folk know, appreciate and enjoy. After some announcements and encouragements, they handed the microphone over to me. The Lord showed me that there were people there with broken hearts. I saw young people weeping while the praise and worship was taking place, especially when Joe Niemand started to sing Psalm 23: "The Lord is my Shepherd".

That's one of the main reasons why I like to sit on the platform, if it's possible, before I speak, so that the Holy Spirit can show me the mood of the people. I saw one young teenage girl, maybe in her late teens, early twenties, in the front row, start to weep, and then I saw a man sitting maybe five rows back, the tears running down his face like a river. I saw heavy hearts there. Yes, people were praising God. They were raising their hands and clapping, but there were heavy hearts and God showed me that it's the broken and the contrite spirit and heart that He will see and hear.

Psalm 51:17 says: "The sacrifices of God are a broken spirit: a broken and a contrite heart, O God, thou wilt not despise" (KJV). In this psalm David was crying out to God after he had sinned and committed adultery with Bathsheba and had had Uriah the Hittite murdered. He was totally broken. The Lord laid it on my heart to share with these beautiful people in Namaqualand that He does not want sacrifices; He wants a broken and a contrite spirit.

I shared that and a few testimonies of what's happened in my own life. I mentioned particularly the young couples who got married in London a few months before, and refusing to leave the church until we performed the marriage ceremony right there and then; something I'll never forget. I shared how things don't always go according to the game plan, like when I collapsed at MMC 09 having had, according to the paramedics, two heart attacks, one after the other. And how God, in His infinite wisdom, used that for His glory and turned the whole conference around and brought a new spirit of tremendous seriousness to the conference.

After that, I made an altar call which astounded me. I made it slow and serious. I said, "Nobody's going to close their eyes and we're not slipping up any hands, we are going to stand up and repent before God." Well, the whole crowd of approximately eight and a half thousand, plus, people stood as one man and repented of their sins. I don't know where they came from, because when I flew in I just saw desert areas, but they were there.

I asked those who were accepting Jesus Christ for the first time publicly to please raise their hands. Seven-eighths of that crowd, a good seven thousand, plus, acknowledged that they were praying that prayer for the first time ever. I was absolutely staggered. It was one of the highlights of my life to see people in this northwestern part of our beautiful country, South Africa, weeping and making right with God and each other. It was a wonderful, wonderful experience.

Afterwards, they insisted on decision cards being filled out. One man told me he couldn't pick up the box of decision cards because it was so heavy. It was an absolute "God-move". I knew beyond any shadow of a doubt that Jesus Christ was totally and completely in control of what took place.

From there we were ushered to a media conference and then back to the bed-and-breakfast. I phoned my dear wife Jill – my intercessor, my best friend – and told her the awesome news. We also told the fellowship at home (the church) what God had done. Another amazing miracle! Yes indeed, we are in a state of revival in South Africa.

That evening we celebrated together with the organizers. We had a most beautiful evening. There was much joy and sharing of testimonies of things that had taken place that one doesn't always see from the platform. We got to bed not far off midnight.

We flew home the very next day. Needless to say, by half past three in the morning I was wide awake again because I was getting ready to go back home. I often struggle to sleep after an experience like that. I don't think there are many people who can sleep when they see how God, in His sovereign love and power, moves people back to Himself.

That morning, early, we got onto the aeroplane and flew back to Cape Town. On the way back I was able to share with the extended team that God is looking for men and women who have a vision and a desire for nothing else but to see God's saving hand move amongst the people.

There was an anaesthetist on the plane who has since become a son of mine in Christ. He has a tremendous burden for the sick. He is also concerned about the system of the world, about the fact that so many organizations are making money out of sick people. He has a heart to see that rectified, and to see Christian hospitals formed, with Christian doctors and nurses who have a desire, first of all, to see people come to Christ, and secondly, to be totally healed physically, spiritually and mentally.

I had the opportunity of sharing with him. I saw him writing vigorously, noting all the Scriptures I was giving him. Scriptures like Proverbs 29:18: "Where there is no vision, the people perish"... about the fact that money is not the issue with God, it's vision; it's having a man who will step into the gap, a man who'll go the extra mile. It was an amazing trip back to the Cape Town airport. What I'm trying to tell you is that it was one of the sweetest weekends I've ever had.

When I got off the aeroplane, I had the privilege of speaking to folks on a one-to-one basis while we were waiting to board the next plane to take us back to Durban. Something that really touched my heart deeply and humbled me was one of our top young South African jockeys. He was flying from Cape Town to ride in some big races in Durban on the Sunday afternoon. My heart was so for the young jockey that I didn't want to speak to him about sport on Sundays, because I could see that this was how he was earning his bread and butter. God will show him in due time what he needs to do about his work situation on a Sunday. At that particular time all he needed was encouragement to keep on keeping on for the Lord – and we were able to do that for him. He said goodbye and I prayed for him that he wouldn't have an accident on those fast, fiery, feisty thoroughbred horses. I believe that God did something in his life.

I want to say to you reading this: please don't major on the negatives in a person's career, or life, or work situation. I've just been phoned five minutes ago by a farmer up in the northern part of KwaZulu-Natal. He leads his workers faithfully in the Word of God, in prayer, in hymn singing and in Scripture reading every morning, and has been doing so for four years. And yet he's struggling, because a number of his people are still involved in ancestral worship and speaking to the spirits. We know that the Bible is clear about that. We cannot serve two masters. Jesus says in Matthew 12:30: "He who is not with Me is against Me; and he who does not gather with Me scatters abroad."

This farmer wanted me to come with my faithful foreman Simeon and share with these people, something which is not possible any more for me because of the time constraints. Yet the Holy Spirit straight away convicted me and prompted me to say to him, "Be careful that you get the right man to come and talk to your people. You don't want someone who is going to come and condemn – and basically elevate the powers of darkness by dwelling so much on speaking against ancestral worship – instead of magnifying the name of Jesus Christ and lifting Him up."

I told this lovely farmer about the fact that when people are taught in the banks to identify counterfeit currency, they do not study the counterfeit. They study only the real thing. Every now and then, the examiner will slip in a counterfeit note and they will recognize it straight away. We need to preach the risen, ascended Jesus Christ, and He will draw all men unto Himself.

A lady was standing next to me while I was talking to that young jockey. She smiled. I was able to greet her while the bus was driving us to the plane and I slipped her a little card that we have printed out, wishing her well. She broke down and started weeping. One of my armour-bearers, my son Dougal, asked her if she was okay. She replied that she was; she was just overwhelmed by the love of God in that bus. It was one of the greatest days that I've had in my life.

We flew home uneventfully, flying first class again, which is a real novelty, something we never expected. The air hostesses treated us so well, like royalty. I suppose any child of God is royal; not through any of our own doing but because He's appointed and anointed us for a time such as this. We got off the plane. While we were paying the parking fees for the car that we'd left at the airport, a young couple came running up to us and said that they watch the *Grassroots* programme every single week. They'd even thought about asking me to marry them. (They'd been married for three months before the actual ceremony.) I was able to give them a big hug and encourage them and pray for them, right in the middle of the reception area.

It was an amazing weekend. We got into the car and drove home. I had that lovely feeling of being a bit punch-drunk. I hadn't slept much. I'd seen God move sovereignly, seen people being saved by the thousands, literally. And then, of course, the individual appointments with people, which is always so special to me.

But then something changed. When I got home, my wife was waiting to see me, as always. My daughter (Dougal's wife) and their little baby boy Jake were having lunch with us. They'd been spending the night with Granny while we men were out in the front line. As they were leaving, the bitter part of this weekend hit me like the proverbial sledgehammer.

About two months ago, I felt prompted to buy Jill a little Jack Russell puppy. She was one of the most beautiful puppies I've ever seen. She was the smallest of the litter. She was brown and white, like Jack Russells are, and she had a little curly tail, which it's apparently unlawful to dock now. But we didn't really worry. We liked her little tail. It curled up and when she strutted around the house it used to stick straight up in the air. She was really a beautiful little dog. She became so affectionate and special to Jill particularly, but also to me. We really fell in love with her. She just brightened up our home. She had a little white stripe that ran right down her nose. We called her Zana. I also happen to have two large bull terriers, a male and a female. They're my dogs. They're very gentle with me but very aggressive towards anything else that moves in that garden.

After we'd had our lunch, I walked with Jill up the garden path to say goodbye to my daughter and son and baby grandson. We were standing outside the garden gate, which obviously needs to be closed at all times because we don't want the dogs running all over the farm. Little Zana had been left out in the front garden. She came around the side of the house and went into the male bull terrier's domain. For some reason, which I'll never know until I get to heaven, she walked right through his territory. I was outside the fence with the family and this male bull terrier attacked little Zana. It took me about three seconds to get through the gate and around the fence to them. Jill was shouting and so was the family. When I got to this beautiful little puppy, she was lying dead. The bull terrier had, in one bite, killed her.

I was absolutely devastated. I picked her up and her last lifebreath poured out in my hands. I didn't know what to do. Her body was just moving, ever so slightly, still warm but totally limp. My wife broke down and wept bitterly. I was totally devastated; it was almost like the whole weekend just collapsed around me. I was saying, "But, Lord, what is happening? What is taking place?"

I didn't even say any more to my son and daughter but took the little body and walked to the back of the garden. I took a spade and dug a hole. Jill came out with Zana's little blanket and an old slipper that she used to sleep with every night and I buried the puppy with her blanket and slipper in the rose garden. I didn't know what to say. I was so angry with my bull terrier. I didn't even go near him. I was heartbroken by this little thing, just minutes ago the life and soul of the home. I can still see those little whiskers sticking out at right angles to her nose and those beautiful little brown eyes, so mischievous and yet so full of joy. And now she was dead. I cried out to God. It brought back some memories of the tragedies that I've had in my life in the earlier years. Again, that Scripture came to me: "Many are the afflictions of the righteous, but the Lord will deliver him out of them all." The bitter-sweetness of life...

I'm writing this chapter the day after it happened. The sun is shining and there are heavy black clouds on the horizon that are full of rain, which we so desperately need at this time. It's a new day. The wind is blowing. My wife has wiped away all her tears. There are people in the Vredendal area who are born again, who woke up this morning to new life, to new opportunities, new beginnings. There are marriages that have been restored by the power of the Holy Spirit as people repented. There are young people who now have vision for their lives. There are others who have been delivered from addictions and from a spirit of hatred and unforgiveness. It's a new day. It's a new day for me and my wife.

However, one thing I do want to stress at this time is that there's no guarantee that, because you're a Christian, you will never, ever suffer any affliction in this world. This world is full of darkness. This world, the Bible says clearly, has the devil roaming around in it like a roaring lion, seeking whom he may devour. We have choices. Today, this morning, I have a choice. Either I can sit down and mourn, be disappointed and angry and ask questions as to why this little puppy is no longer alive, or I can say this morning that people are saved today. Not just a few, but thousands. There are millions who still need to be saved. I can sit down and cry over what happened, or I can get up, dust myself off and press on, knowing that God will show me in His time and in heaven why these things still happen to Christians.

I told the crowd this as well. Jesus never promised us a bed of roses when we gave our lives to Him but He did promise us that He'd never leave us nor forsake us. I think that's the problem with a lot of preachers. They don't preach the whole Gospel. The whole Gospel is: Come to Jesus and He will walk with you to the end of the road. He will not leave you and He will not forsake you. There's nowhere in the Bible where it says: "Come to Jesus and all your problems will be solved. You'll never be tested again."

We are living in a world that is not pure. We are living as it were in a world that is full of darkness and evil, but Jesus said that He has come to be the Light of the world. We need to be the light to those who are now walking in darkness. We are still subjected to bitterness, to pain, to suffering and to persecution; more so actually than those who don't yet know the Lord, because the devil is not interested in those who are not believers. He's more interested in the Christian; to try and break him down. But in Christ we have the victory – and I am choosing to rejoice today that my name is written in the Lamb's Book of Life. I know that God will never allow me to be tempted above that which I am able to handle.

While having my quiet time this morning in my prayer room, and thanking God for all the amazing results which took place after this miraculous weekend, and also just crying out to Him about the pain and the suffering, and the way things sometimes turn out that don't always seem to be according to the game plan, the Lord reassured me. I love the Word of God so much, and really would encourage each one of you to spend lots of time reading God's Word, always getting confirmation. I said to that young anaesthetist in the aeroplane: "At the end of the day, to see your vision fulfilled, you must get a specific Scripture from God through the Word to confirm your vision. Then, when the going gets tough, you will not wilt but you will continue and finish the job, because you'll know that God has seen you through."

This morning I was reading from Mark 16, which gives the account of how Mary Magdalene and Mary, the mother of James, and Salome took spices to anoint Jesus' body and to embalm it. They went down early in the morning to the burial site of Jesus, the tomb where Jesus had been laid after He had been crucified. Again, I can just imagine how heavy their hearts must have been. Their whole lives had basically collapsed before their eyes. Even the disciples had run away. All the plans, all the times that they'd spent with the Master – which must have been so beautiful, so precious, so personal – had been dashed. In their place was fear, confusion, misunderstanding and great depression.

As they walked down the road, they said to each other: "Who will roll away the stone from the door of the tomb for us?" But when they got there, to their dismay, the stone was already rolled away. There was a young man clothed in a long, white robe sitting on the right-hand side of the tomb. They were tremendously afraid and alarmed. He said: "Do not be alarmed, because Jesus of Nazareth who was crucified is not here. He has risen. See, this is the place where He was laid." The angel said to them: "Go and tell his disciples – and Peter – that He goes before you into Galilee: there shall you see Him, as He said to you."

I want to say at this point that this is what really makes me love the Lord so much. He always remembers the finer details. You see, Peter was the one who denied Jesus three times. Obviously the Lord had told the angel: "Don't forget to say 'and Peter'", because Peter would never have gone. He would have felt totally unqualified to go and meet the Lord, because of what he'd done.

But the Lord always remembers the little things. The Lord showed me this morning that no matter how downhearted we might be, as I feel about losing that little puppy so unnecessarily, He would even use this little instance to speak into my life; to remind me that many are the afflictions of the righteous, but the Lord will deliver him from them all. This morning when we were still lying in bed before we got up, my wife Jill prayed, "Lord, please, just take away the pain of seeing that little puppy completely broken physically, and replace it with sweet memories of the joy that she brought us, running around the house, barking, and causing lots of upsets and lots of love and joy." That's what's happened.

As the women of God went down to the tomb and were discussing who was going to help them to roll away this huge stone – a big rock – from the entrance of the tomb, they got there and it was already rolled away. The amazing news was that the Master wasn't there. He is alive!

It's the knowledge that, at the end of the day, the Lord has come to give us abundant life that keeps us going. We, as Christians, must not concentrate on and be focused on the things of this world. We must start focusing on the things which are still coming; the life eternal, when we will be with our Master forever, with other believers who have walked the same roads of pain and suffering. There will be no more pain and suffering in heaven. There'll be no more hurt, no more misunderstanding, no more pain, and no more tears. That is what we look forward to.

Go and tell Jesus' disciples and the doubters, the Peters and the Thomases of this world, that He's not in the tomb any longer. He is in heaven. He is alive and those who love Him are alive with Him. And soon, some of us sooner than others, we will see Him again, face to face, totally restored, totally whole, the most beautiful Person who has ever lived. He will be there to meet you and me on that great resurrection day!

Chapter 26
Let the young men speak

Many years ago, when we started having men's conferences at Shalom, there were an amazing two hundred and forty men at the first one we ever had. Bear in mind that I got the Word from the Lord to mentor (father) young men. I was expecting to mentor maybe five or ten men. However, with no advertising whatsoever, we ended up with two hundred and forty men. At our most recent conference in 2009, there were over three thousand ushers alone. Isn't it amazing how God works if we just give Him time, and are patient? The problem with many of us, especially men, is that we just don't give God that opportunity.

At the end of that first Mighty Men Conference a young man by the name of Clive came up to me. His eyes were filled with tears. He said, "I have an earthly father whom I love dearly, but please Uncle Angus, could you be a spiritual father to me?" That gave me gave pleasure and honour. To this very day, he is still a spiritual son of mine.

After that, God literally opened the windows of heaven, because as I am writing this I can say that I now have more than seventy spiritual sons all over this world. I'm sure that the two hundred thousand men who came to the conference in 2009 in some way look to me as a Dad, because most of them, not all, are younger than me. The difference between those men and my spiritual sons is very much an intimacy thing. The qualification is quite simply this: When those young men phone me, as each one has, or contact me, or grow closer to me through affiliation and by spending time with me, they indirectly ask me to mentor or father them, and obviously I always accept. That's the only qualification; nothing else.

God has given me a tremendous heart for young men; to see them established as prophet, priest and king in their own homes. Maybe it's because I started off in life with a big family, and really do understand and feel with a heart feeling – not just a head knowledge – what it's like to grow up five children, plus our close-on thirty children at our children's home, and the many other young men who have come and stayed at Shalom over the years, whose needs I have tried to supply by putting food on the table, clothing them, educating them and standing with them. It's a tremendous responsibility and a very hard job. Some people don't understand that. Also, to protect their wives, to love them, to cherish them, to discipline the children, to have patience and understanding when things don't go just exactly the way they should, and to give them another chance, just like the Lord's given me so many chances. I have a real heart for the huge task that they have.

Obviously it's almost impossible to be a spiritual father to seventy men on a very personal level. I pray for them by name every day. I write each one a spiritual letter, father to son, once a month. Once a year, we have a get-together; not on a weekend but in the middle of the week. These boys have to make a sacrifice to get here to see me. They come on a weekday. We start in the evening and spend one full day together. That's all. Then they leave and go back to their respective homes and businesses the next day.

This past year I had spiritual sons who had come from Singapore, from the east coast of Australia, from the city of London in England, from North Yorkshire in the north of England, from Bulawayo in Zimbabwe, from Lusaka in Zambia, from the Karoo in South Africa, from Cape Town, from Pretoria, and just about every area in South Africa. They came from every different church denomination, from every racial group and every occupation. They included professional sportsmen, farmers, businessmen, schoolteachers, headmasters, personal fitness trainers, professional musicians, preachers, pastors, CEOs of businesses, property developers, civil engineers and many others, and they all came last week to spend one full day and an evening with me. Afterwards, they went straight back to their busy, hectic lives.

I want to tell you that this meeting is one of the highlights of my life. I have had, and have, the privilege of speaking at huge sports stadiums, auditoriums, tents, etc., but for me personally this has to rank right at the top. We experienced an intimacy during that week like I don't think I've ever experienced before in my life. I don't know why, but when the men started arriving I was more nervous than I am when I have to address a crowd of two hundred thousand men, probably purely because of the expectation that these men have, not of hearing from me, but of hearing from God. I'm coming to the stage in my life where I know that I must hand over the baton. I know that the Lord still has plenty of work for me to do, but the young men must be put in position and take their place; obviously, first and foremost in the home and in the family; then in the church; but also very importantly, in every sector of the marketplace.

They need to be put in place, and this is what happened. We started off on the Monday night. Normally I have a programme organized. This time I had no agenda. We started off together, seventy of us in the little chapel that my late Dad and I built. It's a little thatched chapel on the highest point on the farm Shalom, called Bethel, the House of Prayer. We built the chapel because the Lord gave Jill and me clear instructions when we began this ministry that we must build a place where the Holy Spirit can operate freely.

That's exactly what happened. We started off with Joe Niemand leading us in praise and worship, and then I felt that we needed to introduce ourselves to each other once again because some new spiritual sons had come into the family during the course of the year. So we started, one by one. When these young men began to speak it was, as Jason, one of my sons from Australia said, like a symphony in motion.

I really didn't preach, and I didn't want to because they've heard me preach and it wasn't appropriate. These young men first of all introduced themselves. What I loved was that they spoke very highly of their families: "Married, beautiful lady, two children, one on the way." Then they spoke about their occupation. They began to speak as the Holy Spirit led them. Each man, not knowing where the other man was at, started to speak prophetically – and I mean that in the genuine sense of the word.

I get so tired when people use the word "prophetic" almost as a cliché, with no understanding and no meaning. They weren't aware of what their brothers were going through. But I know every one of them, because I pray for them every day. I know their heartaches. One young son of mine from Zambia, who heads up about sixty churches, is just completing the building of a five thousand-seater auditorium in Lusaka. He lost his only daughter a year ago.

He's got three sons and a daughter, so you could call her my granddaughter. He's really struggling to get over it. She was so special to him and his wife. Other sons there were struggling with marital problems, some with separation or divorce. I know exactly who they are, but the others don't. As they got up and started to speak it was an absolutely divine appointment.

I've entitled this chapter "Let the young men speak". I remember as a young child – and many of you in my age group reading this book will also remember – we used to be told: "Children should be seen but not heard." When I reflect on that, I think it is so sad. There is a place and a time for children to speak. There is indeed a place.

These young men began to introduce themselves. That's all that they were meant to do. During the introduction I interjected because they're very humble sons and would not have given the full extent of what they're doing. I would chip in, like a proud Dad always does, and say that this particular son has the biggest construction business in Durban, a city of over three million people.

Or the next son, a very famous rugby player, but what they don't know is that he's got two gold medals from two World Cup victories. Or this son, who lives in a grass hut in the southern part of the Sudan, a volatile area where two thousand people have been murdered this year by warlords and in-fighting. The only contact he has with the outside world is by satellite connection. Or this son of mine, who is a headmaster of an ordinary, plain, government school, but his results are supernatural. In seventeen years there has not been a matric (school-leaving certificate) failure. Last year eighty per cent of his students got university exemptions. Or another son, an olive farmer, who has been awarded the gold medal in the world championship for the best olive oil in the whole world.

As I interjected and encouraged, these men started speaking – unbeknown to themselves and without offending anybody, because no one knew, apart from me, what their brothers' problems were – of intimate things affecting one another. One man got up and said, "Alcohol is playing havoc among many young farmers." He's an agent for a wool company and inspects wool all over the country.

He spoke about alcohol to two men who said that there's nothing wrong with alcohol. Yet both of those men are divorced because of alcohol abuse. He said, tongue in cheek, "If you can tell me one good thing about alcohol, let's go out and get smashed tonight!" All the brothers and sons laughed. Right behind him another son of mine, who happens to be a wine farmer from the Western Cape, got up. I could see that he was thinking deeply about the testimony of this brother of his. There were no fingers pointed and no condemnation but the Spirit was moving powerfully.

I could feel the presence of God so tangibly as these young sons of mine started speaking. They began to relax. I could hear it in their voices; I could see it in their faces. Nobody was standing on ceremony. There was no need for any man to prove himself. It's a terrible thing (and I've had to repent of it myself), when we expect so much of our sons and we keep saying it's for their sakes. But we know it's not, it's for the sake of our own reputation. These boys had no pressure whatsoever. They didn't have to perform. All they were doing was sharing their hearts. The tears started flowing.

There was also laughter as one young man, a very, very special young man from Johannesburg, stood up. All the farmers, the athletes and the businessmen were sitting there. He said that a few years ago, before they became Christians, he and a couple of friends toured Europe. More as a dare and a laugh, they decided that when they went back to South Africa they were going to start up a crematorium for domestic pets. Of course the whole place went up in uproar and raucous laughter. He said he now has over seventy vets on his books and they recommend all pet owners to get their pets cremated at this crematorium.

Remember, if an animal dies we farmers dig a hole and bury the animal. I suppose though, if you live in a high-rise block of flats and you're on the twentieth floor, it's not so easy. I, of course, had to put in my five cents and made a little joke, and asked, "How much do you charge for budgies? Do you charge any more than you charge for a dog that is to be cremated?" More raucous laughter! This dear son of mine said, "No, Angus, we don't work by weight, we work on emotion!" Nothing disrespectful, I'm an animal lover. I have some beautiful pets of my own. He's actually making a fortune and I'm happy about that. He's also bringing a lot of peace to pet owners' hearts.

The Holy Spirit really began to move and to minister through these men. We saw eyes filling with tears and men bending their heads as they began to weep as the Holy Spirit started talking to them through their brothers. Let the young men speak!

I'm realizing now, as I've come of age, that the duty of a father is to listen more than to speak. You see, dear parent, when your children come to you, whether they are forty years old or whether they are twelve years old, they already know the solution. They know what they have to do. They know what they've done wrong. All they're looking for is an understanding, loving heart.

A couple of nights ago, I was very honoured to be asked to be the speaker at a Gospel concert, where a very well-known international group of singing artists was performing in Durban. I'm a grandfather seven times over now, not even just a father, and have many, many spiritual grandchildren, and I said to one of my spiritual sons, "You know, I don't even know if I'm going to the right place."

You know what this young man of thirty-eight said to me? "You know something? I prayed for you early this morning and God said to me that it's very important that you go. The young people want to have a grandfather appear, that they know who's there. You don't have to dance and bob up and down and jive, but just your presence says to them: "It's okay. I agree with it, it's fantastic." Enjoy it; praise God in the way in which you know best and feel at ease doing."

I went. Smoke was coming up from the platform, there were like sparklers everywhere, flashing lights, and lots and lots of sound, but I want to tell you that I had an experience with the Holy Spirit amongst those people. Those young men from that wonderful band, Third Day, are godly men. They had me pray for them twice before they went on the platform, once just beneath the stage, and once when I met them before the concert started. Young men want to speak and we, the older men, must start to listen.

Coming back to this father and sons meeting – I don't want to call it a conference because I didn't want it to resemble a conference in any way; that's why I didn't want any speakers or any subjects. We just wanted to be there together. By half past ten the first evening I had to stop the meeting. Only two-thirds of my sons had introduced themselves, and I had to say we would come back the next day. Before the meeting, when they were still flying in from overseas and driving from all the corners of this beautiful nation and continent of ours, I wondered how I was going to fill the time. There wasn't enough time, because when they started speaking I couldn't keep them quiet. They were speaking prophetically, one after the other.

One son, who's probably one of the most famous paddlers that the world has ever known, was just sitting there quietly and saying who he is. He has paddled the Amazon River and every major river in the world; he's been up in Alaska, in Africa, and all over. I had to tell them. Another, a young singer, has turned down a contract to go to Nashville, Tennessee, USA, the Mecca of music, especially of country and western music, because he wants to sing for Jesus.

I was amongst such well-known personalities, such mighty men of God, that I felt totally inferior and insignificant. But this is the bottom line. We don't have to do anything any more; we just have to be there for our sons. God has shown me in my life now it's not even so much what I say any more, but who I am. Just the fact that I'm there is enough. All of us need to begin to do that. We need to start being – and doing less.

I had the opportunity to speak for maybe ten minutes and that's the honest truth. If any of you reading this book know me personally, you'll know that's a miracle in itself! I spoke about prayer. Martin Luther said that prayer is the sweat of the soul. Another mighty preacher said: "Prayer is the gymnasium of the spirit." I explained to the young men how difficult it is sometimes to pray, because we need to discipline ourselves.

I asked another son who is a personal fitness trainer, "How long do you believe a man needs to train every day in order to remain fit?"

He said, "A minimum of one hour a day."

I said, "Gentlemen are we praying, not having a quiet time but praying, one hour a day?"

Of course, nobody, including me, put their hands up, so we were challenged straight away that we need to be a praying people and we need to pray more. With that, we closed off and went home.

They were back the next morning. We were ready to start at nine o'clock. Already I could hear a buzz as they were talking to each other, taking each other's addresses, and praying for each other. It was just so beautiful to see.

Robert Murray McCheyne, a Scottish preacher, a holiness man who went home to be with Jesus at the age of twenty-nine – mission accomplished – started a huge revival in Dundee, Scotland. He said about the revival, "Rather than have been an instrument of the Lord, all I was, was an adoring spectator." I can honestly tell you that by the morning after the meeting the night before, all I was, was an adoring spectator. We went straight into praise and worship. From there, we began to repent before God, starting with me. Totally broken, we asked for forgiveness for arrogance, for pride, for fearfulness, for inadequacies.

I want to say to the older men reading this book: you need to start living your life as an example to your sons and daughters. It's got to start with you. In the Middle East, the shepherds lead their sheep. In the West we push our sheep, we drive them with sheepdogs. We need to lead from the front. I had to be the one to start with repentance. God began to talk with me and broke me in front of my sons and humbled me. That opened the door for the rest of them. Remember, many of these young men are very, very successful men in their particular walk of life, whatever their field.

To humble yourself, to get on your knees and to ask forgiveness, takes a lot of courage but it has to start with the father. That's exactly what Jesus did. Remember, He took that bowl, filled it with water, wrapped a towel around Himself and started to wash His disciples' dirty feet. Unless we are prepared to do that, God cannot use us. As I began to repent before God and ask Him to forgive me in so many areas, the prayers started to flow. Once again, I actually had to stop the prayers, because we would never have finished.

We prayed a general prayer of repentance together and then continued with our introductions from the night before. Just ordinary introductions: your name, who are you, where are you from, what's your family consist of and what kind of business are you in? They started again to bring the Word of God through their testimonies. A personal testimony is a very powerful thing because nobody can argue with it; they weren't there when it happened. People can do one of two things: they can either believe you, or disbelieve you and call you a liar. But they definitely cannot argue with you.

As these young sons of mine continued to introduce themselves, the fire of God began to fall again. One son who is an ex-policeman, a huge man, got up and started to weep and share about a miracle of God. His wife woke up in the middle of the night. Her heart stopped beating. He prayed and got hold of me, and I prayed with him. Miraculously, God healed her. The heart specialist could not believe what took place. As he was sharing this with his brothers, I could see the faith level amongst them beginning to rise and I could see their compassion and love for their brother also rising, because he was weeping.

We continued. We were supposed to go out and have a hotdog at ten o'clock. I felt so sorry for the ladies, because the hotdogs were postponed to eleven o'clock, then to twelve, to one, and eventually at two o'clock the Holy Spirit allowed us to go out and have that hotdog. We took our notebooks, went for a walk into the fields and wrote down what God was talking to us about.

We came back into the chapel, where the presence of God was so strong you could cut the atmosphere with a knife. There was such sweetness; a fragrance, a trust, an incredible love, like I've experienced very few times in my life. That is what makes it conducive for young men to offload things in their lives which they cannot speak about to anyone else. We also made a pledge that we would not disclose anything personal about each other in public.

I then spoke about the mantle of God, the transference of the glory of God. I learned a very special lesson that day. When Elisha asked Elijah for a double portion of his mantle, I've always thought that he was asking to perform twice as many miracles as Elijah. That did happen, by the way, but that is not what he meant when he asked for that mantle, that anointing, that portion.

In those days, the Jewish custom was that if a man had four sons he would, before he died, divide up his inheritance into five portions. When he died, his oldest son would get two portions and the other three sons would get a single portion each. This would give the eldest son the legacy, the power and the authority to lead from where his late father had been. It was a real revelation to us.

We also spoke about the fact that God does not give His mantle, His anointing, His blessing, His power, to a man just to go and put it on a mantelpiece, or in a display cabinet for people to see. It's a weapon, the authority that God gives to His sons and daughters for the work of God. I clarified what I believe to be the most important point. I said, "The onus here today is not on the giver but the seeker." You see it was Elisha, not Elijah, who did what was right in the sight of God.

2 Kings 2 tells us that Elijah actually didn't even want Elisha to go with him, to follow him. He obviously thought of him as a bit of a hindrance and a burden. Even the prophets' sons, some forty of them, kept trying to dissuade Elisha from following after Elijah. But he would not turn back. Eventually, because of his persistence and his availability, he received the mantle of Elijah. He took it and struck the water of the River Jordan. It parted in two and he went across, just like his master had done in the past.

As I sat and listened to these men talking about their visions, their expectations and their failures, it was as if a cleansing took place. It was as though a new building was put up. I felt very strongly in my heart that they needed to seek the authority and the love of God, so that they too could continue to do the work the Lord has set for His children to do. That's exactly what happened. I had the privilege of anointing them with oil and praying over them. I could see men just rising up in front of my eyes in stature and authority.

I said: "There are no lone rangers in the kingdom of God. If you want to be used by God to command authority, you have to be submitted to authority, just like that centurion in the Bible who understood about authority. Jesus said He'd never seen faith like that in any Jewish man in Israel. That Roman officer – a Gentile – understood that if he wanted to exercise authority, he had to be under authority. When Jesus wanted to come to his house to pray for his sick servant, he said, "It's not necessary. Say the Word." Jesus did, and the servant was healed."

I really believe that that's what happened with these young sons in Christ. They've gone away, not with any authority that belonged to Angus, but with authority that God gave them because they were prepared to humble themselves in the sight of God, and in the sight of their brethren. One of the biggest problems with us men is a thing called pride. Pride always comes before a fall. The Bible says in 1 Peter 5:5 that the Lord resists the proud but He gives grace to the humble. I saw a measure of humility amongst these young men that I've never seen before in my life.

I really exhort any pastors reading this to let your church members participate. Because they had the opportunity to speak, there wasn't one man in that chapel who didn't get up and say his piece. I would also say to any mothers reading this: Let your daughters speak, so that they too can be part of what God is doing.

I am convinced that the Lord Jesus Christ, especially towards the end of His three-year ministry – which shook the universe, never mind the world – became more of a listener than a speaker. After the Sermon on the Mount, you often find Him going away, departing with His disciples. He must have just sat there and let them talk.

Once He had to rebuke the "Sons of Thunder" (James and John), when they were trying to jockey for positions in heaven. They asked to sit next to the Lord, one on either side. Their mother even spoke on their behalf.

The Lord asked them: "Can you drink of the cup?"

They said: "Yes," and He replied: "You will anyway, but I

cannot guarantee where you'll be seated in heaven, because that is My Father's prerogative."

Jesus was listening to these young men talking. We too need to let the young men speak. Some of the things they say may not be doctrinally correct at the time, but by allowing them to speak, you are giving them a sense of confidence, a sense of belonging. Very slowly and gently, you can quietly correct them and bring them back onto the path. They won't then feel bad about it. If we continually rebuke our sons, continually chastise them, continually discipline them, and never allow them to speak up and say their bit or say what they feel, they will never mature to anything. They will always be those who drink milk and never get into the real meat of the matter.

One of my sons phoned me a day ago, and I know it was as a direct result of that meeting that we had. He asked me whether he should continue by faith and make a new music CD, bearing in mind that he didn't have any finance. I asked how he made the first one, and he said, "By faith."

I said, "Don't stop!"

He already knew what he was going to do. He just wanted his spiritual Dad to stand with him in agreement. He didn't ask me for any money. He doesn't expect me to give him any money, because I don't have any. What he wanted was affirmation. That's all, a sounding board.

There's nothing I love better than when my sons come to me and ask, "Have you got five minutes? Please, jump in the pick-up with me. I want to show you something." They take me to their strawberry fields or their cattle herds or their forests, and ask:

"What do you feel?"

"What do you think about that?"

They already know the answer. They are much better farmers than I ever was, but they just want Dad to have a look and see, and maybe for Dad to say, "Well done, son. I think that's absolutely amazing." That's all they want to hear. You can see their faces light up. It's like a young man who's been selected to play a sport for his country. He can have thousands and thousands of admirers and fans clapping and shouting his name, but unless his own personal Dad, Mom, brothers and sisters are there, it doesn't really mean too much to him.

I feel at this point that I need to say to some Dads reading this book: be careful that you don't break the spirit of your son. One silly word can destroy him for ever. I remember watching a movie called *8 Seconds*. It was the true life-story of one of the world champion rodeo bull riders, Lane Frost. When it starts off, you see a little boy riding sheep and his Daddy is helping him. He grows into a young teenager and becomes an amazing rider. His Dad was also a former rodeo star but never quite got to the top. This young man went all the way to the top and became the world champion, but his father was always pushing him, always saying:

"You can do better."

"Let's see what happens when you become the provincial champion."

When he became the provincial champion, he said, "Let's see what happens when you become the national champion."

He became the national champion. "Let's see what happens when you become world champion."

Bull riding, by the way, is a fearful sport; it literally makes other contact sports child's play. You're riding an animal that weighs close on two tons; it's got a strap around its middle that makes it come out of that chute very angry. It wants to get the rider off its back. And for those who don't know the finer details of a beast, its skin moves, unlike that of a horse. The skin moves backwards and forwards and from side to side. The bull is so wide that you can hardly get your legs around it.

You have one piece of rope that you need to hold onto for dear life, and they pull it so tight because the animal blows itself up in the rodeo chute. As the chute is opened, it deflates itself and you end up with half a metre of slack rope that doesn't help at all, so they make the rope so tight that the bull can hardly stand the pain. You've got spurs on and you have to spur that animal continually while you're on its back, otherwise you're disqualified. Some of those bulls have horns and they will turn around and literally attack you.

The clowns are probably the bravest men in the rodeo. They run around trying to distract the bull from the rider when he eventually gets thrown off. There are also men on horses, very brave riders and horses too, who try to protect the bull rider from the bull when the rider is dislodged.

Lane Frost became the champion bull rider of the whole world. He was so excited. He was happily married to a young lady who was a world champion barrel rider. She rode horses and was a champion in her own right. His father, his Dad, who meant so much to him, came up to him when he was champion of the world but, instead of congratulating him and saying, "You've done something I could never do," he said, "That's wonderful. Well done. Now let's see how long you can keep the title!"

His son was so devastated by that remark that he went off the rails. His marriage got into trouble and he started drinking. It was extremely sad. A couple of years later, he was gored to death by a bull at a rodeo. I think his Dad realized then what a mistake he'd made.

Praise God that our God is not a condemning God; He's a forgiving God. I thank God for the fact that He forgives and forgets. There are many fathers and mothers who know that if they could live their lives again, they wouldn't do it the same way. You know something? There's nobody more forgiving than a child or a young son. All you have to say is sorry. That's all that repentance means: Sorry. I won't do it again.

We were able to hug each other in those meetings. My own father was a man I esteemed greatly. I loved him. When he was seventy and I was forty, he would say "Jump!" and I would ask, "How high?" That's how much I respected, loved and feared my Dad. He came from the old Scottish tradition and the closest I could get to my Dad was a handshake. But before he died, I had the privilege of leading him to Christ. After that I could hug my Dad unashamedly in front of everybody. Please do the same. I make it a point to hug my sons whenever I see them, whether it be in the street or at church, in the workplace or on the sports field. That's all they want. They want that affirmation.

Let the young men speak!

Chapter 27
New ideas

I always used to joke with my older son, who's a tremendous entrepreneur. He came home from university one day and said, "Dad, I want to grow strawberries on the farm."

I said, "Well, that's not agriculture. That's market gardening."

Again, I was having a go at him. That's not at all the way to do it. Sarcasm is the lowest form of wit, simply because it's always at someone else's expense. We need to be very careful with our children because we tend to continually do that – and it breaks them down. It does not build them up.

I reluctantly allowed him to go ahead and grow his strawberries. I want to tell you that that is probably the single biggest and most effective part of our farming operation at the moment. This young man employs between two hundred and thirty to two hundred and fifty seasonal pickers at a time. Although he's been through his challenges, he has done exceptionally well and he is progressing from there.

I love to tell the story about when Henry Ford's board of managers came together with him and suggested that the Model T Ford, that famous vehicle invented by Henry Ford, should be painted in different colours. Tongue in cheek, he replied, "It can be any colour… so long as it is black."

I told that to my son Andy once, and he said, "Yes, Dad, but that was the beginning of the downfall of the Ford Empire, because all of the other car manufacturers painted their cars in different colours. And if you go out in the street today, you'll see that Fords are in many different colours."

New ideas... We need to allow the young men to run. We need to pass on the baton – I say that figuratively – and let them run, whether it's in the market place, or at home.

On another occasion, I went to have supper with that same son a couple of years after he got married, and his little baby was there. I, being a very impulsive man and always wanting to get on with things, said, "Come on, let's pray, let's have lunch. " With a big smile on his face, and he wasn't being ugly or vindictive about it, he said, "Dad, remember, this is my home. We'll eat when we decide to eat." I must say that I took it on the jaw. I didn't like it very much at the time but I realized afterwards that I was totally out of line. Young people do things differently from us.

One of the areas in my life where I've come of age in these last few months has been to realize that young people have a lot more creative ideas than we have. It's terribly sad for me to see a father trying to compete with his son. I still cannot understand how that can be, how even when a father and a son are playing a sport together, the father will be totally put out because his son has beaten him. Surely, if we are to be good fathers and good leaders, we need to pass the baton on? In order for us to do that, however, our children must be encouraged to excel, exceeding anything that we've ever done. If that doesn't happen, the onus is surely not on the child but on the teacher.

We need to grow old graciously and we need to hand over, so that those new ideas which are being birthed in the young men and women by the Holy Spirit may reach their full potential. I've come to realise that the less I try now and the more I rest in God, the greater the success I'm experiencing, particularly in the ministry which I am doing at the moment. There is plenty of room for everybody.

This huge move of God that's taking place amongst men in our beloved South Africa at present is due solely to the influence and the participation of young blood, of young ideas. After the first Mighty Men Conference when we had two hundred and forty men, the young men literally took over. At our most recent conference that we had just a few months back, where we had close on two hundred thousand men, I can honestly say that I had the easiest job of all. All I had to do was to speak at the different meetings. The young men did everything. They did the logistics, the planning, the financial budgeting; they organized the transport, the accommodation, the water, the showers and the toilets. They literally organized everything.

One man said, tongue in cheek, because the one in 2010 was to be our last Mighty Men Conference, "What are you going to do with yourself after that?" I had to say to him, humbly, "It takes only one weekend of my entire year, this men's conference." But for the young men with the young ideas, it takes a full year to prepare everything. If I had not allowed the young ideas to be implemented, it would never have got off the ground.

At the end of the day, it's all about bringing glory to our heavenly Father. Even as He gave complete authority to His Son, our Saviour, Jesus Christ, we too need to do exactly the same thing. Don't tell your son or daughter that you love them. Show them that you love them. How can we do that? Not only by word of mouth but by demonstration; by releasing them, by giving them the baton, by giving them the authority to go ahead – and when they fall down not to castigate them, but rather to pick them up, dust them off and let them run again. The greatest investment that you'll ever make on this earth is your children, your young people. I just wish that I'd learned that lesson even thirty years ago.

As I write this, my son is coming up the road on a quad bike with his son, my grandson. What a sight it is to behold! This young man is married to my youngest daughter. At the age of twelve, he gave his life to Jesus at a crusade that I held in Pietermaritzburg, a city not far from the farm. I never even saw him in the crowd. He went back home and led his father, his mother and his two brothers to Christ. About twelve years after that, he came and asked for my youngest daughter's hand in marriage. Today he's a Christian leader in our community and he's got lots and lots of ideas for his future.

He's got two little boys and he's bringing them up in the fear of the Lord. I trust that he's not making as many mistakes as I made in bringing up my sons. We need to let young people go free, to be free as the wind, to hear from the Holy Spirit. The only directive that we can give our young people is that whatever idea, whatever vision, or whatever dream they have, there is no problem as long as it lines up with the Compass of Life (the Bible). If it does not add up or tie in with the heart of God, then we need to gently but firmly dissuade them. If they know that our heart is for them, they will gladly obey.

You can take a horse to water, they say, but you cannot make it drink. I know that, I'm still riding horses. A young man, or a young woman, who has a vision, a dream, or a brand-new idea, will come to you for confirmation, as a sounding board. They will come to you and to me to seek our approval and then away they'll go and attempt great things for God and expect great things from God, in the same way that William Carey, the great missionary to India, did.

He was a man who had new ideas, yet the Baptist Union at the time couldn't see them and told him that if India needed to be saved, and God needed to save India, He didn't need him. How wrong could they be? He left with his wife and his young children, never to return to England. He buried his children and his wife in India and never turned back. He began to translate the Bible into Sanskrit, Hindustani, Chinese and other languages, and literally turned Asia around for Christ. A man who was nearly stopped by the long white-beards, because he had new ideas! God forbid that you or I should ever do a thing like that again.

Chapter 28
The reality of God

Joseph Parker, a nineteenth-century English Congreg-ationalist preacher, once said: "If we as the church do not get back to spiritual visions, glimpses of heaven and an awareness of the greater glory and life, we will lose our faith. Our altar will become nothing but cold, empty stone, never blessed with a visit from heaven. *This is the world's need today – people who have seen their Lord.*" (Extract from *The Lost Art of Meditation*, as quoted in *Streams in the Desert*.)

Mankind realizes that we are living in the last days and there's a tremendous hunger in the world today for people to find their spiritual place in life. People are desperate to meet the real God. In their desperation, they are trying all kinds of pseudo-mystical encounters in their search for God. Yesterday I was speaking to a dear friend who said that he's very concerned about the springing up of all types of mystical groups; of people who say that because they have been on a certain course with a certain group, they have the power to heal. People are opening up their homes so that children can come for spiritual massages, and there all kinds of other strange doctrines in these end times.

Things are coming to a head now and people want to know about God, our Creator. They want reality. They are sick and tired of the plastic presentations, the froth and bubbles, and the commercial presentation of the Gospel of Jesus Christ. They are desperately seeking men and women who can offer them some kind of alternative to the life they are living at the moment, which is an absolute rat race, lacking so badly in the area of spiritual content. It's almost like the difference between going to a fast-food outlet and buying food which smells good and tastes good but seems to have no substance, or going and getting a good plate of Granny's home cooking, which is solid, nutritious and delicious to the taste – and once you've eaten it, you feel you can take on the day.

The world is absolutely starving to meet people who have seen the Lord. It goes right back to the time just after Jesus' death and resurrection, where the Bible says that wherever Peter, James, John and the other disciples walked, the people marvelled that these uneducated men were making such an impact on the world – and they perceived that they had been with Jesus.

They say that when the great revivalist Charles Finney entered into the factories, where there were large numbers of people working in boring, uninteresting, unrelenting job situations that offered no stimulation, people would come under the conviction of the Holy Spirit just through the presence of the man of God. He spent many hours on his own in the presence of the Lord and he had a great capacity to love following an experience in the forest, where he said that the love of God penetrated his soul to such a degree that he cried out to God: "Lord, if You don't stop, I'm going to die!" When he walked up those assembly lines, the people could sense that presence of God in his life and would fall to their knees and repent and ask for forgiveness.

Oh my dear friend, how the world needs to see that again. One thing I have come to realize is that the only thing that people really desire of any speaker, any preacher, or any man or woman of God, is not their eloquence in preaching or presentation of the Gospel, or even their good works, or the amazing abilities or giftings that God has given them. They simply want to meet men or women who have walked with God. It's like a fragrance that they meet. That's why, when Moses came down from Mt Sinai, he literally had to wear a veil over his face for three weeks because of the glory of God that was exuding from his very being.

People are desperate for God. They are not desperate for experiences. They are not desperate for any kind of showmanship. They are desperate for the presence of God. That is something that cannot be conjured up. It's something that cannot be manufactured. It's something that cannot be learned. It's something that comes through spending time with the King of kings and the Lord of lords Himself, the Maker of heaven and of earth. There is no short cut.

In my own life I have realized that if we need to be used of God, we have to spend time with God. The more time we spend with God, the more effective we will become. The less time we spend with God, the less effective we will be. We're not even talking about gifting or ability. It's not like someone who wants to learn to play a violin and must join a music college to learn how to play, or someone who wants to learn to be a great athlete and must go to a certain training camp and be schooled by the top Olympic coaches in the world. It comes out of a relationship, a desire to have a friendship with the King of Glory.

In Matthew 17:1–9 we read how Jesus took the three disciples, Peter, James and John, up a high mountain where he was transfigured, and it was there that the disciples saw the glory of God when our heavenly Father came down to speak with His Son. Moses and Elijah were present at that same meeting. It changed those disciples' lives forever and gave them a new dimension of who Jesus really was.

It's like that upper room where Daniel, that wonderful ambassador of God, spent time praying relentlessly to his Maker, the Lord. Daniel received strength and inspiration and a power that even King Nebuchadnezzar, the most powerful man in the world at that time, desired to have but couldn't. When Daniel was eventually thrown into the lions' den, the very lions themselves would not touch him because of the presence of God.

My friends, I've heard that story about Daniel in the lions' den many times. I want to tell you that the fact of the matter is that those lions that were in the den with Daniel were ravenous, half-starved, but never touched him the whole night. Yet those same lions, when Daniel's accusers were thrown into the same den by Nebuchadnezzar the next day, literally tore the accusers apart and ate them before they hit the bottom of that pit.

We've really got to seek God more sincerely than ever before if we expect the Lord to use us as instruments to influence others. We are very familiar with the wonderful Scripture in Colossians 1:27, which says, "...Christ in you, the hope of glory." The only way that we're going to get Christ in us is by spending time in His midst, by spending time in His presence, by disciplining ourselves and by spending not only quality time but also quantity time with the King of kings.

I really do wish that I had known these truths thirty years ago. It would have saved me so much blood, sweat and tears. That's why the great apostle Paul could say in Philippians 3:10: "That I may know Him, and the power of His resurrection..." When I look back on my past years of walking with the Lord, it seemed to be hard work every time I attempted to do something for God and the actual results seemed to be negligible. However, when I've spent time waiting, with almost minimal effort, on the King of Glory, the results have been astronomical.

One good example of that is the Mighty Men movement, which was literally birthed through spending time with God. I've said it so many times before, but I need to say it one more time: A good idea is not always necessarily a God-idea, and a need does not always justify a call. The way the world works is that if something is working, why change it? And if it's having a wonderful effect, keep it going.

As I write this book we are preparing for our last men's conference at Shalom and we are expecting no less than four hundred thousand men. With that type of result, surely the natural, worldly tendency would be: Why stop? If it's working, why not keep it going? But you see, God started it, and God has given me clear instructions to stop it. It would be futile for me to try and keep it going, for whatever reason, even if it's with the best intentions in the world.

We've got to start doing what God tells us to do. In God's economy, two and two often equal seven. It just does not make sense in the natural, and yet supernaturally it works every time. Think of the early disciples, who did things that didn't make sense, yet they always had miraculous results.

I think too of the story in the Bible where Elijah went to Zarephath. When he came to the city gate, there was a widow gathering sticks. He called to her and said: "Please, bring me a little water in a cup that I might drink." He was thirsty. God had told him to go to that town and that he would be fed there. He said: "And please bring me a morsel of bread in your hand."

She must have looked at this man of God, and she said:

"As the Lord your God lives, I do not have any bread, only a handful of flour in a bin, and only a little oil in a jar. You can see I'm gathering up a couple of sticks so that I can go and prepare a meal for myself and my son so that we can eat it. And then we will lie down and die together."

Elijah said to her (and he says to you and me – and sometimes it doesn't make sense – you don't have anything left): "Do not fear. Go and do as you have said. But first make me a small cake and bring it to me out of the flour that's left, and afterwards make some for yourself and your son." It must have been awesome. He said: "The bin of flour shall not be used up, nor shall the jar of oil run dry." She'd just told him that she only had enough for one cake but he was talking faith into her life.

So often God tells us to do something that doesn't seem right in the natural; it seems, actually, like suicide. It seems ridiculous. At the moment we are experiencing drought symptoms here in our area. It's already well into November and there hasn't been any decent rain yet. In fact, we've started having forest fires now. My word of encouragement this morning on a radio programme to all the farmers was: "Plant your seed. There is no point in keeping it in the barn. It will not grow there. Do it as unto the Lord and do it by faith – and you'll give God the opportunity to bless you."

If that widow had not used the remainder of her flour and oil to give the man of God something to eat, if she'd refused, she would have made one more cake out of that flour and she and her little son would have lain down and died. But she didn't. She obeyed the man of God. She heard what he said. He said: "If you make that cake, your flour and your oil will not run out until the Lord sends the rain." She went away and did according to the word of Elijah. She and her household ate for many days and the bin of flour was not used up, nor was the jar of oil dry. According to the Word spoken by the prophet of God, the Lord honoured her.

There are so many things I wish I'd known when I was younger. It would have saved me so much heartache, so much pain, so much depression and anxiety, worrying about things that have never actually happened; putting away things for a rainy day, and it's never had to be used. I really want to exhort you to hear the Word of the Lord and to sow a good seed. God will water it and add an increase to it.

People often come to me and say, "You've done lots for the Lord; you've given lots to the Lord." I really don't see that at all, and I mean that from the bottom of my heart. I don't feel that I've done half as much as I could have. I don't feel that I've given half as much as I could have. I really mean that with all of my heart. That widow gave the man of God everything that she had. God honoured that heart attitude and that physical giving.

I will never forget watching Steven Spielberg's film, *Schindler's List*, an awesome but horrific story about the Holocaust, which greatly impacted my life. Of course, Spielberg himself is a Jew.

The film was based on a true account of Schindler, a German, who was a playboy of note. He was an industrialist, a member of the Nazi party during the Second World War. He had friends in the Gestapo and he knew exactly what they were doing: murdering God's people; loading rail cattle trucks full of men, women and children every day, and sending them to the gas chambers and burning their corpses in incinerators. Over six million Jews and sympathizers died during that time; probably about the most horrific single act that's ever taken place on the face of the earth.

Yet Schindler had a heart for the Jewish people and the people in his factory. He was responsible for saving over one thousand Jews. He is esteemed greatly by the Jewish people, in fact there's a special cemetery in Jerusalem, just outside the old city in Israel, where his grave is. I think he's about the only Gentile that is buried there; truly a friend to the people, the children of God.

Right at the end of the movie, you see all the real folk flashing by on the screen with all their descendants – so it became many more than a thousand because they married and had children. This huge crowd of people came past, and each one put a small stone on top of his grave in Jerusalem. They were simply paying tribute to the man who was responsible for saving their lives. There was an old accountant who put his arm around Schindler and thanked him so much for what he did for the people. He said, "Well done! You saved over a thousand Jewish people."

Schindler started to weep and he said, "I could have done so much more. I could have sold my car and I could have bought a couple of people with that. I could have sold this, and I could have sold that, and I could have sold my gold watch."

But, you know, the bottom line is that he used what he had at the time. He made a tremendous impact on God's people. As I've come of age, I've realized that there's no good in crying over spilled milk, over things we haven't done in the past. We can't redeem those things. However, what we can do is redeem the time we have now, and not waste valuable time and money on things which are of no consequence in this world.

Again, the Lord has reminded me that this life we are living is passing by so quickly. Three score and ten years, with ten years extra if you've got the strength, the Bible says. If I had my life to live over again, I would do things differently. But I don't have it to live again. The life that I'm living now is not the dummy run, it's the real thing. And after this it's judgment time and eternal life; it's home-time and I can't wait! But until then, I intend to use every drop of blood and every bit of energy that I have to lead people to Christ, to comfort the downhearted, to heal the sick and to set the captives free.

We've just had two little baby girls under the age of three, one severely burnt in a fire, come into our children's home. One of these little ones made me cry because she said that all she wants to do is to see Uncle Angus because she watches me on our TV programme *Grassroots* every week. This little thing is a toddler. She came to me in church yesterday morning and put her arms around me. She's my little girl and I'm her Dad. What a privilege and honour!

Just do what you can with what you've got. God will do the rest. Remember the widow. Remember the oil and the flour. God will multiply it.

Chapter 29

Revival

When I looked up the *New Collins Concise English Dictionary* to find out the exact meaning of the word "revival", one of the meanings is a reawakening of faith. Another is to be brought back to life. Yet another, which I think is so fitting, is to flourish again. At this time in my life I am seeing people flourishing again, and it brings great joy to my heart.

Edwin Orr says, "Revival is times of refreshing." David McKee says, "Revival is new beginnings." That great preacher Dr Martyn Lloyd Jones said, "You can't stop a revival any more than you can start one. It's all in God's hands." Maybe that's why it's so special. John Blanchard said, "Man can no more organize revival than he can dictate the wind." Again, Martyn Lloyd Jones says, "A revival never needs to be advertised. It always advertises itself."

Like never before, that is what I'm experiencing everywhere I go, and I honestly believe that revival is actually upon us in this beautiful nation of South Africa. I'm about to embark on a trip down to Cape Town. We are having a meeting tomorrow in a place called Worcester, the *Boland* town in the Western Cape where the Andrew Murray revival started in 1860. That revival spread right through South Africa and around the world, and I'm believing for nothing less than that.

There's a hunger and openness about the things of God, especially among men, like I've never experienced since I gave my life to Christ in 1979. Everywhere I go, men are speaking about Jesus. To think that sportsmen – men of great note and calibre in their particular sport – are speaking about revival and acknowledging Jesus Christ when they win a competition, is something I am very excited about.

Where else in the world have you seen or heard of a huge stud bull sale where, when the auctioneer has welcomed all the buyers and the sellers, he stands aside and lets a minister come up and bring the Word of the Lord? Where have you ever heard that in your life before? Yet that is exactly what I saw a couple of months ago. And not only in one place – in numerous places.

I was invited to be the main speaker at the SA Grain Board Conference, a huge conference. Bear in mind that maize meal is the staple diet of the continent of Africa. The men at this conference were the main players in the food-producing sector of South Africa. I was given a free hand to speak about our Lord Jesus Christ in my address. This was not a church meeting; this was a secular, food-producing conference. I can truly put this down to one thing only, and that is revival. Once again I remembered the words of the great revivalist Charles Finney: "Where there is no Mr Amen and no Mr Wet Eyes in an audience, there is no revival" – and I can assure you that these men were saying "Amen" wholeheartedly when I was speaking!

Revival has been compared with and referred to as a mighty roaring wind. That's what happened in the room when the Holy Spirit came down upon the disciples. They were cowering there for fear of their lives, and it changed them instantaneously into giants for God.

As I'm writing, I have just observed something which is so beautiful. It is a very wet day today on the farm. There is a heavy mist turning into a light drizzle. Everything is sopping-wet, green, fresh, and it is quite cold, probably about eight or nine degrees. I'm watching two of our horses, tails up in the air, galloping full-tilt around the paddock. The wind is blowing through their manes. I'm concerned that they won't be able to stop when they come to the end of the paddock because of the wetness, but it doesn't seem to worry them at all. They are running like the wind, like they've been created to do by God. The horse's main defence mechanism is to run, but they love running.

It's just so refreshing for me to watch this. I really believe the Holy Spirit is showing me that that's how revival is. It's something that is free, it is exciting, invigorating, refreshing – and it's even a bit dangerous as we just don't know which way it's going and what's going to happen – because it's totally out of man's hands and absolutely in God's hands.

Oh my friend, to see God take broken people and restore them and make them run like the wind, is something that renews and rejuvenates my heart. When I'm feeling tired and sometimes a bit down because of the workload, to get a letter, or a phone call, from a man whose life has been turned around by the power of God through the Holy Spirit, is like fresh, sparkling, effervescent water. Drinking that water makes me feel totally refreshed and renewed. I received one such letter after the last men's conference and I have permission to share it with you:

Dear Uncle Angus,

My name is James Visser. I just want to thank you so much for your constant obedience to God. You will never be able to comprehend the difference that you are making in people's lives through God's enabling, especially mine.

I came to the Mighty Men's Conference 2009; I was listed in the Saturday Tribune *as one of the famous people that attended the Conference. Quite a joke really, I was only listed because my friend's dad works there. I was World Champion Jet Skier when I was 18 (I'm 23 now), but I'm certainly not famous.*

I gave my life to Jesus when I was 16 years old, and soon after that I became a professional jet skier, travelling the world quite a lot, having a lot of fun, and I was able to use it all as a great witness for Jesus. But it was never viewed as much of an achievement by most of my family and their constant disappointment in the fact that I didn't have a "real" job (even though I earned more money than most of them), and their negative words towards me took a toll on my thinking and I started to slip into self-depression.

This progressed until last year when I was considering ending it all. I heard that you were coming to preach at Hillcrest Christian Fellowship on Sunday the 1st of June last year 2008, and I promised God that I would hold out till then. I remember crying on my bedroom floor the night before begging God to say something to me if he had any reason for me to live at all.

The next day when you were preaching, I was sitting all by myself in amongst a sea of people I didn't know. I knew God was working through you, it was obvious, but then you stopped mid-sentence, pointed directly at me and said, "My son, if you're thinking about committing suicide, I tell you don't do it. There are no short cuts to Heaven." I now know that it's true, one word from God really can change your life; it changed mine, it gave me hope.

Today I've got a new fire in my heart for Jesus. I'm an intern this year at our local church, and I'm able to go out once a week with a missionary to the Muslim communities to tell them about Jesus, I'm able to go out with Campus Crusade for Christ, I've been blessed to go on mission trips to Zimbabwe, Mozambique, and around SA, and we've almost finished designing a Gospel tract to try and spread the Word even more. I've been able to share about Jesus in many places and a couple of churches (I'm not sure if I preach, I just think of it as telling people about my best friend, Jesus). I've never felt more alive, and to think, just one year ago I almost ended my life, but your obedience to God stopped me, and for that I can never thank you enough, and especially I can never thank God enough.

Sir, thank you so much for all that you have done to help me, thank you for your obedience to God.

Your son in Christ,
James Visser

I think the most beautiful thing about this present-day revival is that no man can take credit or touch God's glory in it. It is a "Godthing". As the internationally-known Christian speaker John Blanchard said, revival can no more be dictated by man than man trying to dictate the wind. It's God, from the beginning to the end, and He gets all the glory. All I can say is: "Lord Jesus, take Your glory, and thank You that I have lived in a time when I have been able to observe this taking place in my own life and around about me."

When you see more men going to church than women – almost – then you know that God has done something supernatural. l remember growing up and going to church as a young boy. All we saw there were women and children, maybe the odd one or two old gentlemen, and that was about it.

Recently we had a men's breakfast in Amanzimtoti, which was organized by a twenty-three-year-old young man whose uncle had died two years before at a Mighty Men Conference. The uncle had wanted to go back and start having men's breakfasts. This young man took up the torch and organized it. Over five hundred men arrived on a working day, on a Friday, at the Civic Centre in Amanzimtoti to hear the Word of God. These were working men, strong men, young men – and to see them responding to the Gospel of Jesus Christ was truly nothing short of miraculous.

The men asked Duncan Campbell, leader of the Hebrides revival, about his experience; why he thought that God had only spared him to be part of one revival. He said quite straightforwardly that he knew the reason – his physical body would not have been able to endure a second revival. There's a power, an unction that literally drains one in these revivals. It drains one completely, because one can basically only take so much at a time. It's just too big; too enormous; too miraculous.

After these meetings I feel totally worn out, absolutely exhausted, but there is a joy and a fulfilment in my life that no other event can even come close to. I am an avid sportsman. I love sport, but I want to tell you that I've never been to any rugby or soccer match, not even a World Cup Final, where I have experienced anything like the tangible presence of God when He visits a group of people.

I think of South Africa's most famous rugby stadium, Loftus Versveld up in Pretoria, where we saw seventy-two thousand people approximately; men, women and children, meeting in the presence of Almighty God. Coming to the end of the praise and worship session, just before I started to speak, the music leader stopped all the musicians and led us in singing the Lord's Prayer in Afrikaans. I swore that I heard angels' wings fluttering above us. It was the most reverent, most beautiful time I think I have ever experienced in my life. Not one child made a noise, not even a baby was crying. These people began to worship their God as they sang: "Our Father, who art in heaven, hallowed be Thy name..." I had a taste of what I think we're going to see and experience with the King of kings when we get to heaven one day.

As I come towards the end of this book, I can honestly say that I have come of age. I've grown up. I think of that beautiful chapter in 1 Corinthians 13, the passage on love, possibly the most famous chapter in the Bible. It says: "When I was a child, I talked like a child; I thought like a child, I reasoned like a child. When I became a man, I put childish ways behind me. Now we see but a poor reflection as in a mirror; then we shall see face to face. Now I know in part; then I shall know fully, even as I am fully known."

I can honestly say that God has given me new eyes and new values. That comes through the hardships of life. It had to happen at that last Mighty Men Conference. I look forward to one more this year. I believe it will be possibly one of the greatest moments we've ever seen. By faith, we are expecting to at least double the number that we had in 2009. I don't know what God's going to do at this conference, but I know it will be supernatural. He will get all the glory, as He did last year. Like never before, God's given me a more sensitive spirit to tell the good news to the lost.

Men and women are crying out for God all over the world. Today a phone call came through to me. A young man sitting in the Kruger National Park wanted to end his life and phoned and asked if he could speak to me. He got my address through the South African Broadcasting Network, the television network. I was able to SMS him and say that I'd speak with him next week. He replied to my SMS, which tells me that he's still alive, and I thank God for that. We'll talk next week about things that pertain to everlasting life.

Of course, revival always comes at a price. If it came cheaply, it wouldn't be worth anything. There's always a price to pay. Jesus Christ had to die on the Cross of Calvary, so that you and I could have eternal life. There's nothing cheap about the Gospel. It's expensive. We must be prepared to go the extra mile for the Lord. If it means sleeping in strange beds, if it means travelling, then we must do it. If it means working extra hours, then it must happen. If it means going without for the sake of the lost, then it must happen. But it must happen voluntarily, willingly and joyfully.

If it means that one must be misrepresented and misquoted, then so be it. My prayer for each one reading this book, and for myself, is that we would not compromise God's Holy Word for anything or anyone. My sincere prayer for each of us is that we would finish the race strongly. That Scripture found in Philippians 3:12 comes to mind: "Not that I have already attained, or am already perfected; but I press on, that I may lay hold of that for which Christ has also laid hold of me." The Lord has called you and me to do a job for Him. Let us not fail. Let us run the race and finish strong for Him, so that very soon we can hear those wonderful words: "Well done, thou good and faithful servant! Come and enter into thy rest."

Chapter 30
First things first

Last night I returned from Worcester, the town in the Western Cape that the Lord chose to use as the starting point for one of the greatest revivals that this world has ever seen. It started in a little church called the *Sendingkerk*, the Mission Church of the *Nederduitse Gereformeerde* (Dutch Reformed) church. In the 1800s the minister – and indeed his father before him, who had been praying for many years for revival – was Dominee Andrew Murray. He was born of Scottish parents in South Africa but was educated in Aberdeen, Scotland, where he got his MA in Theology.

I believe he then went across to the Netherlands, where he continued with his theological education before coming out to South Africa, where God used him very powerfully in the revival that was to come. He wrote over two hundred books, many of them still in print today. He was a man who walked extremely close to God; he preached holiness, grace – not good works – and God used him amazingly.

The story goes that one night he was preaching at the *Moederkerk* (the Mother Church); the main church in the centre of Worcester. One of the elders was walking past the *Sendingkerk*, where the youth group was meeting and he heard a tremendous noise going on inside. Some people were crying, some praying out loud, some on their knees, some on their faces before God, some standing up. The elder walked straight on past the church and must have run up to the *Moederkerk* and told Dominee Murray that there was a tremendous noise going on down amongst the youth at the Mission Church, and that he'd better get down there.

Dominee Murray went down to try and stop the noise. He went in and asked the youth leader what was going on.

He said, "It's God! It's God, Dominee!"

Dominee Andrew Murray said, "God is an orderly God. He doesn't act like this. Tell these young people to be quiet!"

He said, "I can't!"

Dominee Murray said, "Well, let's start singing the hymns."

The two of them, the dominee and the youth leader, tried to sing a hymn. It didn't work, because the kids ignored them. That evening, when a young Fingo girl had stood up and begun to pray out loud to God, a mighty wind had blown through that church. It was the start of the revival. Years later, the students still used to tease Dominee Andrew Murray and say: "Dominee, please tell us about the time when you tried to stop the Great Revival!"

I stood inside that little church last week. The front of it has been leased out, and it is now a café called The Pardon Café. Isn't that a beautiful name? I asked the proprietor if a group of us could go through to the back. I looked up at the high ceiling and tried to imagine what it must have been like when that mighty wind blew through that church in 1860. As I write, this year, 2010, it is exactly a hundred and fifty years since the beginning of the revival.

From there, we all went out and got into the cars. There was a tremendous sense of expectancy in the air. They took me out to the Nape Valley, to Andries Rabie's farm, where he grows olives. What a lovely young man of God! He's the biggest olive oil producer in Southern Africa. His family has been there since the 1700s and the Rabie Mountain is named after them.

We had half an hour to rest, then we got dressed and went to the agricultural showgrounds in Worcester for a Christian meeting. I want to tell you that it was one of the most amazing meetings I've ever attended in my life. First of all, having studied revival (it's my subject, my passion; it's what I love), I don't think Andrew Murray ever saw so many people gathered together in that town where the revival started, simply because there just wasn't that huge a population in those days. But in this small town in the middle of the rural area (the *Platteland*, as they say in Afrikaans); a farming area where there are vineyards, dairy farms and mixed farmers, we saw no fewer than about twenty thousand people packed into that arena. The expectancy and the excitement were tangible. You could have cut the atmosphere with a knife.

They had put a little caravan at the back of the main stage for me. We'd no sooner got there and prayed than the meeting started. A young Afrikaans woman, Riana Nel, got up and led the praise and worship. Joe Niemand, whom God is using powerfully in the Christian music industry at the moment, got up and sang his heart out.

Then it was over to me. I brought a shortish message and basically just spoke about the greatest sin in the Bible being the sin of unbelief. I mentioned that God takes donkeys and turns them into racehorses. I told them that there's nothing too hard for those who believe. I also told them to stop saying that revival is coming to South Africa; we are in revival!

On a Saturday afternoon, when most South Africans

are either playing sport, fishing, hunting, or watching the Springbok rugby team play a very important test match, I wouldn't have expected to see anybody here ten years ago. Yet the place was packed to capacity. The thing that really touched my heart was that it wasn't just white people. It wasn't just black people. It wasn't just coloured people. It was everybody mixed together.

Right from the outset, the fire came down. At the end, before we prayed for the sick, I asked all those who wanted to repent of a heart of unbelief, and to recommit their lives to Jesus Christ openly, to please stand up. The whole stadium of approximately twenty thousand people stood as one man like a regiment. I prayed a prayer and they followed after me, and I could feel the presence of the Holy Spirit come down on that meeting.

I did something I haven't done before. I said, "All those who have prayed the sinner's prayer publicly for the first time in their lives, please remain standing. The rest, please be seated." I was totally overwhelmed and emotional, because just about the whole stadium remained standing. These are people who go to church! They had obviously never before publicly accepted Jesus Christ as their Lord and Saviour. It was a very emotional moment.

The organizers of this meeting had had seven thousand, five hundred commitment cards printed out for first-time commitments, which, when they told me, I thought was very courageous and ambitious, and a real faith move. I want to tell you that those cards were snapped up, and there were still thousands of people left who couldn't fill in a card. I estimate that over ten thousand people made first-time commitments on Saturday afternoon, 21 November 2009. Truly one of the highlights of my life!

One thing that God has impressed upon me very strongly since I collapsed at the Mighty Men Conference is to do first things first. It's no good teaching a man how to have a better marriage; how to manage his finances correctly; how to be an ambassador for Christ; how to live life with the joy of the Lord; how to treat your fellow man, unless he has been born again. Romans 10:9 says that if you confess with your mouth, "Jesus is Lord" and you believe in your heart that He has been raised from the dead, you will be saved. That's what those people did. I believe that because they put first things first, all the other things are going to fall into line in due course.

I had been talking about the twelve couples in Britain who earlier in the year had been married in our revival meetings. They were dressed in their jeans and their casual clothes, not expecting it to be the best day of the rest of their lives. I had been talking at that meeting in Britain about the power of God and the conviction of the Holy Spirit for people to do things in the correct manner. They came forward, repented of their sins, and then they got married.

I told the people in Worcester about one young man who had literally pulled me back into the church at the City Temple, where he was with his beautiful girlfriend on his arm. Both of them, Johan and Christina, were weeping and asked me to please marry them before I left. That was what persuaded the other four to come up. In the morning service before that (coincidentally in Worcester, England), seven couples had come up, asking to be married.

When I'd finished telling the story – and I think there were lots of wet eyes in the stadium – I was astounded. Up onto the platform came the very two people I had been speaking about! Johan and Christina have come back to

South Africa. He was looking so handsome; Christina was looking absolutely beautiful.

They were doing things God's way. They had been born again, had got married, come back to set up home in their beloved South Africa and Johan was looking for work. He's an accountant. While he was on the platform, I asked him whether he had found a job and he said he didn't have one yet. I stand to be corrected, but they told me that when he went off the platform, he already had a job offer! Some man in the crowd had offered him a job.

My dear friend, if you put Jesus Christ in your life, if you put first things first, you can rest assured that all these other things will be added unto you. I have come to realize that you can preach about whatever you like, but until someone has made a public confession of their faith, it is invalid and of no consequence. There is definitely a place for Bible instruction. There is a place for ten rules to a better lifestyle; five laws to a successful marriage; six points to relating to your children, and so on, but Jesus Christ must be foremost and prominent in every single teaching instruction that we receive. I think the problem with lots of churches and men of God is that they presume that everybody knows Jesus Christ when they start to preach or speak. Of course, there couldn't be anything further from the truth.

I was speaking at a huge convention of one denomination some two months ago. These men and women were leaders of go-ahead churches. At the end of the session, I felt the Holy Spirit say to me, "Make an altar call to call people forward to give their lives to Christ."

I thought: "Lord, this is totally ridiculous. I mean, these people are leaders in their churches!"

Nevertheless, I did what the Holy Spirit told me to do.

About ten or fifteen people came up and made a first-time commitment to Christ. It's not good enough to say: "My parents were Christians; I grew up in a Christian home." The Lord has no grandchildren. Each one of us has to meet Him, just like Nicodemus did, one-on-one. When that happens, then all heaven breaks loose in your life. There's something about making a public confession that cements your faith and gives you courage.

I think of Paul, in my humble opinion probably the greatest of all the apostles. Every time he opened his mouth and made a statement that Jesus Christ is indeed the Son of God, he got severely beaten. He got chastised. He got thrown out of town. He got humiliated. But he carried on doing it. The amazing thing is that every time he did it, he got stronger.

Peter, who was such a coward that he couldn't even own up to the slave in the high priest's courtyard that he was a follower of Jesus Christ, ran away. One of the saddest verses in the Bible is when Jesus looked upon Peter, and Peter wept. Then he ran away. Yet, when he was filled with the Holy Spirit, and truly born again, he spoke to a large multitude of people and three thousand souls gave their lives to Christ on one day.

That's what I've found in my own life, too. The more I speak about Jesus, the bolder I get, the more courage I seem to have and the more power I seem to command. I'm not talking about walking up and down the street with a big placard saying: "The world is coming to an end. Repent, otherwise you're going to burn forever," or something like that. I'm talking about being unashamed of the Gospel. One of my favourite Scriptures in the Bible is Romans 1:16: "For I am not ashamed of the Gospel of Christ, for it is the power of God to salvation for everyone who believes, for the Jew first and also for the Greek [Gentile]."

That's what happened last Saturday afternoon. Over ten thousand people stood up and publicly confessed Jesus Christ as their Lord and Saviour. After that, we prayed for the sick and we are still waiting to hear about the miracles that will be coming in as people trusted God for physical healing as well.

As I walked off the platform and sat in the tent, some very tragic testimonies came through, but I know God is more than able to meet each one. A man came in weeping, saying that his son-in-law, who is a policeman, had shot his three baby children because he was jealous of his wife. He was weeping but he prayed the prayer and forgave his son-in-law for what he did, and he is believing for his son-in-law to know Jesus Christ as his personal Lord and Saviour before he dies.

There are so many needs in this world. Before we start speaking about doctrine, before we start becoming concerned about theological issues, we need to make sure that a man's heart has been touched. Unless a man is born again, the Bible says, he will never see the kingdom of Heaven. Why is it that we're so busy teaching and standing on things like adhering to the Sabbath, being baptized, being confirmed, going through all the membership laws, when the person has not yet given his life to Christ? It is truly putting the cart before the horse. Then we wonder why these people don't understand.

When I gave my life publicly to Jesus Christ on 18 February 1979, and after I'd told three people (and have never stopped since), I began to seek, of my own free will, the things of God. That is: baptism, church membership, communion, and all those other important facets of the Christian life, but those things were of no consequence to me before I accepted Christ as my Saviour. I've realized that with the short time that we have in this life, for this life is indeed but a vapour, people need to know, first and foremost, what it means to accept Jesus Christ as their personal Lord and Saviour.

As I finished praying for those people, one of the ushers came running into the tent to say that one of the most prominent men in that town had just filled in a commitment card and had publicly accepted Jesus Christ as his Lord and Saviour. This usher was more blown away by that than by anything else. He could not believe that this man would ever do a thing like that. Yet the man has nailed his colours to the mast. He has decided that, for him, from now on, it's going to be the Lord. That is going to give him tremendous liberty.

My prayer is that the people would follow up these new converts. But even if they don't follow him up, I believe that once a man has publicly accepted Christ as his personal Saviour then he himself will go and seek that fire and warmth from other believers.

The thing that amazes me more than anything else when preaching at a revival meeting is the change in the presence and the countenance of the crowd. It is something that is very hard to explain. Large crowds and rural people tend to be very conservative by nature, and sometimes even sceptical about these large meetings. Bear in mind that for some of them the largest meeting that they've ever been into is in the local church – and now they are confronted with a huge crowd like you get at a rugby or soccer match.

They are also sitting next to people of different colour,

different gender and different cultures, so there's a huge amount of reserve. When the message, the undiluted Word of God, is preached in simplicity, there's a sense of openness as the Holy Spirit comes down and begins to minister to people individually. Once the sinner's prayer has been prayed, you're looking at a totally different crowd. I cannot explain it in words. There's joy, there's faith, there's relief, there's peace, there's inner healing and – most of all – just absolute, undiluted happiness. Only the Holy Spirit can do something like that. Then we start to pray for the sick and the needs of the people.

But first things first!

Chapter 31

I believe in miracles

Many years ago, in fact in 1979, when I gave my life to Christ, one of the first paperback books that I ever read was a book by Kathryn Kuhlman called *I Believe in Miracles*. Kathryn Kuhlman died in 1976 but that book impacted my life like few books ever have. It was miraculous. It was exciting. I couldn't put it down. It strengthened and increased my faith dramatically, because it was like an account of what the living God is doing at the moment. Remember, Kathryn Kuhlman was a maize (sweetcorn) farmer's daughter from somewhere in the Midwest in the USA.

She started off as a young evangelist and fell in love with a married man, who was also an evangelist. I think he had two little children. He divorced his wife in order to marry Kathryn Kuhlman. They were married for eight years. Her ministry spiralled downwards and was a total and complete disaster during that time. When they realized that they were living in sin, they got divorced and she never married again. Many years later, she said in an interview with Jamie Buckingham, the famous author who was doing her life story: "No one will ever know what this ministry has cost me."

She chose to go God's way. She repented of her sin and the Lord Jesus Christ used her in a very, very powerful way with signs, wonders and miracles. She never laid her hands upon people. She had a ministry in the word of knowledge. She used to have giant meetings each week in an industrial hall, where there'd be about ten thousand people packed in. She would start to preach, and then stop and say: "There's someone in the top left-hand corner. God has shown me that He is healing you of cancer of the spine." Then there'd be somebody in the front right-hand corner: "God is healing you of eczema." As she carried on like that, people would start coming forward, totally healed.

When I read that book, it was like a revelation again to me that the Lord Jesus Christ is indeed the same yesterday, today and forever (Hebrews 13:8). I share this story with you because last Sunday I was asked to hold a service in my hometown of Greytown, a little town with a population of ten thousand. There is a Scripture in the Bible that says that a prophet is not without honour, except in his own hometown (Matthew 13:57). It was therefore with quite a bit of apprehension that I accepted. Most of the churches in Greytown closed their doors and came together in a big tent on the local common park grounds. There was a lovely, quite substantial crowd which had gathered, especially when one thinks of the size of the town.

The praise and worship were beautiful. Then I had my chance to get up and preach. It was advertised as a healing meeting, so there were many sick people there and quite a few people in wheelchairs. I saw some people who were obviously suffering from cancer, with scarves around their heads to cover the effects of the chemotherapy they were having.

We spoke about the greatest sin in the Bible being the sin of unbelief. About ninety per cent of the people in the tent repented of not trusting God enough, of having a heart of unbelief. I prayed for first-time commitments and was quite surprised to see the huge number, hundreds of people, who responded to the Gospel.

After that, I began to pray for the sick. The Lord started laying certain diseases on my heart. I called out people who had skin problems and about thirty, maybe forty, people came out. The elders of the local churches anointed them with oil and I prayed the prayer of faith. I made another general invitation to those who were battling with anger, unforgiveness in their heart, to come forward. Again I was amazed at the number who flocked to the front. We anointed them with oil. This carried on.

I felt the Lord telling me to ask those with hearing problems to come forward. There must have been maybe twenty, thirty, people who came to the front. One little girl, Amy, perhaps between eight and ten years old, stood there. I prayed for her and said, "I can sense like a popping in your ear. " I could see the way she was swallowing. My wife was sitting in the front row and she also noticed it. It was just like when a person tries to clear their ears when they're in an aeroplane and they're coming in to land. With that pressure in the aeroplane, it causes one's ears to pop. She was clearing her ears. I said, "And now? How do you feel?" She said that she could hear.

I asked her to go and stand at the other side of the tent, maybe thirty, forty metres away, to face the canvas, away from me, and to respond when I called her name. I called her name from about thirty paces away, and she spun around. The people started clapping. They were getting so excited. I moved further back, stood on the platform, and lowered my voice even more. She responded instantaneously. Everybody clapped, and I could sense the people's faith level starting to rise.

I want to say something that I've learned. Faith is

contagious. It's catching, just like doubt and fear are also contagious. We need to start to walk and operate in the faith realm. If we're going to finish this race strong, if we're going to mature and grow up as Christians and come of age, we really need to begin to walk the faith walk. Faith, remember, is the substance of things hoped for, it is the evidence of things not yet seen. As St Augustine said, faith is to believe what you cannot see, and the reward of that faith is to see what you believe.

I prayed for a lady sitting about two or three rows back who had come with those extended crutches that fix themselves around your upper arm to support you. I know exactly who she is. Her brother-in-law comes to our church. She'd been in a terrible car accident and had been paralysed. She told me that she had tremendous back pain. We prayed the prayer of faith and I anointed her with oil. I took the crutches away and she started walking. Folks, she was struggling to walk because I don't think her leg muscles had been exercised since the accident, but she said to me, "The pain in my back has gone. There's no pain." She carried on walking. She walked right around the tent and sat at the back. By this time, the Holy Spirit was moving in a sovereign way.

We prayed for a lady who had come with her husband all the way from Johannesburg, some six hundred kilometres away. She'd had a freak accident. She'd been walking down a pathway on a sidewalk. A cyclist had knocked her over. She'd bashed her head on the concrete and as a result she couldn't speak. She hadn't spoken since July 2009. That was five months. She stood up on the platform, a fine-looking woman probably in her mid-forties. I could see that she was very tense. Her husband was standing next to her. He was fighting back the tears.

"Do you love Jesus?"

She nodded her head.

I anointed her with oil, prayed the prayer of faith, took the mike and put it by her mouth. I said, "I want you to repeat after me: 'I love Jesus.'"

She said it absolutely distinctly, without fault. Well, the whole tent erupted.

After that, I asked her husband, "What is your name?"

He said, "My name is Terence."

I said, "I want you to say: 'I love you, Terence.'"

She said, "I love you..." She struggled a little to get her tongue around the word 'Terence' but, sure enough, it came out.

I asked her how many children they had.

"Two children." She named them. She said that she loved them and the people applauded. I want to say that it really encouraged me no end.

Then a lady I've known for many years, who lives in town, came up. She had just had a cataract removed from one of her eyes. The specialist had said: "The other eye is finished. It's beyond repair. Just forget about it, because you'll never see out of it again."

We anointed her with oil, prayed the prayer of faith, and I asked her to put her hand over the good eye, the eye that she could see out of, the eye that had had the cataract removed. And, with the other eye open, I put my hand in front of her face and asked, "How many fingers do you see?"

She said, "Five."

I then put a finger away and asked, "How many?"

"Four."

"Three."

"Two."

And then, with the fist: "None."

By this time the tent was really absolutely praising the name of Jesus Christ. I went down the healing line. There was a lady sitting in a wheelchair who had had a stroke. I prayed the prayer of faith, and without any effort, she got out of the wheelchair and just started walking, straight away. Her husband was later seen pushing the empty wheelchair out of the tent towards the motorcar.

I prayed for a man standing in the line. He also had one eye he couldn't see out of. I prayed, and he just started crying, "I can see! I can see your hand in front of me. Jesus, Jesus!" He just kept calling out that name which is above every other name.

As we say at Shalom: One genuine miracle equals a thousand sermons. Apparently everybody in Greytown was talking about that service on the Monday morning. No doubt they are still talking about it, maybe some negatively. But it doesn't matter. They are still talking about it. That's the thing that excites me more than anything else. I don't even mind what people say, as long as they're talking about Jesus.

I want to exhort you to believe in miracles. I want to exhort you to trust the name of Jesus Christ, because it's in that name that the power is found. I firmly believe that in these last days the Lord Jesus Christ is going to manifest Himself through signs, wonders and miracles such as have never, ever been seen before. The Bible tells us that the latter rain will be greater than the former rain, because the time is short and is becoming more critical. The Lord is coming back very soon. There is no time to waste.

When people of other faiths see these miracles, they

cannot dispute the fact that Jesus is real. There is no other god that heals. There's no other faith that can heal. Only that name, which is above every other name, can heal the brokenhearted and set the captives free. In Mark 16:17, the Lord says that these signs shall follow the preaching of the Gospel. "In My name..." the Lord says: We will lay our hands upon the sick and they shall recover. We shall cast out demons in His name, set the captives free, and heal the broken hearted.

I get so excited when I see these miracles happen. It also wears me out. Towards the end of the meeting, I was so tired that they had to put a chair on the platform for me to sit on, and I had to literally reach out and lay my hands upon the people as they walked by, as I had promised them I would do.

Remember, the power and the healing is in His name. It's got nothing to do with me, or anybody else for that matter, but He is looking for men and women who will trust Him. The sad thing for me is that there are many who won't do it, because "What if?" If we really think about it, it makes no difference. If we have died to self, it should not be a concern to us about "What if...?"

"What if they're not healed?"

"What if the miracle doesn't take place?"

"What happens if...?"

God has told us to lay our hands upon the sick and to pray the prayer of FAITH. Not just the prayer, but the prayer of faith – and I think that that is where the key lies. Many people pray the prayer but they don't really believe it's going to happen. So it doesn't. We need to pray the prayer of faith and believe God for that great and mighty miracle.

Chapter 32
Turnaround

In the previous chapter I spoke about the miracle of divine healing. I want to speak now about the elements. This is so exciting for me because I am a farmer. My wife says that you can dress me up in a three-piece suit, or in a tuxedo, and I'll still look like a farmer. That I take as a tremendous compliment. Farmers are so often misunderstood and misrepresented in the world today. In some places they are often regarded as the oppressors of the poor – the land owners – and yet farmers are the ones who produce food and work extremely hard, often for a very low return. However, there is no other place that I would rather have brought up my children than in the country and on a farm.

From an early age, I've showed them the miracles of God's hand in the elements. It's a funny thing, people talk about teaching little children about the birds and the bees, about Mother Nature, about how babies are born. I never had to do that with my children. They saw it happen in front of their eyes. They saw a cow come into season and they saw a bull mount the cow. They would ask me, "What's happening?" and I would explain it to them. They would say, "Oh. That's good," and they would just take it in their stride. There was nothing embarrassing about the situation. When a cow was giving birth to a calf, the children would often not only be watching but helping me in assisting the mother in birth. Again, the same question would be asked, "What's happening, Dad?" and I'd be able to explain to them the miracle of birth.

Of course we would also explain the other realities of life: things like death, when a horse breaks a leg and we have to put it down, or when an animal comes to the end of its productive life and we have to sell it off. We spoke as well about bushfires, droughts and floods. There were also times when the children would sit around the kitchen table with Mom and with me, and we'd pray and ask Jesus to send the rain. The Lord would, of course, always answer that prayer of faith; the rain would come and their faith would be built up.

As a result, all of my children have a living experience and a relationship with Jesus Christ as their Lord and Saviour. It so encourages me to see them do the same things with their children. I have seven grandchildren as I write this book. It's so beautiful to see them praying over their food and thanking Jesus for the fact that they've got food to eat. They also pray for the weather patterns.

I'll never forget flying down to Port Elizabeth and going to a huge indoor gymnasium in Uitenhage, and asking the Lord Jesus Christ to send rain at a very critical time when the farmers literally had nothing, nothing whatsoever, to feed their cattle or sheep. I saw young schoolchildren stand together and pray, asking God to send the rain.

Nor can I forget the day when, as I walked out of that meeting, two little girls started weeping as I walked past them. I don't know why they were crying, but I know that the Lord was touching their hearts. What joy it was for me to hear the next day that it had been raining in that area! It poured with rain. I thought of those two little girls who'd extended their faith to Jesus and asked Him to send rain for their dry land. Even in their most dire straits, they will never, ever forget incidents like that when they are older and they have families of their own. They will always remember how the Lord undertook for them. That's why I think that it's so important to introduce miracles, signs and wonders to young believers.

Kathryn Kuhlman's book *I Believe in Miracles* was such an encouragement to me. It gave me hope to believe in a living God. I once read an article which said, "If you take the miracles out of the Christian faith, you have nothing left." It's true. I see it time and time again. Young people are sick and tired of being preached to. They get enough of that at school and university. They want to see the power of God in action. I'm not talking about froth and bubbles. I'm not talking about calling things out of the air. I'm talking about real, down-to-earth, genuine miracles. When they see that, you don't have to say any more. They never forget those incidents.

The Harley Street heart specialist, Dr Martyn Lloyd Jones, a Welshman with an incredible preaching ministry, was invited to be the minister at Westminster Chapel. Apparently one is only offered that position by invitation. He said, "Miracles are not meant to be understood. They are meant to be believed." That's exactly how it is.

It's so sad when you meet people who say that miracles went out with the Book of Acts; that when the disciples died, the miracles came to an end. That is a total untruth, an absolute lie. I can honestly give testimony to the fact that I have seen, experienced and tasted the miraculous. They say that there are none so blind as those who will not see.

The Lord's Word, the Holy Bible, is full of miracles. In the New Testament, right from the nativity, it's just one miracle after another. The very facts of the holy nativity – Jesus being born of a virgin in a little dusty town called Bethlehem, His cot a manger (a feed trough); his mother a young girl of maybe not even fifteen or sixteen years old, who had never, ever known a man – is that not a miracle?

Just the other day I was reading in the Bible about Peter, who was placed in chains by order of King Herod in Jerusalem. He had an armed guard on either side of him. The angel of the Lord appeared to him in the middle of the night and said, "Stand up!" The chains fell off. He walked out through the door, which miraculously opened. The next thing he was in the street and the angel left him (Acts 12:3–10).

How is it that we read these accounts in the Bible, and we believe them because we've been told those stories from when we were young, but then when we hear of a woman who was unable to speak, and whom the Lord touched and healed through His servants, and her speech was returned to her, people question: "Was that really true?"

I suppose the same thing happened in the Bible. Remember the young boy who was born blind? Jesus prayed for him and he regained his sight. The Pharisees, the "churchmen", came to his parents and asked, "Was he really blind when he was born?" They, being afraid of the pressure from the church, responded by saying, "Well, ask him." They were too afraid to tell the truth that he had been blind from birth. The young man turned around and said, "Listen, I don't know who this man is, but I once was blind and now I can see." Then, tongue in his cheek (and good for him!), he asked the churchmen, "Why? Do you also want to serve Him? Do you want to follow after the King? Do you want to follow after the Lord?"

How do we get faith to believe for these miracles? It's in the school of sorrows that our faith grows stronger. You only need faith when you can't do something on your own. That's why Jesus said that it's easier for a camel to pass through the eye of a needle than for a rich man to enter into heaven.

We're not saying that there's anything wrong with riches. Not at all! But when we rely on our money and not on God, then we think that we don't need miracles. But when we're lying on our deathbed, or when we've just been given the pronouncement that we have terminal cancer and have only a short time to live, that is the time when only a miracle from God will suffice. All the money in the world cannot help. The finest physicians can tell you what's wrong with you, but they can't heal you. That is the time when we have to exercise our faith and cry out and call upon the name of the Lord.

That's what happened to Bartimaeus, the blind man (Mark 10:46–52). He had no Plan B. He was disregarded by society. He was sitting in the dust on the side of the road and he heard that Jesus, the Healer, was coming down the road. He started shouting at the top of his voice: "Jesus, Son of David, have mercy on me!"

The people – and isn't this how it always works? – turned on him and told him to shut up, to keep quiet. He took no notice of them, because he knew that they hadn't helped him up till then anyway, and he shouted even louder.

Then the Healer, the Prince of Peace, Jesus Christ, stopped in His tracks. He turned around and asked: "Who is calling My name?"

Isn't it amazing how the people changed completely? Straight away they shouted out: "Bartimaeus, the Lord is calling you!" They picked him up and led him to Jesus. He stood in front of Jesus with his eyes closed, and probably his hands stretched out in front of him.

Jesus did a very strange thing. He asked Bartimaeus: "What is it that you want Me to do for you?" Isn't that amazing?

I remember visiting a place called Hornchurch in London, England, many years ago. A lady wheeled herself up to the front for prayer. I anointed her with oil and prayed the prayer of faith. She said that she was in extreme agony, that her back was killing her. When I'd finished praying, her face lit up and she said, "The pain is gone. Thank you so much." She praised the name of the Lord, turned her wheelchair around and started wheeling herself back to the place where she'd been before. I said to her, "But, madam, don't you want to walk?" She smiled and said, "No, thank you." That's why, before I ever pray for a sick person, or a person who has a need, I always ask them an obvious question: "What do you want Jesus to do for you?"

Jesus asked Bartimaeus that very question. Bartimaeus replied: "Oh *Rabboni* (Teacher), oh that I might see!" The Bible says that Jesus immediately healed him, and he followed after Jesus.

We do need to make our requests known to God. That's why it is so important at a healing meeting for the people to come forward and give testimony and ask God to heal them. That's why I always ask the people at a healing meeting to please be quiet and attentive, and also to be praying. It's not just my faith or the sick person's faith, but the faith of all of us together.

Apparently Kathryn Kuhlman would not tolerate any noise at all in her meetings. Even if a baby was crying, she would stop the meeting and ask them to take the baby out. I have a problem with that, because I love children, but I do understand exactly what she meant. She wanted everyone to have their full attention and their full concentration on what God was about to do in a miraculous way.

People have come to me on occasion and asked me to please pray over their hands, because they also want to lay their hands upon the sick so that they recover. I've said, "I won't pray for your hands, but I'll pray that the Lord will break your heart, so that that you'll have a heart of compassion for those who are suffering or are in pain, and for those who are struggling. That compassion, that love and those tears, God will use to heal the sick."

I think motive is so important when praying for people in need. The motive must be pure. The motive must be simply to give God all the glory; and that people will recognize that Jesus Christ is the Son of God through the miracle that takes place. Secondly, for the individual concerned, that they might have relief and the opportunity to start all over again. Of course the greatest miracle of all has got to be the miracle of new birth, of new life. That is the main purpose I pray for the sick. When they see those miracles, they turn to God.

When praying for the sick we don't want to deal with the symptom, we want to deal with the root problem. Often a sickness will come about in someone's life through unforgiveness, through anger, or through fear. When that's dealt with, the person automatically recovers. For example, sometimes I've wanted to pray for someone who is suffering from migraines or rheumatoid arthritis and – not in every case, but often – the Holy Spirit will stop me and I'll ask, "Do you have unforgiveness against somebody? Has somebody hurt you in the past?" The person will inevitably break down and weep, and say, "Yes." Normally it's somebody very close to them. We ask them to forgive that person. They struggle to do it, but as soon as they do, you can see a release, and healing overcomes them. You can see that peace coming over them and they immediately start to change.

To see the miraculous turnaround in a man is what keeps me on the road and keeps me preaching all the time. After this last men's conference, I got a letter from a lady who said that her husband came to the Mighty Men Conference. He was an alcoholic, a cocaine addict, he had a foul mouth, he had wasted all their money, he was lazy, he didn't work, and they lost their house and their car. This was a young woman with children.

In one weekend, from a Friday night to a Sunday morning, the Lord Holy Spirit intervened and turned that man's life upside down. He went home to his family, broken and repentant. He went and bought himself a Bible first thing on the Monday morning. Only God can do that. No man can do that. No fancy preaching can do that. No fancy fellowship can do that; just an encounter with the living God, exactly as happened to Saul of Tarsus on his way to Damascus. He was going there to hunt the Christians – and he became Christ's greatest apostle!

This man went home and bought a Bible, found a job, broke off all ties with his fellow drinkers and druggies, and he came home every day. This all happened in the space of two months. She said he has not touched any drugs or alcohol. He reads his Bible, prays with the family, and is a completely reformed man. Surely that is the greatest miracle of all?

Here is a copy of the letter his wife wrote me after the

conference, which she gladly shares with the readers of this book:

Hi there

I am not sure where else to send this email to. I NEED to tell how GRATEFUL and BLESSED I am, my entire life has changed since my husband went to MMC this year. My husband did not even own a Bible, he was amongst other things a cocaine addict and we all know what this comes with, gambling, fraud, etc, etc. I can't go into this it is too painful and will take up pages and pages. To make a long story short, after losing EVERYTHING, house, family, job, EVERYTHING, he was talked into going to MMC. It feels like I am still dreaming; that this isn't my husband and that my husband is still going to come back. He hasn't touched drugs, alcohol, doesn't curse, since MMC, which is now over 2 months. He has a job for the first time in years, which he is on time for every single day, we go to church as a family, he ONLY listens to gospel music (used to be rave, rap, etc, etc). God has not only blessed him (and saved him) but me and my children have been blessed with the most WONDERFUL husband and father anybody can ask for. I can't even begin to understand how this is the same person??

I am FOREVER grateful and I now just pray everyday that God delivers my husband from temptation, all evil and evil friends for the rest of his days. He is not even in contact with ANY of his friends. I don't know how much more to thank God, I go on my knees every day; I praise him all the time. THANK YOU AND GOD BLESS

THANK YOU FROM THE BOTTOM OF MINE AND MY CHILDRENS' HEARTS.

As I have come of age, and have had the privilege of seeing and doing many wonderful things in my life, the altar call is still, for me, the greatest miracle. To see people come forward – men and women, boys and girls, of all types, all ages, all works of life, all creeds, all classes, all colours – and bow the knee and ask God to forgive them, and to give them a second chance to start again, is the greatest miracle of all.

It's for that reason, and only that reason, that I leave my precious wife and family and spend so much time on the road. I'm a very happy and contented farmer. For over thirty years, I went home every night and slept in the same bed. But when I met the Man from Galilee, the Miracle-Worker, my life was changed, forever.

Chapter 33
Losing the way

I was watching the biography of a young film superstar by the name of Heath Ledger on television the other night. He was a young Australian actor, a fine-looking man, very much a man's man and a brilliant actor. I first saw him acting in one of the supporting roles with Mel Gibson in the film *The Patriot*, where he played the part of a young frontier boy fighting against the English when the Americans were trying to get independence from Britain. He died in the battle.

I was then very disturbed to hear that he took the part of a homosexual cowboy in *Brokeback Mountain* and I wondered how he would have worked through that one, having an affair with another man. In the biography they spoke about him playing the part of the Joker, a psychopathic, mass-murdering, schizophrenic clown with zero empathy, in the movie *Batman: The Dark Knight*.

Being a very keen actor and wanting to give of his best, he tried as much as possible, according to the narrator, to get right into the minds and hearts of these characters that he portrayed. The next thing, he was found dead in his apartment, at the age of twenty-eight. He had been separated from his young partner and his little baby. They said that he battled for a long time with insomnia before he died. He just could not sleep.

When I saw the programme on television, my heart was really sorely troubled. I realized again how important it is that we know in whom we trust. This young man must have been going through hell trying to re-enact characters who had huge psychological and spiritual problems. I'm no psychologist, but I can imagine that that young man must have really grappled with who he was. He possibly lost his identity and indeed his way. Right at the end of the biography, they showed the funeral. All of his friends held hands and ran, fully-clothed, into the sea, because apparently he loved the sea. Possibly he was a good surfer.

My heart was so saddened because of the number of people who seem to have lost their way. The tragedy is that it's not just young people; it's also the older generation who are getting ready for retirement. I always say that I cannot find the Scripture in the Bible where the Lord speaks of retirement. There is no retirement for a child of God. In fact, people just grow wiser (hopefully) and more purposefully directed and orientated; more mature.

Moses was eighty years old when he was called to do probably the biggest job that any man has had to do in the history of the world; to lead God's chosen people out of Egypt, away from the strongest military leader of his time. He had no weapons and he had no game plan, but he had a directive from God and he had the faith to do it. He was eighty years old. Definitely not a young man!

He took approximately two and a half million people through the Red Sea, which opened supernaturally for him, and led them through the desert for forty years. I have personally been to that desert and I can assure you that it is genuine desert. I never saw a green shoot, a green leaf, or a tree anywhere; just sand and stone and cliffs and gullies. Nothing else. He was definitely not retired at the age of eighty.

You hear of a business executive; someone who has been a mover of men and mountains most of his life, a CEO of a huge organization, who is working towards his retirement. At the age of sixty, sixty-five, he gets the golden handshake, buys the beach cottage of his dreams and does the thing that he loves more than anything else, fishing at the seaside. For the first week of his retirement he gets up bright and early every morning, tells his wife he's taking his fishing box and will be bringing fresh fish back for lunch, and off he goes. He enjoys it immensely.

He does that for a week, maybe two, then he gets tired – and perhaps more to the point – he gets bored. He doesn't want to fish any more but he's got nothing else to do. He's still too young and his mind is still too sharp just to sit all day reading the newspaper. He begins to get depressed. He starts to lose his way. He starts thinking of other things to do. He offers his services, but he's already retired and he can't find any temporary work anywhere.

Slowly but surely, he begins to get disenchanted with life. He doesn't get up as early as he used to. He doesn't train any more, because he's got nothing to train for. His eating habits start falling by the way, his body begins to take strain, he starts getting depressed, and the next thing we see an obituary in the newspaper that John Smith, having retired two years ago as CEO of that large company, died of a heart attack in his beach cottage. He left behind a wife, three children and five grandchildren.

That is not an unusual story. What happened? I firmly believe that he lost his way, like the foolish farmer in the Gospel of Luke who, when the Lord had blessed him with a mighty crop, said he would pull down his barns, build new ones to store all his grain, and then he would sit down and eat, drink, and be merry. But the Lord said to him: "Foolish man, do you not realize that even this very night your soul will be required of you?" (Luke 12:16–21).

I remember that at the age of thirty-two I'd basically arrived, as they say. I'd left Zambia in Central Africa at the age of about twenty-nine. I'd sold a three and a half thousand-acre farm, four tractors and two hundred and fifty head of beef cattle. I'd been doing six thousand broiler chickens a month; growing watermelons for the Chinese, who were building that great railroad from Zambia through to Dar es Salaam in Tanzania; and also supplying them with pigs. Our children were coming to school-going age and my wife, having grown up in a boarding school environment, refused point-blank to send our children to boarding school, for which I am eternally grateful to her. We were not even Christians at that time but she said, "None of my children are going to be leaving the house." So we left.

We sold up everything and came down to South Africa via Swaziland. We started on a piece of overgrown wattle bush. We built a house in three weeks. There were no cellphones in those days, no electricity, no water and no lights. We started with nothing. We had three children and one on the way. Jill was already six months pregnant. Young people today talk about having a large family when they have two children! I'll never forget that wife of mine having to get into the car and go to the next-door neighbours with two plastic twenty-litre buckets to get water for drinking, washing and preparing the kids for school the next day.

In the meantime, I was trying to learn to speak Zulu, the language of the local people. I was trying to find out where one bought fertilizer. I was trying to put together a tractor which I had brought out from Zambia in pieces in the back of my truck; trying to establish a seed contract with the local seed company. We literally worked night and day together.

We built the house and moved into it. We managed to set up a lighting plant and had our own electricity. I dug a hole in the ground and water came out. We put a little pump, a windmill, on that spot and pumped water up to our house. Jill had long hair that went right down to her waist. The first night that we got the shower rigged up and got hot water (which we managed to heat by means of an old donkey-boiler; a forty-four-gallon drum that we built a fire underneath), that young wife of mine, who wasn't even thirty years old at that time, stood in that shower I think for about an hour and she just let that water wash her. She had the most glorious shower.

We planted that crop of maize. We put every cent, every penny that we had, into that crop of seed maize. God was so gracious to us – and I didn't even know Him at that time – and we reaped an absolute bumper crop. As a result, we were able to pay back all the money that we'd borrowed, we were able to connect up our telephone, and to purchase another tractor and continue clearing the bush. We had money to pay wages. We'd been accepted in the district, our oldest children were settled in school, Jill was starting to make friends and this was the time for us to literally eat, drink and be merry. But that was when I lost my way.

As a young man, I had come back from Australia to Zambia and had worked for a couple of farmers. I had taken that money and bought into a partnership and eventually bought my partner out. Then my family and I travelled all the way down from Central Africa, across the mighty Zambezi on a pontoon, in the middle of a bush war between Rhodesia (now Zimbabwe) and Zambia; through Rhodesia into South Africa across the Limpopo River; then into Swaziland, where we lived out of boxes while we were waiting to find a farm in South Africa.

Not having enough money to put down a deposit on a farm, we bought a piece of overgrown bush. I had worked seven days a week, having said to myself, "I'll show them that I can do it again!" By the grace of God, with me not even knowing it at that stage, He allowed me to succeed. But then it was like I came to the end of the road. I was only thirty-two years old but I kind of thought to myself: Well, what else is there to live for? That is when I came to the crossroads of my life.

I always like to use the illustration of a motorcar with the accelerator pedal pressed hard to the floor, the engine screaming, about to explode and not being able to turn off the ignition key. That's exactly where I was. I was so programmed; I was working so hard. We had arrived, as it were, and all that there was, was that there was nothing else. I should imagine it's like when a man climbs Mt Everest and when he finally gets to the top, that's it. When a man makes the Springbok rugby side and he gets his blazer and his colours, that's it. Or a man wins the Wimbledon singles, or the British Open golf championship, and that's it. When a man wins, that's it. There's got to be more! That's exactly what I realized. There's got to be more to life than this.

That's what happens to that CEO when he loses his way. All his life he's been working; working for that beach cottage, for those days when he can stand on the seashore and fish. The day has finally come. He does it for a few weeks, maybe even a couple of months. And then, after that, he says to himself, "There's got to be more!"

I met a man once who'd worked his whole life in a factory. He became the factory manager. He was a lovely gentleman. He became a very dear friend of mine. His whole working career he worked for one thing only; to go back to the family farm and to build the house of his dreams – which he subsequently did. When he came to retirement age, he moved back to the house and began to get everything in order; the garden, the house which he'd been working on over the years every free weekend that he had, every public holiday. By the way, he deserved every part of it.

But then I heard that he was sick with a terminal disease. I was devastated to hear that he only had three weeks to live. He'd been in his beautiful home for, I think, only three months. I went to visit him one day. As I got out of the pick-up he was sitting on the verandah. He'd lost a tremendous amount of weight. I could see that the man was dying. Not knowing what to say to him, and trying to make small talk, I said to him, "John," (that wasn't his name) "what a wonderful job you've done. What a beautiful home you've built!" Tears started running down his face. He said, "Yes, Angus, but what for?"

I think what I'm trying to say is that there's got to be a purpose for living on this earth. It's got to be bigger than just making money. It's got to be bigger than getting married and having a family. It's got to be bigger than realizing your sporting opportunities, or getting to the top of the ladder in your corporate world. It's got to be bigger than just this life. That's what I've come to realize.

The CEO of that huge enterprise, the one who went fishing every day and eventually gave up and died, didn't realize that God had prepared him for such a wonderful and exciting life. God had been educating him through commerce and industry to be able to touch and impact many lives in this world that's so full of poverty and ignorance and hunger and lack of education. He was sitting there with all that gifting but he didn't know how to use it, because he hadn't met the Man from Galilee; the Man who understands what this life is all about, because He is God. He came down from heaven to show you and me how to live a life that is totally fulfilled; in fact He says in John 10:10 (KJV): "I came that they might have life, and that they might have it more abundantly."

Fortunately that young farmer who came from Zambia went, in desperation, to a little church in Greytown on a Sunday morning. There was a visiting group of laymen that included building contractors, farmers, housewives, nursing sisters, and others. Each one of them got up into the pulpit and explained how Jesus, the Carpenter from Nazareth, had changed their lives forever. I sat there with my mouth hanging open. I could not believe what I was hearing. It was the first time in my life that I'd seen grown people weeping unashamedly, speaking about how God had put broken marriages together again, speaking about men who'd lost vision and how God had restored their vision and given them a reason, a genuine reason, to live.

After a simple altar call, Jill and I, with our children, went forward and committed our lives to Christ. That was the turning point in my life. From that moment onwards, I had a reason to live. From that moment onwards, I had found my way once again. I want to say to you that I am more motivated now, more excited about life now than I have ever been in the past. I have a reason to get up in the morning. I have a reason to keep fit, hence the fact that I jog every day.

I have a reason to preach the Gospel, because I love people, especially young people, and I want to give them as much help as I can. I want to explain to them what it means to live a fulfilled life; to aim at a goal and a vision, and then to see it come to pass. Wherever I go, I love to pick up young and older people and challenge them to get back into the race; to get back on target and to find their route; to find the purpose for which God has ordained them and brought them into this beautiful world. All of a sudden, my eyes are open. I'm starting to see beauty that I never saw before. When I go walking, jogging or riding my horse, it's like I see a new world; new opportunities, new challenges, a new reason to get out of bed in the morning.

Age has got nothing to do with vision. I've met some young people who are so disillusioned with life that they talk and act like old fogies – and I've seen some older people who are absolutely on fire for God. I'm thinking particularly about Aunty Peggy O'Neill, who wrote the foreword of this book. She is now permanently in a wheelchair and she's had many personal tragedies in her life but her eyes are more sparkly and more on fire now than ever before. I correspond with her regularly and visit her and her co-worker, Moyra. And do the two of them know how to pray! They pray for every door that God has opened for me, from writing a book to making DVDs; they pray for me when I come back from a trip overseas, from a campaign, or a men's conference. Praying for me is sheer joy for them – and to hear about the people who have come to Christ because of feature films that have been made by faith, is what keeps them going.

We need to find our way. Jesus says that He is the Way, the Truth and the Life and that no one will come to the Father but by Him.

Right now, I'm busy walking around the perimeter of the farms on which we are going to host the biggest men's conference that I've ever dreamed of. I want to tell you that whereas in the past, as a young, strong-headed, stiff-necked, independent Scotsman from Africa who always wanted to do things his way – and when the challenge came could not sleep at night – I am now sleeping like a baby.

The budget for this mammoth operation is inconceivable when you think that I don't have anything to back it up with. I've ceded my farms, my businesses, to my family and Jill and I live in a rented house (for which I refuse to pay rent), on one of my sons' farms. I feel like that fish eagle. I feel free, I feel exhilarated when I get up in the morning. I can't wait to see what God's going to do and how He's going to do it. Because He has to; nobody else can. But I've learned over the years that God always, always, responds to faith. This vision was birthed in my heart by the Holy Spirit and will be concluded by the Holy Spirit. And Jesus will get all the glory!

The Bible says that where there is no vision, the people perish. Whether you're leaving school, whether you're receiving your retirement package, or whether you've been boarded because of ill-health, you can make it – and you will succeed if you know where you're going.

There's that beautiful illustration in John 14, where Jesus said: "I'm going to prepare a place for you. And if I go, I'll come again and take you with Me."

Thomas asked: "But, Lord, where are You going? And how will we know how to get there?" We could add to that Scripture: "Because, Lord, we've lost our way."

That's when Jesus told him: "I am the Way, and the Truth, and the Life."

The Lord has a habit of not using the strongest, or the most qualified, or the men or women that you and I would use to do His work on earth. He often picks the youngest, like He did with King David. He picks the humble, the uneducated and the unqualified person to do His work. I've often thought: "Lord, why do You do that?" I believe it's so that, at the end of the day, when all has been said and done and the work has been accomplished, people will say: "Surely that was God! Because that man or that woman could never have done that thing..."

So be encouraged. Get back on the road. If you don't have a reason for living, ask God to show you a reason. And He will! If you don't have a purpose in life, ask God to give you one, and your life will be fulfilled like never before.

Many years ago, when God told us to start a children's home to take care of those who have no home, we had no money, we had no support in any way, and we had very little idea of what to do. But we had heard of some prefabs that were being thrown away by the local high school because they were totally worn out. We offered to dismantle them and throw them away for them. Obviously, the headmaster gladly agreed.

We took our old lorry, the same truck that brought us out of Zambia, got some young men together, unbolted those prefabs, brought them to the farm, resurrected them, painted them, plugged them, fixed them up, and put old carpets on the floor to cover the holes. And, the day that we stopped, the day that we finished rebuilding the skeleton of the children's home, the door opened and the Lord started sending babies. Today I can proudly say that our first baby is now a young man and has just been accepted into university. He's going to study a computer science course, starting literally in a week or two's time.

I remember driving home from church in the pick-up on a Sunday morning when I was still a young farmer and they were babies, some of them still in nappies. The older boys would sit next to me in the front and say, "Dad, one day we'll be driving the pick-up and you'll be sitting next to us." I would smile and say, "Yes." You know something? It's happening, and it's happened in the twinkling of an eye.

As I write this, I remember that the Lord said that life is but a vapour. It's here today, it's gone tomorrow. It's like the grass of the field. Right now I'm walking past a grassy meadow. This meadow will be cut down in a short time and be turned into hay and fed to the cattle. Do not waste valuable time sitting and having a pity party and saying, "Woe is me. What can I do?" That is exactly how the devil wants you to be. He wants to take you right off that road which leads to fulfilment and eternal life. And he will succeed if you allow him to!

Remember, in order for evil to abound, all that good men have to do is nothing. I would encourage you to rise up, mighty man, mighty woman of God, whether you are sixteen years old or sixty-six years old, and put your hand to the plough. Don't look back, and you'll live a life that will be so exciting. Maybe for some of you reading this book, this will be the beginning of the most exciting chapter of the rest of your life here on earth.

How big is God? That is a very real question. I want to tell you that my God is so big and so magnificent, so miraculous, so majestic, that there is nothing, absolutely nothing, which surprises me any more. He is waiting for you and me to answer His call. It will probably start right at home base, where you are at the moment. He will test you and allow you to be tested severely sometimes. But, if you pass that test, when He sees that He can trust you with His name, with His Son's name, with integrity, with honesty, and with obedience, He will open the windows of blessing and He will use you, literally, to move mountains.

He will use that vast experience that you have gained over a lifetime. He will use that gentle spirit that's come about through the fiery trials of life. He will use the humility that you have now received by being constantly put through the trials and tribulations in this world. He will use you, because He sees that there is no more arrogance, no more self-centredness, in your life. He will use you, because He sees you are not interested any more in what people think of you because you have come of age.

Rise up, have done with lesser things. Put your hand in the hand of God and start to walk with Him on a road that is full of excitement, of purpose, of satisfaction and fulfilment. Don't look to the left, don't look to the right. Don't even look behind you. This is the road that will lead you to eternal life.

Chapter 34

People

At the end of the day, when we sit down and sum up our life's journey and assess what is important in life and what's trivial, we realize there's only one thing that matters, and that is people. People, not things, are what count in life. It must be so distressing when a man has lived his whole life chasing a dream, running down the wrong road, down a cul-de-sac, then having to turn around and come back again, only to find he's run out of time; or building that great white tower of concrete and steel, only to know, at the end of your life, that it's a total waste of time. I'm not saying that it's wrong to be a builder. What I am saying is that it's wrong to put bricks and mortar – things – in place of people's lives.

I think that one only realizes these things when one comes of age. It was only when I collapsed that, all of a sudden, important things in life started to count and mean something to me, and the trivial things in life meant absolutely nothing. We're talking basically about getting our priorities in order. The Bible is very clear on this: What does it profit a man if he gains the whole world and loses his soul? The answer to that is: absolutely nothing.

Our children's home at Shalom Ministries was very small when we started off many years ago, and we now have twenty-seven children. Our oldest boy has just finished his first year at Music College. He's writing his own music in

Zulu and English, singing at weddings and at parties for Jesus. He sang the South African National Anthem on his own at Absa Stadium (Kings Park) in Durban, South Africa, in front of fifty-five thousand people. I was so proud of that son of ours. As time has gone on, that children's home is starting to mean more and more to me. In fact, it means a lot more to me now than the day that we got a Word from God to start it, to make a home for His children.

Jill reminded me the other day of a little baby who came to our home. When she arrived, no one knew her name and they called her Pretty. Little Pretty only stayed with us for a couple of months, because she was very sick. But she stayed with us until the day that she died and went home to be with her beloved Creator.

A thought that Jill shared with me, that actually brought me to tears, was that that little soul came into the world not knowing anybody, and nobody knowing that she even existed. She lived and she died and went to heaven, and not a soul knew who she was. Jill reminded me that Jesus knows little Pretty, because He created her. He gave her life and then, in His infinite mercy and love, made a decision to take her home to be with Him again. We have no doubt that we'll see her in heaven one of these fine days.

I thought again about the importance of family; the importance of people. Our priority has to be people, not things. As you read this book, maybe you're feeling a bit lonely and a bit out of sorts? Spare a thought for little Pretty. Not one of us needs to remain in that frame of mind.

As I'm dictating this chapter I'm walking down a farm road on a beautiful Sunday afternoon. It's misty, there's been some lovely rain, there's a bite in the air and there's not a soul anywhere to be seen. There's no work happening, because it's just after Christmas. I realize that the beauty that the Lord created for you and me is absolutely wonderful, but without people it actually doesn't mean much.

God has given me such a love for people. He has reminded me of the importance of a person's life. What value do we put on a life? We can't, because a life is priceless. The Lord created us so that there is only one of that kind in the universe. Each one of us has a unique set of fingerprints, a unique character, a unique personality and a unique spirit. We need to remember that, and not be so careless when we deal with one another, because that franchise is absolutely priceless; more priceless than the finest china, the finest crystal. China and crystal can always be remade but that person cannot.

In two days time I have to meet a man who's just lost his wife in a terrible car accident. This man is middle-aged, he's been married for over thirty years and he is absolutely devastated. He is badly wounded. They're bringing him to me, and I don't know what to say to him. I've never walked that road. I've walked many others, but not the road that he's walking at the moment. I can only think that it would be as devastating as having your arm and your leg cut off by a chainsaw or something, and then still trying to live. To live with your partner for over thirty years, and then instantaneously just not have him or her there any more must be a very, very hard road to walk.

I'm going to extend the love of Jesus Christ to this man and tell him about a Friend who sticks closer than a brother; then I'm going to trust that the Holy Spirit will do the rest of the work. That balm of Gilead, that ointment which one spreads over those wounds – and slowly but surely they start to heal – is the only thing that will help him. It's the only thing that's helped me through my different trials.

On that point, I would encourage you to extend lots of love to those who have been hurt. You can go to counselling courses and to Bible studies and they'll give you all the relevant Scriptures and all the information that you need to speak to someone who has been severely hurt in this life. But what I've found over the years is that it's not so much the Scriptures, it's not so much even the godly counsel, it's the love of God that people are craving. Many a time when I've taken a funeral, or been to a hospital to visit someone who's very sick and approaching death, they're not interested so much in the Scriptures, because often, due to their pain, they cannot even hear what you're saying, or understand what you're saying. What they need is love. They need God's love, through you, towards them. They need the reassurance that they are not alone. Sometimes, to put your arms around them, to hug them and hold them close to you, and also to weep with them, has more healing power, and is more consoling, than all the theology that you can find. We need in these last days to ask God to give us a tremendous heart for the lost.

I have studied and read up on many of the great men and women of God who have gone before us. Each and every one of them was motivated to leave their comfortable homes and families and people and go to an unknown destination in a far-off country, with a foreign language and people of different colours, cultures and creeds. Just like Hudson Taylor, who went to China to preach the Gospel to the Chinese; or William Carey, who went to India to preach the Gospel to the Indians; or David Livingstone, who came to share the good news with the black people of Africa, we too need to be motivated just by the undiluted love of God in our hearts.

Jeremiah said: "There's a fire in my bones which constrains me to preach the Gospel." Paul said: "Woe unto me if I do not preach the Gospel." Our beloved Lord Jesus Christ came down from heaven to earth because of the love that He had for people, His creation, you and me, the whosoevers in this world. In Romans 10:13, the Lord says that whosoever calls upon the name of the Lord shall be saved. The most important thing in my life – and the thing which I have discovered – is that, outside of people, there's nothing worth living for. Nothing at all. My only regret in life is that it took me so long to realise that it's all about people.

I was invited to go to a funeral on our farm just two weeks ago. The mother of one of our tractor drivers had passed away and gone to heaven. Nellie Zondi was ninety-six years old. In good Zulu tradition, the funeral had started on the Saturday morning and had gone on right through until the Sunday. They asked if they could have the final service in the little thatched chapel which my late Dad and I built thirty years ago on our farm. We said that that would be totally appropriate and a great honour for us.

They asked us to please come and pay our respects and to say a few words, which I duly did. I saw people, mostly elderly people, paying tribute to this dear old soul with a passion for God in their hearts. In typical Zulu tradition, before you testify you normally sing a song and do a small dance. As each one got up, that's exactly what they did. Then they gave heartrending testimonies of the goodness of God, and how God had used their friend, a gentle lady. Every one of them agreed that she was a humble, gentle and caring person.

When I got up to give a testimony, I saw all these white-haired old men and women and felt totally unworthy and out of my depth. Nevertheless, I had been asked to please say a few words. I remember an old Red Indian proverb: When an old person dies, it is like a library burning down.

The church was jam-packed with folk paying their respects. Again, by tradition, the Zulu nation has a tremendous respect for their senior citizens and for people who are older than them. Unfortunately, that seems to be forgotten in the western nations. But most of the Zulu people still esteem old people with great respect and reverence; something that really endears the Zulu culture to me. I was able to tell the younger people that they need to take the opportunity of receiving counsel and advice from older people while they are still alive. Because, once they die, all that knowledge, all those hard lessons from the school of life, go with them. I could see the young people taking note of what I said.

As I'm dictating this, the last chapter in this book, I think of my late Dad. A country blacksmith, he didn't know too much about farming but he knew lots about life. Many a time, after my Mother had passed on to be with the Lord, I would go up in the afternoon and sit on the verandah with my Dad and ask him questions. I was a budding farmer and we were running a very effective farming operation but invariably his answers would be just what I wanted to hear. We would talk about the cereal crop that I'd planted, about the cattle, about the tractors, about the horses, the sheep, and we'd talk about the farming programme. But, at the end of the day, we always came back to people.

People make farming effective and profitable. That goes for every business. So often, we get it back to front. The product we're producing, whether it be beef, milk, butter or maize meal, almost becomes more important to us than the people who are producing it. That is such a silly, basic mistake. You know something? Some of the cleverest people in the world are guilty of that. They might have built up an empire, but if they haven't built up the people, the infrastructure to run that empire, it never lasts.

That saying: There's no fool like an old fool, is so true. When people have white hair, they're supposed to be clever and wise. Yet I've often seen men of my age group, and older, who have become almost childish in their ways. They're more concerned about the money than they are about the people. As a result they lose the people, and then they lose the money.

That doesn't only happen in big organizations. I've seen it in family enterprises, family businesses – especially farming – because that's where I've spent most of my life. Men who have had beautiful farms but who, for whatever reason, would not release them to their sons... Eventually, they lose their sons, because they have to get on with their lives. They might emigrate overseas, or go into a completely different type of industry. Then, when age catches up and the old man can't farm any more, and he can't run the business, he has nobody to hand it over to and he sells it. He puts the money in the bank and buys a house, and he sits there, a very lonely, frustrated, old man.

I've done many things wrong in my life, but one thing I thank God that I did do right was to hand over my farms to my sons some years ago already. The farms are in their names. They are farming them and officially I am staying on their farms. Right now I'm walking around one son's farm and looking across at the other son's farm. They are making a better success of their farming operations than I did of mine. I'm so proud of them.

It's all about people. We need to put people above our personal ambitions, above our selfish ideals, and start to prefer our children to ourselves. You know what happens? It's like when you put your hand out for that little bird. He comes and settles on your hand to eat those crumbs in your hand. If you close your fist, you'll catch him and he'll eventually die in your hand. But if you open up your hand, he'll fly away and bring back some of his friends. That's what happens when you hand things over to people and trust them. It comes right back to you again.

My sons are happily married. They have children of their own. We have now become a community. The church, which my wife and I started on this farm, is now being pastored by one of my spiritual sons. Just a couple of days ago, when I was sitting in the service as one of the congregation on Christmas Day, and the church was full almost to overflowing with over five hundred people seated there, I was so proud of what God has done through my spiritual son and daughter. When we hand over and allow other people's visions to come to fruition, when we prefer others to ourselves, God automatically honours us.

I heard a story about Sir Edmund Hillary and the Sherpa, Tenzing Norgay, who both climbed to the top of Mount Everest. Obviously, one of them had to get to the top first. Was it Tenzing, or was it Edmund Hillary? They never told anybody until many years later. Finally, the newspaper men and the writers managed to get it out of them. I still can't remember, and it doesn't actually mean anything to me, which one actually got to the top first. They both got to the top and that's all that counted. But, from that moment onwards, there was, I believe, a great deal of disagreement and unpleasantness between the two parties and their families. The bottom line is: What does it matter?

I was talking to my younger son the other day. He was a very good rugby player and we were talking about people's reputations; about how long people remember other people's feats and records. Later, my son went over to our children's home and was speaking to the young boys who love rugby. He was speaking about the South African rugby captain and the famous South African rugby players of five or ten years ago. Not one of those young men knew who they were.

Everything in this life passes by. You can't remember the beautiful maize crop you had five years ago. You can't remember that brand-new motor car you bought twenty years ago. You can't remember that barn or building you built twenty years ago. You can't remember records, or world championships, or worldly accomplishments. But you can remember people. People will always be a part of you. That's the way that the Lord has made us. I remember an old man who used to tip his hat every time we drove past a group of donkeys standing at the side of the road. When I asked him, "*Oom* Johannes, why do you do that?" he said, "Because they carried my Master." I've never forgotten the old man for that.

I remember when I was foolishly burning a firebreak on one of the boundaries of our farm many years ago. There is a huge wetland which runs about one and a half kilometres along one of the boundaries of our farm. I was burning a firebreak in the middle of winter. A gust of wind blew the fire into the vlei, which had been bleached snow-white by the heavy frost and was as volatile as high octane. This meant that the whole district had to man their boundaries. In desperation, I was trying to wade into the water with three- to four-metre reeds blazing across the top of the wetland.

A man who had come to stay with me, an incurable alcoholic, was so desperate to see that I didn't hurt myself that he was shouting. He ran in and literally pulled me out of that blazing inferno. He said, "Don't go in there! There's nothing you can do about it!" We were able to radio all the neighbours from our pick-up, which was parked right next to the firebreak, and warn them so that no one else burnt out. That fire burnt for two or three days afterwards. But the thing that I remember is not the fire. I remember the man that I was trying to help pulling me out of the fire and saying, "Angus, there's nothing you can do about it. Don't lose your life for this."

Many years before, that same wetland was on fire. I was trying to put the fire out with a little tractor and a water cart. I had my older son Andy, who could only have been about eight or nine years old at the time, with me. The fire turned around a few times and came at the tractor and nearly set the tractor – and me – on fire. Then it would get pushed away from the other side by another gust of wind.

Eventually, when everything was burnt-out, black, I stopped the tractor and looked around. There was my little son sitting on the mudguard. I said to him, "Andy, what are you doing on the tractor?" I hadn't seen him there; I wasn't even conscious of him being there. "Why didn't you jump off the tractor when you saw the flames just about to engulf us?" He said, "Dad, I didn't want to leave you. I wanted to stay with you. If you were going to go, I was going to go with you." That young boy is now forty years old and I've never forgotten that statement. People are more important than farming land or tractors.

Jill and I have had a very exciting life, right from the first day that we met up until now. We've seen the power of God move so mightily in our lives and in the lives of those who have been with us, mainly our family. We've been through fires and droughts, through floods and hailstorms. We've been through personal tragedy. We've seen people come and people go. We've seen folks come and say that God has sent them to join us at Shalom, and then, when things didn't work out quite the way they expected, we've seen them turn their backs on us and leave us.

But I want to tell you more about one person who's been with us from the beginning, and is still with us today. She is one of my intercessors. She's an old lady, well into her eighties. She's become a spiritual mother to me. She lives in the old-age home in Greytown. She used to live with us on the farm for maybe ten or fifteen years. But, because she needs more care now, she's relocated to the old-age home in town, fifteen kilometres away. I still visit her as often as I can. She still wants to know everything that I'm doing. She prays about everything, and when I visit her she mostly just sits and listens to me. She hardly says anything. Then, right at the end of my one-hour discourse, Tortoise O'Neill will make one profound statement which will answer all of my questions, put to rest all my fears, keep me humble and keep me going.

She has seen them come and go in this ministry that God has given me. She has seen groups of people gather together to try and stand against me, and she's seen those groups being dispelled through prayer. She is the one who can tell me anything she likes. She'll never offend me and she'll never get me angry, because I know how much she loves me. She has no hidden agendas. Unlike so many others who have come to Shalom over the years, she has no personal ambitions. God has kept her until now and I believe a lot of it is because God knows that I need her to help me fulfil the work he has called me to.

Tortoise O'Neill's co-worker, Moyra, also lives at the old-age home in Greytown. This dear old lady came to Shalom with her husband, an ex-rancher, who went to be with the Lord many years ago. I was pulling out tree stumps, clearing virgin land for cultivation, when this little motorcar pulled up on the side of the road. The driver turned off the engine and out got this old man, who subsequently became a father to me. There was steam coming out of the bonnet as the little car was boiling.

He and his wife came and joined us. They were PEOPLE who stood by me and my wife and family through thick and thin. They were pensioners. They didn't have much to offer; in fact they had nothing to offer in material terms, but everything to offer when it came to love, when it came to reassurance, and when it came to faithfulness and steadfastness. I am so looking forward to seeing Uncle Jimmy when I get to heaven. His dear wife Moyra and Tortoise O'Neill pray for me every single day – and I think most of the day. There's no money that can buy that kind of prayer and love.

Invest your time and your energy in people. I'm not talking about the famous or the rich. I'm just talking about whoever God puts in your pathway. Henri Nouwen was a Catholic priest, an intellectual, an academic, and a preacher. He was very much sought after and he taught theological students all over the world. God said to him: "I want you to stop everything you're doing."

Pretty much like God said to me when I was preaching and He said that I had to mentor young men. As I'm writing this book, we're preparing to welcome the no less than four hundred thousand men that we're expecting in a few months time. That came out of God telling me that people are more important than things. I thought that God was using me in ministry before, as I had campaigns booked all over the world. I cancelled all of them to mentor people; especially young men. As a result, a men's ministry has unfolded which I believe is unprecedented anywhere in the world. All the glory goes to God.

Henri Nouwen was told to stop his ministry and go to a home for people with learning difficulties up in Canada. There were about ten or fifteen people in that home, that's all. Henri was quite proud of the fact that he was an academic, a very clever man, yet it was through this home that God taught him his greatest lesson. He used simple people, grown people with the mindset of a five- or six-year-old child, PEOPLE with learning difficulties, to speak to Henri.

He tells the story of how he took one of the patients, Bill, with him on one of his preaching tours. He had Bill sitting on the platform while he was busy speaking to an auditorium full of intellectuals. Maybe five or ten thousand, I don't know. Bill was a fully-grown man, with the mind of a small boy. He was sitting back and listening to Henri Nouwen lecturing. Henri was struggling. I don't think he was making too much headway with the crowd, but he was still delivering his paper.

There was a tap on his shoulder. He turned around and there was Bill standing next to him. Henri excused himself from his audience and asked Bill, "What do you want, Bill?"

"I want to speak to the people."

Henri didn't know what to do. He said, "Okay", and stood back and gave him the mike.

Bill was about to start speaking when he looked up and saw the enormity of the crowd. Just like any little boy of maybe three or four years old, he got stage fright, started to cry and put his head on Henri's shoulder. Henri obviously comforted him and let him be seated. God's ways are not our ways, and God's thoughts are not our thoughts. That act had more impact on the crowd than the whole lecture of this academic. I don't think there would have been a dry eye there. When God calls us (each one of us, by the way) to put people as a priority, we need to obey and do whatever He says.

The same thing happened to me at the last Mighty Men Conference. I'd worked out, after thirty years of preaching, exactly how we were going to address this huge gathering of men, the biggest gathering I've ever seen in my life. We knew that the glory of God was going to visit us, because we'd had many confirmations. One of my spiritual sons, the famous singer, Joe Niemand, flew all the way down from Johannesburg to tell me that very thing. We didn't know how it was going to happen – whether it was going to come through the music, through the camp-fires, maybe, or even through the preaching – but we knew that the Lord was going to visit us. We never, ever dreamed, not in a million years, the way He was going to do it.

Basically, He took me right out of the picture in order to allow His glory to come down. I collapsed after the second service, on the Saturday morning, and my son Andy caught me in his arms. After being rushed home, I collapsed a second time, and was actually dying. But the prayers of millions of people all over this world saved me. God gave me a new heart. That impacted those men more than if I'd preached the best sermon of my life.

Stephen Hunter was one of the many men at the conference who were praying for me when I collapsed. God gave him an awesome vision of what was happening in the spiritual realm at that time. On the Thursday after MMC 09, he posted this account of his experience on a Christian web-site. It is included with his permission.

A new beginning!

What a Mighty God we serve! I have to share something with all of you men who were at MMC 09. You may recall the anxious moments we all experienced when brought together at the stage on Saturday afternoon to pray for Angus, who fell ill. Just after we formed small groups to pray for Angus – (May I add that the presence of the Holy Spirit was tangibly there – very powerful prayers. GOD WAS LISTENING VERY INTENTLY TO ALL OUR CRIES!). Suddenly there was a cloud that moved before the sun. It became slightly cloudy. As I looked up (I had dark glasses on) I saw an image that I believe God showed me. Looking into the sun, the cloud haze around the sun had an image of a FOETUS. Yes, absolutely and very definitely, I believe God showed me that what was happening at that moment (Angus being struck down) was a life-changing moment for him, as well as for the MMC now and in the future. THIS IS THE BEGINNING OF NEW THINGS! The FOETUS will grow!!! How exciting to look

*toward the future and have promises like these. Certainly we
are men of Promise and a country of promise.*

*Coincidentally, at the evening service Andy reminded
us that what happened on Saturday is also a reminder
that we have to mature as men (it is not about Angus).
We cannot stay immature and keep on asking to be fed
like babies. We need to take the baton and run. Shalom
Farm is just a blessed meeting place for our men to be
refilled with new passion and drive for God's work to be
done in this country and in the world.*

TO JESUS BE ALL THE GLORY!

We don't know how God works and it's not for us to try and
figure it out. One thing I have realized though is that God
always uses people. He used one person, Moses, to bring
the children of Israel out of Egypt. God used one man to
deliver the Israelites from the Philistines. His name was
David. He used one man to bring salvation to this earth. His
name was Jesus. Yes, He was God, but He was man as well.
And God wants to use you, and He wants to use me.

The question is not whether you are able, the question is:
Are you available? I have come to realize that God always
honours faith. God always uses faithful men and women
to do His work, not men and women of great learning or
great natural ability, but men and women who are prepared
to believe Him and do whatever He says, no matter how
ridiculous it might seem at the time.

Again I ask: How big is God? He's as big as you'll allow
Him to be. One of the saddest stories I've ever heard was
when I was preaching in Sweden some years back. A lady

came to me, tears running down her face, and said, "Angus, please pray for us in Sweden, because we keep Jesus in a matchbox in this country. Every now and again we open the matchbox and let Him out, just a little bit." They have everything that anyone could ever want in that country. It's one of the most beautiful countries I've ever seen, with the most beautiful people. But, without Jesus, there is no hope.

I think the most precious thing to have in this life, and which money definitely cannot buy, is a good friend. Next to the Lord Jesus Christ, my best friend is Jill, my wife. We've been together now many, many years. The longer we are together, the better friends we become. To the younger people reading this book, I'd like to say that the physical aspect of marriage is very important. You must fall in love. There must be a physical attraction to your loved one. But, at the end of the day, marriage is so much more than mere physical attraction.

My children are now grown up and married, with their own children. However, even though I'm privileged enough to say that they all live within a few hours distance from our home, they have their own families now and things change. That's the way the Lord meant it to be. But it doesn't make it any easier. At the end of your life you find that you end up like you started – just the two of you. That's why it's so important to cultivate and develop that friendship. It's not to say that you need to live in each other's pockets. Not at all, but you do need to respect one another and love one another, have things in common and work at your friendship.

There's no such thing as a naturally blessed marriage. Every marriage has to be worked at in order to succeed.

Husbands, you need to love your wives more and more, especially in their senior years. Wives, you need to submit to your husbands more and more, even as you grow older together. The only way you can ensure that that relationship, or any friendship for that matter, succeeds, is through the relationship that you have with Jesus Christ. The closer you become to God, the nicer the person you become. The more you take on the character of God, the friendlier you become, and the more friends you'll have. The more time you spend with God, the more value you'll put on people, and you'll respect and love them that much more.

They asked George Müller, who started the children's home in Bristol, England in the 1800s, why he took care of so many children and what motivated him. He basically said it was not even for the children's sake – although he loved them – but more for God's sake that he did it. If you love the Lord Jesus Christ with all your heart, your marriage will work better, your friendships will be stronger, your business will be more likely to prosper and life will be sweeter.

Like the great apostle Paul, I can honestly say at the end of my life: "For to me, to live is Christ, and to die is gain" (Philippians 1:21). Right now I am living life to the full, enjoying every moment of it, still learning lots and still making lots of new friends. I am ready for great challenges, but the second that the Lord calls me and says that it's time to go home, I have my bags packed as it were, and am ready to relocate at a moment's notice.

In Revelation 22:20, the second-to-last verse of the Bible, John writes: "He who testifies to these things says, 'Surely I am coming quickly.'" John responds: "Amen. Even so, come Lord Jesus!" As I told the men at MMC 09 after the Lord miraculously healed me, I have written in the margin of my Bible: "Keep short accounts with God and with man, for the time is now very short."

Epilogue
Coming to the best stretch

Off went Buchan-Hare with a weak wave of his hand
And a flip of his tail
Looking meaner and leaner than ever before
His Master, he knew, he could not fail
The end was in sight – he'd even the score.
Rounding the bend, he could see up ahead
Peggy-Tortoise and Co, leaping and cheering
with banners that said:
"You've done it, you've done it, you've done it!!"
Your trophy you'll find in the Master's hand,
He will present it to you when before His throne you stand.
"What is my trophy?" Buchan-Hare asked
with shaky voice.
"Oh, you'll have the pick of the crop –
it will be your choice."
"All I need now, dear Lord, is 'Well done',
a pat on the back and a smile,
But my Father, please, don't ask me to go
another mile!!!"

"Even to your old age and grey hairs I am He,
I am He who will sustain you. I have made you
and I will sustain you and I will rescue you."

Jesus said in a loud voice: "If anyone is thirsty,
let him come to Me and drink. Whoever
believes in Me, as the Scripture has said,
streams of Living Water will flow from within him."

"If your enemy is hungry, feed him; if he is thirsty, give him something to drink. In doing this you will heap burning coals on his head."

"And we pray this in order that you may live a life worthy of the Lord and may please Him in every way, bearing fruit in every good work, growing in the knowledge of God."

"I saw you, Angus, walking carefully along a ploughed furrow, where the cabbages are planted. You were taking one careful step at a time. God is preparing a path for you to walk along. It will be as rough as that furrow. You are to take one careful step at a time – be very cautious of the steps you take."

"Being confident of this, that He who began a good work in you will carry it on to completion until the day of Christ Jesus."

"Finally brothers, whatever is true, whatever is noble, whatever is right, whatever is pure, whatever is lovely, whatever is admirable – if anything is perfect, excellent or praiseworthy – think about such things."

"And my God will meet all your needs according to His glorious riches in Christ Jesus."

"I know what it is to be in need, and I know what it is to have plenty. I have learned the secret of being content in any and every situation, whether well-fed or hungry,

whether living in plenty or in want.
I can do all things through Him who
gives me strength."

"If anyone sets his heart on being an overseer,
he desires a noble task."

"Keep watch over yourself and all the flock
of which the Holy Spirit has made you
an overseer."

"The Lord will guide you always, He will satisfy
your needs in a sun-scorched land and will
strengthen your frame. You will be like a
well-watered garden, like a spring whose
waters never fail."

As Time Passed By
Buchan-Hare began to wonder
And on this mystery he would ponder and ponder
How come Peggy-Tortoise was always ahead?

To this day, on this bothersome question,
No light can he shed!!

You've done it, you've done it, you've done it!!
The Lord and I are proud of you.

Love,
Peggy